I0080565

Bibliographies of Modern Authors
ISSN 0749-470X
Number Five

The Work of
ROBERT REGINALD

An Annotated Bibliography & Guide
Second Edition, Revised and Expanded

by
Michael Burgess
California State University, San Bernardino

R. REGINALD
The Borgo Press
San Bernardino, California □ MCMXCII

THE BORGO PRESS
Publishers Since 1975
Post Office Box 2845
San Bernardino, CA 92406
United States of America

*   *   *   *   *   *   *   *

Copyright © 1985, 1992 by Michael Burgess

Library of Congress Cataloging-in-Publication Data

Burgess, Michael, 1948-
  The work of Robert Reginald : an annotated bibliography & guide / by
Michael Burgess. — 2nd ed., rev. and expanded.
     p. cm. — (Bibliographies of modern authors, ISSN 0749-470X ; no. 5)
  Includes index.
  ISBN 0-8095-0505-3. — ISBN 0-8095-1505-9 (pbk.)
  1. Reginald, R.—Bibliography. I. Title. II. Series: Bibliographies of
modern authors (San Bernardino, Calif.) ; no. 5.
Z8736.47.R43 1992   87-6306
[PS3568.E4754]
016.8093'876—dc19   CIP

SECOND EDITION

CONTENTS

Introduction: "Comet's Don't Slow Down," by William F. Nolan   5
Preface: "It Was Twenty Years Ago Today...," by Dr. Fran J. Polek   8
A Robert Reginald Chronology   9

A.   Books   17
B.   Short Nonfiction   66
C.   Short Fiction   82
D.   Editorial Credits   83
E.   Documents   110
F.   Catalogs   113
G.   Book Production and Design   124
H.   Unpublished Works   127
I.   Juvenilia   130
J.   Public Appearances   132
K.   Secondary Sources   136
L.   Honors and Awards   142
M.   Miscellanea   144

Quoth the Critics   152
Afterthoughts: "Harvesting the Vineyards of Obscurity," by Robert Reginald   166
Afterword: "Robert Reginald: Force Majeure," by Jack Dann   168
Title Index   171

Dedication

For My Mother,

BETTY JANE KAPEL BURGESS,

Who Wanted One of Her Very Own

INTRODUCTION

"Comets Don't Slow Down"

by William F. Nolan

The amazing Robert Reginald—who also writes under the names Michael Burgess and Boden Clarke—wears many coats. Publisher, author, librarian, editor, bibliographer, cataloger, book designer, historian, genealogist, and scholar—as well as an expert on current political affairs, and one of the nation's top authorities in the field of science fiction—he is all of these. He has also been responsible for a veritable flood of books on a wide variety of subjects relating to his many enthusiams.

In 1987 he was presented with the $2500 Meritorious Performance and Professional Promise Award by California State University, San Bernardino, where he currently works as a full professor and librarian.

Tracking his many projects is like trying to follow a comet across the heavens. Reginald is working on literally dozens of projects at any given moment, moving as writer or editor or publisher from one to another, as a hummingbird darts from flower to flower.

The secret of Reginald's uncanny ability to work on so many books at once has to do with the fact that he has learned how to crowd thirty-six hours of work into a twenty-four-hour day. I picture him plugged directly into a bank of computers, a sandwich in one hand and a manuscript in the other, having mastered the mystic art of combining food, sleep, and work into one unbroken cycle. When they split the atom, they produced R. Reginald, a phenomenon who is most certainly atomic-powered.

If you think I exaggerate with such dramatically bold assertions, then I suggest you simply begin sifting through the pages of this book, and you'll see what I'm talking about. A few basic Reginald statistics should silence any lingering skeptics:

♦ Since 1970 he has written or edited sixty books of his own, under several bylines, including one that was so large (1,200 8" x 11" pages) that it had to be broken into two volumes for publication.

♦ He has published nearly 140 short nonfiction pieces, scattered over several dozen professional publications.

◆ He has been responsible—as author, editor, or publisher—for the publication or distribution of roughly **1,250** volumes in the last two decades, including 130 from Borgo Press, more than 150 from Newcastle, almost 200 from Arno Press, and many others.

◆ During this same period, he edited **three** magazines or journals, **fifteen** monographic series, and **three** publishing companies, and has influenced the development of several others.

◆ As part of his editorial duties, he prepared copy for at least **eighty** publisher or series catalogs, and designed **twenty-six** books for other companies.

◆ Here's the clincher: *during this entire period, from 1970-1991, Reginald was an academic librarian at California State University, San Bernardino*, where, by the way, he contributed dozens more documents, position papers, policy manuals, etc.

He has done all this over the past two decades, having launched his professional career in 1968, at the age of twenty, with an academic article on science fiction.

In popular terminology, he was born an "Air Force brat," at Itazuke Air Force Base near Fukuoka, Japan, in February of 1948. His father, a career officer, was reassigned to Oakland in 1949.

As early as 1956, at the age of eight, young Reginald demonstrated his creativity by winning second prize in an essay contest, and five years later, at thirteen, was turning out a series of histories in Latin as class papers.

By 1964, at Spokane, Washington, he was Features Editor on his school newspaper, and had embarked on what has become a lifelong study of his family's genealogy. A year later he achieved a high SAT score, and was awarded a scholarship to Gonzaga University, where he majored in English and classical Greek.

After attending his first science-fiction convention in Berkeley, California, in 1968, he began his first book project, *Stella Nova*, a "who's who" of science fiction authors, compiled through direct-mail questionnaires. He completed the book at the age of twenty-one, and moved to Southern California that summer, to complete his graduate degree at USC.

That same year, 1969, was a pivotal one for Reginald. When he met Doug Menville at a Hollywood bookshop he had no idea of the mass of material they would eventually produce together as an editorial team.

He graduated from SC in August of 1970, several months after his first book was published, accepting a position at Cal State San Bernardino. With Menville, he produced two film histories, and edited nine anthologies and three series for Arno Press. On his own, he produced two major bibliographies for Gale Research Co. during the 1970s.

In 1975 Reginald decided to start a publishing company, and almost simultaneously met the girl he would marry a year later—Mary Alice Wickizer. As Mary Burgess, she has worked shoulder-to-shoulder with Reginald in developing The Borgo Press and associated imprints, and in co-editing and supervising the growth of the company.

It's not my intention here to chronicle Reginald's many achievements exhaustively—this book does that better than I ever could—but rather to pay tribute to the man and his work, both of which are worthy in their own right. Suffice to say that here is a one-man factory of projects and ideas, an individual of boundless energy and high purpose, who loves the world of books and bookmen with an abiding passion, whose output is awesome in its scope and impressive in its dedication to quality.

Reginald has achieved miracles of productivity in the past without sacrificing quality; he will achieve equal miracles in the future.

Comets don't slow down.

—William F. Nolan
Agoura Hills, California
July 27, 1990

PREFACE

"It Was Twenty Years Ago Today..."

by Fran J. Polek

Of the young Michael Burgess I met some years ago at Gonzaga University, when I was a newly-minted Ph.D. and he was a super-energetic, chock-full-of-ideas Honors student, my pleasurable memory is clear. Michael came to me at the age of twenty with an idea that I at first felt was twenty years beyond him (I was soon to learn that one should never underestimate the verve, acumen, and professional know-how of R. Reginald): to produce his first book, a bio-bibliography of science fiction writers, as his senior Honors project. Mike, with his characteristic gusto, managed somehow to send questionnaires to over 500 authors and editors.

I remember that Gonzaga helped Mike to the tune of $100, found in some obscure financial cubby-hole. So with a little cash, and his own indefatigable enthusiasm and dynamism, the book was completed twenty years ago last Spring, and published in 1970. 483 bibliographies were included, and 308 biographies. *Stella Nova* (later to become *Science Fiction and Fantasy Literature*) proved to be a significant contribution to the advancement of science fiction scholarship, and Mike's first ship was launched, to be followed by entire fleets as the years rolled by!

Mike was kind enough to mention my more than modest contribution in *Stella Nova*'s introduction. The truth of the matter is that Michael—by sharing his vision and dedication—gave far more to those of us fortunate enough to know him at Gonzaga than we were ever able to give him. And a constant pleasure in my life has been watching Mike achieve one writing and publishing triumph after another. This is an exceptional person, with an exceptional career.

—Dr. Fran J. Polek
Professor of English
Gonzaga University
Spokane, Washington
March 19, 1990

8

A ROBERT REGINALD CHRONOLOGY

1948 Michael Roy Burgess born February 11th at Itazuke Air Force Base, near Fukuoka, Kyushu, Japan, oldest child of 1st Lt. Roy Walter "Walt" Burgess, a career Air Force officer (who was the second son of Roy P. Burgess and Edna Josephine Mathews); and Betty Jane Kapel (the second daughter of Andrew Kapel [originally Andrej Kapel] and Anna Kosnick [originally Ana Krsnic], Slovenian immigrants). The author is a tenth-generation descendant on his father's side of William Burges, who died in Richmond (later King George) Co., Virginia, in 1712, and an eighth-generation descendant on his mother's side of Jurij Krsnic of Hrovaca Ribnica, Slovenija.

1949 Walt Burgess reassigned to Oakland, California (January).

1951 Stephen Andrew Burgess (first brother) born May 5th at Oakland. The author's earliest memories, of his father being absent in the Korean War.

1952 After returning from duty in the Korean War, Walt Burgess is sent to Westover Air Force Base, near Holyoke, Mass.; the family rents a house in Fairview, Mass.

1954 Walt Burgess transferred to NATO base near Izmir, Turkey. Prior to leaving, the family travels across country to visit author's grandfather, Roy P. Burgess, who dies suddenly on September 28th (aged 64 years), one week after the family's return to Massachusetts.

1955 Spends the summers of 1955 and 1956 traveling in Europe with his parents, visiting Italy, Switzerland, Greece, Paris, Austria, and southern Germany.

1956 Receives second prize in an essay contest, a photo album.

1957 The Burgess family returns to the U.S. (Summer), Walt Burgess having been assigned to McConnell Air Force Base, near Wichita, Kansas. The Burgesses live at 1815 South Old Manor Road.

1959 Andrew Kapel (grandfather) dies May 9th at Spokane, Washington, aged 79 years.

1960 The Burgesses move to 536 Calhoun St. in Wichita. Mark Eugene Burgess (second brother) born July 8th.

1961 Attends Chaplain Kapaun Memorial High School. Begins compiling lists of monarchs and rulers of the world. Produces as class papers a series of Latin-language histories on the ancient states of Asia Minor.

1963 Maj. Walt Burgess retires from the Air Force. The family moves to Spokane, Washington (June), living at E. 34 Euclid. The author transfers to Gonzaga Preparatory School. His father buys a service station, Walt Burgess Chevron.

1964 Serves as Features Editor and reporter for school newspaper. Discovers on local paperback rack a "nonfiction" study of sexual mores with the byline "Michael Burgess" (the book was actually written by the well-known historical novelist, Noel B. Gerson); signs his name "M. R. Burgess" thereafter. Begins asking his immediate relatives everything they know about the origins of both sides of the family, thus initiating a lifelong interest in genealogy. Works as gas attendant at his father's station, Walt Burgess Chevron (beginning in October), and uses his first check to begin his collection of science fiction paperbacks. Scott Alan Burgess (third and youngest brother) born April 14th.

1965 Scores in the 99½th percentile on SAT test. Receives a one-year full-tuition scholarship to Gonzaga University, which he enters in September (Honors at Entrance), majoring in English and minoring in Classical Greek. Joins the incipient Honors Program at Gonzaga. Travels each week to downtown Spokane to haunt the local bookstores, steadily building his collection at the rate of 1000-1500 books per year. Begins collecting information on Eastern Orthodox Church patriarchs, after he finds several published lists in the Crosby Library at Gonzaga.

1966 Family moves to two-storey house at N. 3316 Lidgerwood in Spokane. At about this time, deliberately adapts his handwriting to a more unique "printed style" partially derived from Greek, and also alters his signature, eventually dropping all but his last name as his official *nom de guerre*.

1968 Celebrates 20th birthday (February 11th), which he regards as the beginning of his professional career. First professional article, a critical history of science fiction, is published under the byline "R. Reginald," the first appearance of the author's pseudonym in print. Makes decision to use this name on all future publications. Attends first science fiction convention, Baycon, at Berkeley, Calif., over Labor Day weekend, where he meets Edmond Hamilton, Leigh Brackett, and Emil Petaja, and has idea for first book, a bio-bibliography of science fiction writers, while talking with

Petaja on a bus. Begins this project, *Stella Nova*, as a senior Honors project in October, sending out questionnaires to five hundred authors and editors.

1969   Completes his first book and graduates from Gonzaga in May with an A.B. (Honors) degree. Summoned by the Draft Board (June) to take a pre-induction physical, which he fails due to his nearsightedness; his 1-Y classification allows him to continue his education. Awarded Title II Fellowship to work on a master's degree in Library Science at the University of Southern California. Rents a room from a Black engineer in the crime-ridden Adams District of Los Angeles. Attends St. LouisCon, the annual World Science Fiction Convention. Meets Douglas Menville at a book store in Hollywood, the Sunset-Vine Bookmart, owned by Alfred and Joseph Saunders. Locates his surviving great-uncle, George Osmer Burgess, who leads him to other cousins of the Burgess family. An active effort to piece together the Burgess lineage begins. Walt and Betty Burgess buy the Royal Crest Motel in Medford, Oregon. Grows a mustache during this period.

1970   Graduates from USC with a Master of Science in Library Science degree in August. Accepts a position as librarian at the California State College, San Bernardino Library, beginning September 1st. Publishes first book (May) under the imprint, Unicorn & Son, Publishers. Proposes several projects to Gale Research Co., and is given two contracts, one for a comprehensive bibliography of science fiction, one for a bibliography of the mass market paperback from 1939-1959, work on which has already begun. Becomes Associate Editor of *Forgotten Fantasy* magazine, a new business venture of the Saunders brothers, with Menville as Editor. During his first six months in San Bernardino, rents an apartment at 1415 E. Date Street.

1971   *Forgotten Fantasy* folds after five issues (June). A second Saunders venture, Newcastle Publishing Co., Inc., begins, with Menville and Reginald as joint editors. The first eight releases of this trade paperback line appear in July. Becomes Periodicals Librarian at Cal State, when the Library is moved to its new five-storey building (September). Moves to a duplex at 379 Edgerton Drive in San Bernardino, on Little Mountain, which he calls "Hill House." On a summer trip to Spokane, meets several distant cousins, Paul, Forrest, and Ray Burgess, all interested in the Burgess genealogy; while on vacation, begins growing a beard, which he retains to this day. Publishes the only issue of *The Burgess Bulletin*, a genealogical newsletter devoted to the history of the Burgess family.

1972   Completes work on his twenty-year bibliography of the paperback. Gradually abandons his work on the Burgess genealogy as he becomes more involved with writing and publishing. With Douglas Menville, is active in developing the Newcastle paperback line.

1973   *Cumulative Paperback Index, 1939-1959*, published under the joint byline
        "R. Reginald and M. R. Burgess" by Gale Research Co. Begins work on
        Science Fiction and Fantasy Literature. Proposes The Newcastle Forgotten
        Fantasy Library, a series of classic reprints of imaginative literature, to
        Newcastle, with Menville and Reginald as joint editors. First volume in
        this series, *The Story of the Glittering Plain*, by William Morris, published
        in October. Begins submitting bibliographies of books published by
        SFWA members to *SFWA Bulletin* (through 1974).

1974   Proposes science fiction reprint series to Arno Press, with Menville as co-
        editor. They immediately offer a contract. Steve Burgess (brother) marries
        Gina Rae Mann on March 16th. Awarded tenure at Cal State (effective
        September 1st).

1975   *Science Fiction: 62 Books* published by Arno Press (April); the series in-
        cludes a revised version of the author's first book, now called *Contempo-
        rary Science Fiction Authors*, and an anthology, *Ancestral Voices*. Re-
        ceives first large royalty check from Gale Research Co. and decides to start
        publishing company, The Borgo Press, whose books Newcastle agrees to
        distribute. Meets future wife, Mary Alice (Wickizer) Rogers (June 3rd),
        and Mary's children, Richard Albert Rogers and (Mary) Louise Rogers, at
        a Christmas dinner.

1976   Borgo Press releases its first two titles, *Robert A. Heinlein: Stranger in His
        Own Land*, by George Edgar Slusser, and *The Beach Boys: Southern Cali-
        fornia Pastoral*, by Bruce Golden, in April. Second Arno Press series, *Su-
        pernatural & Occult Fiction: 63 Books*, co-edited with Douglas Menville,
        is published, with four anthologies co-edited by the author. *The Attempted
        Assassination of John F. Kennedy*, an alternate-world fantasy, is published
        under the byline "Lucas Webb." Marries Mary Alice Wickizer Rogers on
        October 15th (his parents' 31st wedding anniversary) at Highland, Califor-
        nia, and moves to Mary's two-storey house at 6970 Perris Hill Road in San
        Bernardino.

1977   Publishes *Up Your Asteroid! A Science Fiction Farce*, under byline "C. Ev-
        erett Cooper." Success of *Star Wars* prompts Times Books, a sister com-
        pany of Arno Press, to phone with an offer for a history of science fiction
        films, if it can be completed in time for the Christmas trade. Reginald and
        Menville "bang" the book out in a six-week period in August and Septem-
        ber, Reginald also designing and typesetting the book. *Things To Come:
        An Illustrated History of the Science Fiction Film* is published in Novem-
        ber. Third Arno Press series sold.

1978   Celebrates 30th birthday (February 11th). *Lost Race and Adult Fantasy Fic-
        tion: 69 Books* (co-edited with Menville) is published by Arno Press, with

12

four anthologies. Sells fourth Arno series, *Science Fiction and Fantasy Criticism*, a proposed 50-book set of original and reprint nonfiction volumes. Responds to ad in *Los Angeles Times* and begins series of assignments for Irving Wallace's *People's Almanac*. Neil Barron proposes a review magazine to Borgo Press. Promoted to Senior Assistant Librarian at Cal State, and moves to Technical Services, where he works as Chief Cataloger and Assistant Bibliographer. Proposes the J. Lloyd Eaton Conference to Eleanor Montague, University Librarian at the University of California, Riverside; George Slusser later develops the project.

1979   Begins publication of *Science Fiction & Fantasy Book Review*, with Barron as Editor and Reginald as Publisher, in February. *Science Fiction and Fantasy Literature: A Checklist, 1700-1974, with Contemporary Science Fiction Authors II*, published in October. Article on The Borgo Press appears in *Paperback Quarterly*. Two critical articles appear in *Survey of Science Fiction Literature*. Allison Renae Burgess (niece) is born November 28th at Portland, Oregon, to Steve and Gina Burgess. Participates in first annual J. Lloyd Eaton Conference in Science Fiction and Fantasy (University of California, Riverside), which he had proposed with George Slusser.

1980   A year of transitions. The review magazine is shut down in February, due to rising commitments elsewhere. *Science Fiction and Fantasy Literature* nominated for Hugo Award as Best Nonfiction Book of 1979, and selected by *Choice* magazine as an academic book of the year. Completes fourth Arno series, but Arno suspends operations later in the year before the set can be published. Kevin Hancer publishes *The Paperback Price Guide* from Harmony Books; Reginald takes action to force an acknowledgement of its antecedents in *Cumulative Paperback Index*. The last book in the Forgotten Fantasy Library is published (October), and Reginald ceases direct editorial involvement with Newcastle due to rising commitments elsewhere. Reaches tenth year of service with Cal State (September 1st). At the second annual Eaton Conference, presents the first of an annual series of Milford Awards for Lifetime Contributions to the Publishing and Editing of Science Fiction.

1981   *Science Fiction and Fantasy Awards* published. Last article for *The People's Almanac* published. Promoted to Associate Librarian (*i.e.*, Associate Professor) at Cal State (June). Takes two-year research leave of absence without pay from Cal State (beginning July).

1982   *The Holy Grail Revealed*, cobbled together from a manuscript by Patricia and Lionel Fanthorpe, is published by Newcastle (April); *If J.F.K. Had Lived*, a rewriting of *The Attempted Assassination of John F. Kennedy*, also released in April. Settles dispute with Kevin Hancer, who agrees to put

Reginald's name on the title pages of future editions of *The Paperback Price Guide* (the Second Edition of which is published in September).

1983 Serves as Consulting Editor for *Survey of Fantasy Literature*, and pens thirteen critiques for that publication. Publishes *The House of the Burgesses*, a genealogy of the author's family, and (as co-author) his wife's genealogy, *The Wickizer Annals*. Also published: *Tempest in a Teapot: The Falkland Islands War*, with Jeffrey M. Elliot (August). Returns to Cal State in September. Enters 10,000,000th bibliographical record in the international OCLC cataloging data base (Oct. 11th), for which he receives wide acclaim. Awarded bronze plaque by OCLC at California Library Association meeting in Oakland (December).

1984 Promoted to full Librarian (*i.e.*, full Professor) at Cal State (June), a few weeks before the school is upgraded to university status. Awarded paid sabbatical leave for school year 1984/85, the first given to a librarian at that school. Publishes the cataloging manual, *A Guide to Science Fiction and Fantasy in the Library of Congress Classification Scheme* (August), the first to appear under his real name, Michael Burgess. Begins new series, Bibliographies of Modern Authors, all of the books in which he either writes or edits; first volume in this series, *The Work of Jeffrey M. Elliot*, released in December, under the name Boden Clarke. Decides to split his publications in the future under three names: Burgess (general reference, history, and cataloging manuals), Clarke (Eastern Orthodoxy, bibliographies, and current affairs), and Reginald (books on science fiction, and books for other companies). Pens nine fictional articles and charts for *The Dune Encyclopedia*. Obtains all remaining stock of and rights to *The Paperback Price Guide No. 2*. Richard Albert Rogers (stepson) marries Sheri LeeAnn Clark (July 7th). Anna Kosnick Kapel (grandmother) dies February 18th in Spokane, Washington, aged 91 years.

1985 Returns to Cal State (September). Publishes *Lords Temporal and Lords Spiritual*, a chronological checklist of Eastern Orthodox church patriarchs (May); *Futurevisions: The New Golden Age of the Science Fiction Film*, with Douglas Menville (October); and three bibliographies, *The Work of R. Reginald*, *The Work of Julian May* (with T. E. Dikty), and *The Work of Bruce McAllister* (as uncredited editor). Edna Josephine "Jo" Mathews Burgess Mobley Fellman, last surviving grandparent, dies June 26th in Portland, Oregon, aged 86 years.

1986 Publishes two bibliographies, *The Work of George Zebrowski* (with Elliot), and *The Work of Charles Beaumont* (with William F. Nolan), and has three critical articles published by *Twentieth-Century Science-Fiction Writers, Second Edition*. Step-granddaughter, Whitney Louise Rogers, born July 6th. Named to CSUSB Campus Scholarship Committee. Mark Burgess (brother) receives his Doctor of Veterinary Medicine degree from Oregon State University (July).

1987   Appointed to state-wide Librarians' Task Force of California Faculty Association, and named Founding Editor of the *LTF Newsletter*, the first issue of which is published in October (through 1989). Presented $2500 Meritorious Performance and Professional Promise (MPPP) Award by Cal State (June). Publishes *Mystery and Detective Fiction in the Library of Congress Classification Scheme*. Given second two-year research leave of absence without pay, which begins in December (to last through February 1, 1990). Stepdaughter, (Mary) Louise Rogers, marries Dr. Richard Reynnells (May 6th), and moves to Laurel, MD. The Borgo Press moves into remodeled offices at 6980 Perris Hill Road, San Bernardino (Fall). One hundredth article published.

1988   Celebrates 40th birthday (February 11th). Publishes *A Guide to Science Fiction and Fantasy in the Library of Congress Classification Scheme, Second Edition*; *Western Fiction in the Library of Congress Classification Scheme*, his fortieth published book; *California Ranchos*; *The Work of William F. Nolan*; and the second issue of the *LTF Newsletter*. First two professional genealogical articles appear in *Kentucky Ancestors*, and another in the National Genealogical Society *Newsletter*. Nephew, Andrew Ryan Burgess, born October 31st in San Jose, California, to Steve and Gina Burgess. The Fall, 1988 Borgo Press catalog is the first in five years to be fully annotated, being distributed to 10,000 libraries worldwide; it includes 750 active titles in over 1200 bindings. The Borgo Press occupies remodeled shipping facilities at the rear of 6980 Perris Hill Road, San Bernardino (December).

1989   *The Arms Control, Disarmament, and Military Security Dictionary* (with Jeffrey M. Elliot and Mary A. Burgess) is published by ABC-CLIO (June); other books published include the edited volumes, *The Work of Colin Wilson*, *The Work of Chad Oliver*, *The Work of Reginald Bretnor*, *The Work of Ian Watson*, and *The Work of Ross Rocklynne*; the third issue of the *LTF Newsletter* is published in May, at which point the author resigns from the Librarians' Task Force. Step-grandson, Dustin James Rogers, born April 27th at Fontana, CA; step-grandson, Russell Edward Reynnells, born May 24th in Maryland. Begins work on a much revised and expanded second edition of *The House of the Burgesses*, and on the Supplement to *Science Fiction and Fantasy Literature*. The Borgo Press publishes its 100th original title.

1990   Returns to Cal State (February 1st), where he completes two decades of service (September 1st). Publishes *The Work of Pamela Sargent*, *The Work of George Zebrowski* (Second Edition), *To Kill or Not to Kill*, *The Work of*

Charles Beaumont (Second Edition), *The Work of Dean Ing, Hancer's Guide to Paperback Books, Third Edition.* The 1990 Borgo Press catalog exceeds a thousand active titles for the first time (at 1,063). The author's biography appears for the first time in *Who's Who in America.*

1991   Publishes *Reginald's Science Fiction and Fantasy Awards* (Second Edition), *The Trilemma of World Oil Politics, The Work of Louis L'Amour, The Work of Katherine Kurtz, The Work of Brian W. Aldiss, Lords Temporal and Lords Spiritual* (Second Edition); pens seven essays for the Third Edition of *Twentieth-Century Science-Fiction Writers,* and reworks the "Reading List" in the book's Introduction.   The Borgo Press acquires Brownstone Books, The Starmont Contemporary Writers Series, one book from The Starmont Mystery Guides Series, Sidewinder Press, and St. Willibrord's Press as new imprints, and also initiates the imprint Burgess & Wickizer.   Scott Burgess (brother) receives Master's Degree in Computer Science from Rutgers University (May).   On sabbatical leave from Cal State (Fall Quarter, 1991), during which time he completes a 467-page, three-year project, *A Reference Guide to Science Fiction, Fantasy, and Horror,* and most of the work on the Second Edition of *Science Fiction and Fantasy Literature.*

1992   Returns to Cal State (January 6th).   Borgo Press releases its largest catalog to date, eighty pages in size, and the first to have a four-color cover; some 1425 titles are featured.   Completes the massive supplement to *Science Fiction and Fantasy Literature* for Gale Research Co. (April).   *The Work of Robert Reginald: An Annotated Bibliography & Guide, Second Edition,* a much expanded version of the 1985 book, is published by The Borgo Press.

A.

BOOKS

A1.   *Stella Nova: The Contemporary Science Fiction Authors*, non-bylined.
Los Angeles: Unicorn & Son, May 1970, [348 p.], spiral-bound paper.
LC 79-282012. Cover by Bill Hughes. [bio-bibliography]

The author's first book, begun after the author attended Baycon (the World
Science Fiction Convention) in September, 1968. Upon returning home,
he proposed the idea to his faculty advisor in the Gonzaga University Honors Program, and received two semesters' academic credit for this senior
project during the 1968/69 school year.

The book was intended to be a "Who's Who" of science fiction and
fantasy, compiled through direct-mail questionnaires, with bibliographies
of the authors' books in chronological order. Ultimately, 483 bibliographies were included, with 308 biographies. 108 copies were produced
from offset masters; of these, ten were reserved for the author and his
friends. More than half of the copies were sold to libraries, leaving
roughly forty-five books in private hands. The book later served as the basis of several other publications, and has proved to be a standard resource
book for all later biographical directories of science fiction authors.

CONTENTS: Bibliographical Information; About the Cover Artist;
Foreword; Introduction; Contents; Symbols and Abbreviations Used; Stella
Nova: The Contemporary Science Fiction Authors; Addendum; Index of
Books Included in This Work; List of Pseudonyms. A typical entry includes: author's name, bibliography of the authors in chronological order
by publication date, biography (as provided by the author himself), and
sidelights or comments by the author.

See also the revised edition (A3).

SECONDARY SOURCES AND REVIEWS:

1.   *AB Bookman's Weekly* 76 (October 28, 1985): 3086.
2.   Aldiss, Brian W. "Afterword: The Day Equality Broke Out," in *Best
SF: 1970*, edited by Harry Harrison and Brian W. Aldiss. New
York: G. P. Putnam's Sons, 1971, cloth, p. 222. Also: New
York: A Berkley Medallion Book, 1971, paper, p. 222. Also: as:

The Year's Best Science Fiction, No. 4. London: Sphere Books, 1971, paper, p. .

3. Anthony, Piers. *Bio of an Ogre: The Autobiography of Piers Anthony to Age 50.* New York: Ace Books, 1988, cloth, p. 195-196.

4. Anthony, Piers. *Hasan.* New York: Tor, A Tom Doherty Associates Book, 1986, paper, p. 241.

5. Ash, Brian. *The Visual Encyclopedia of Science Fiction.* London & Sydney: Pan Books; New York: Harmony Books, 1977, paper, p. 331.

6. Barron, Neil. "Bibliographies, Indexes, and Teaching Aids," in *Anatomy of Wonder: Science Fiction,* edited by Neil Barron. New York & London: R. R. Bowker Co., 1976, paper, p. 363.

7. Briney, Robert E., and Edward Wood. *SF Bibliographies: An Annotated Bibliography of Bibliographical Works on Science Fiction and Fantasy.* Chicago: Advent:Publishers, 1972, paper, p. 17.

8. Currey, L. W., and Marshall B. Tymn. "Reference Sources for Science Fiction," in *AB Bookman's Weekly* 76 (October 28, 1985): 3086.

9. Menville, Douglas. *Forgotten Fantasy* 1 (April, 1971): 47-48.

10. Tymn, Marshall B., Roger C. Schlobin, and L. W. Currey. *A Research Guide to Science Fiction Studies: An Annotated Bibliography of Primary and Secondary Sources for Fantasy and Science Fiction.* New York & London: Garland Publishing, 1977, cloth, p. 10.

11. Tymn, Marshall B. and Roger C. Schlobin. *The Year's Scholarship in Science Fiction and Fantasy: 1972-1975.* Kent, OH: Kent State University Press, 1979, cloth, p. 49.

A2. *Cumulative Paperback Index, 1939-1959: A Comprehensive Bibliographic Guide to 14,000 Mass-Market Paperback Books of 33 Publishers Under 69 Imprints,* by R. Reginald and M. R. Burgess [joint by-line]. Detroit: Gale Research Co., September 1973, xxiv, 362 p., cloth (ISBN 0-8161-1050-3—does not actually appear in book). LC 73-6866. [bibliography]

ab. Detroit: Gale Research Co., 1980?, xxiv, 362 p., cloth. Second printing.
b. San Bernardino, CA: The Borgo Press, 1990, xxiv, 362 p., cloth (ISBN 0-89370-022-3). The Borgo edition consists of remaindered copies of the original book with a Borgo imprint label placed over the original Gale imprint on the title page.

A three-year project begun in 1970, the CPI attempted to list every mass-market paperback published during the first two decades of paperback publishing, from 1939-1959 inclusive. The book has been acclaimed as the "paperback collector's Bible," and later became the basis for *The Paperback Price Guide* (see A20).

CONTENTS: Introduction, Abbreviations List, Publisher Specifications [providing lists of stock numbers used, book height, edge color, numbering system, price codes, total books published], Author Index [providing author, title, publisher, stock number, year of publication, and original price], and Title Index [providing title and author only].

SECONDARY SOURCES AND REVIEWS:

1. *Bibliographical Society of America Papers* 69 (January, 1975): 143.
2. *Booklist* 71 (December 1, 1974): 389.
3. *Catholic Library World* 46 (April, 1975): 402.
4. Clareson, Thomas D. *Extrapolation* 15 (May, 1974): 157-158.
5. Ferman, Edward L. *The Magazine of Fantasy & Science Fiction* 47 (August, 1974): 58.
6. Lee, Billy C. *Paperback Quarterly* 1 (Spring, 1978): 39-41.
7. Lerner, Fred. *SFRA Newsletter* no. 32 (September, 1974): 2.
8. *The Library* 5th ser. 29 (June, 1974): 245.
9. Patten, Fred. *Delap's F & SF Review* 3 (June, 1975): 7-8.
10. "Reference Books of the Trade," in *Literary Market Place* (1978): 419.
10. "Reference Books of the Trade," in *Literary Market Place* (1982): .
11. Sheehy, Eugene P. *Guide to Reference Books, Ninth Edition.* Chicago: American Library Association, 1976, cloth, p. .
12. Tymn, Marshall B., Roger C. Schlobin, and L. W. Currey. *A Research Guide to Science Fiction Studies: An Annotated Bibliography of Primary and Secondary Sources for Fantasy and Science Fiction.* New York & London: Garland Publishing, 1977, cloth, p. 6.

A3. *Contemporary Science Fiction Authors, First Edition*, compiled and edited by R. Reginald. Science Fiction: 62 Books. New York: Arno Press, April 1975, [xii], 368 p., cloth [violet] (ISBN 0-405-06332-6). LC 74-16517. [bio-bibliography]

ab. New York: Arno Press, 1976 (?), [xii], 368 p., cloth [violet]. Includes the abbreviations list on p. [xii] accidentally omitted from the first printing.
ac. New York: Arno Press, 1978 (?), [xii], 368 p., cloth [blue-green]. Includes the abbreviations list on p. [xii] accidentally omitted from the first printing.

A revised edition of A1 (q.v.). The index to book titles has been completely reworked, the book repaginated, and a new introduction added, with minor corrections of other errors and omissions. Other contents remain the same. The abbreviations list was accidentally omitted from the first printing. At least three distinct printing variations are known, and two different colors of the binding stock.

SECONDARY SOURCES AND REVIEWS:

1. Aldiss, Brian W. *Science-Fiction Studies* 2 (July, 1975): 173-174.
2. Allard, Yvon. *Paralittératures*. Montréal: La Centrale des Bibliothèques, 1979, cloth, p. 442-443.
3. Barron, Neil. "Bibliographies, Indexes, and Teaching Aids," in *Anatomy of Wonder: Science Fiction*, edited by Neil Barron. New York & London: R. R. Bowker Co., 1976, paper, p. 363.
4. Brown, Charles N. *Locus* no. 185 (Feb. 29, 1976): 9.
5. Currey, L. W., and Marshall B. Tymn. "Reference Sources for Science Fiction," in *AB Bookman's Weekly* 76 (October 28, 1985): 3086.
6. Delap, Richard. *Delap's F & SF Review* 3 (June, 1975): 8.
7. Hall, H. W. *SFRA Newsletter* no. 45 (November, 1975): 5-6.
8. Lerner, Frederick Andrew. *Modern Science Fiction and the American Literary Community*. Metuchen, NJ & London: The Scarecrow Press, 1985, cloth, p. 103.
9. Lupoff, Richard A. *Algol* no. 27 (Fall, 1976/Winter, 1977): 34-36.
10. Mullen, Richard D. *Science-Fiction Studies* 2 (July, 1975): 181.
11. Tymn, Marshall B., Roger C. Schlobin, and L. W. Currey. *A Research Guide to Science Fiction Studies: An Annotated Bibliography of Primary and Secondary Sources for Fantasy and Science Fiction*. New York & London: Garland Publishing, 1977, cloth, p. 10.
12. Tymn, Marshall B. and Roger C. Schlobin. *The Year's Scholarship in Science Fiction and Fantasy: 1972-1975*. Kent, OH: Kent State University Press, 1979, cloth, p. 49.

A4. *Ancestral Voices: An Anthology of Early Science Fiction*, edited by Douglas Menville and R. Reginald. Science Fiction: 62 Books. New York: Arno Press, April 1975, [298] p., cloth (ISBN 0-405-06305-9). LC 74-16508. [anthology]

   b. *Ancestral Voices: Classic Tales of Science Fiction*. Mercer Island, WA: Starmont House, 1992, [160] p., cloth. An abridged version of the original.
   bb. *Ancestral Voices: Classic Tales of Science Fiction*. Mercer Island, WA: Starmont House, 1992, [160] p., paper. An abridged version of the original.

c.   *Ancestral Voices: Classic Tales of Science Fiction.* San Bernardino, CA: The Borgo Press, 1992, [160] p., cloth. An abridged version of the original, with the Borgo Press label stickered over the Starmont imprint on the title page.

An anthology of nineteenth- and early twentieth-century science-fiction stories, reproduced facsimile from their original sources (usually, single-author story collections).
CONTENTS: "A Glance Ahead, Being a Christmas Tale of A.D. 3568," by John Kendrick Bangs; "The Third Eye," by Robert W. Chambers; "The Space Annihilator," by Harle Oren Cummings; "A Corner in Lightning," by George Griffith; "The Lizard," by C. J. Cutcliffe Hyne; "The Romance of the First Radical," by Andrew Lang; "The Red One," by Jack London; "Beyond the Spectrum," by Morgan Robertson; "Impossibility: A Study of Reason and Science," by James F. Sullivan; and "Love and a Triangle," by Stanley Waterloo. The last page of the Griffith story was accidentally omitted by Arno.

SECONDARY SOURCES AND REVIEWS:

1.   Clareson, Thomas D. "The Emergence of Science Fiction: The Beginnings to the 1920s," in *Anatomy of Wonder: A Critical Guide to Science Fiction, Second Edition*, edited by Neil Barron. New York & London: R. R. Bowker Co., 1981, cloth, p. 69.
2.   Clareson, Thomas D. "The Emergence of Science Fiction: The Beginnings to the 1920s," in *Anatomy of Wonder: A Critical Guide to Science Fiction, Third Edition*, edited by Neil Barron. New York & London: R. R. Bowker Co., 1987, cloth, p. 37.
3.   Contento, William. *Index to Science Fiction Anthologies and Collections.* Boston: G. K. Hall & Co., 1978, cloth, p. 174, 464.
4.   Lupoff, Richard A. *Algol* no. 26 (Summer, 1976): 40.
5.   Mullen, Richard D. *Science-Fiction Studies* 2 (July, 1975): 194-195.

A5.   *The Attempted Assassination of John F. Kennedy: A Political Fantasy*, by "Lucas Webb." San Bernardino, CA: The Borgo Press, September 1976, 47 p., paper (ISBN 0-89370-204-8/ISBN 0-87877-204-9 [Newcastle distribution]). LC 76-40282. [novella]

ab.   San Bernardino, CA: The Borgo Press, February 1979, 47 p., cloth (ISBN 0-89370-104-1).

An alternate history of the world in which George Washington was chosen first elected monarch of the United States, under the title "Lord President," thereby altering the history of Europe; and in which Kennedy was never assassinated. Reginald postulates a world order where the old monarchical structures have been maintained, largely excluding the republican form of government, although the Western democracies have evolved much as they did in real history. The pseudonym was chosen serendipitously from a *San Bernardino Sun* marriage announcement (someone named Lucas marrying someone named Webb), and bears no relationship to the pseudonymous "Lucas Webb" who wrote two novels in the 1960s. Later rewritten as *If J.F.K. Had Lived* (see A23).

SECONDARY SOURCES AND REVIEWS:

1. Patten, Frederick. *Delap's F & SF Review* 3 (March, 1977): 24-25.

A6.   *Alistair MacLean: The Key Is Fear*, by Robert A. Lee, anonymously edited and co-authored by R. Reginald. The Milford Series: Popular Writers of Today, Volume Two. San Bernardino, CA: The Borgo Press, October 1976, 60 p., paper (ISBN 0-89370-203-X/ISBN 0-87877-203-0 [Newcastle distribution]). LC 76-29047. [literary critique]

   ab.   San Bernardino, CA: The Borgo Press, February 1979, 60 p., cloth (ISBN 0-89370-103-3).

Faced with a distribution deadline for a title previously announced, Reginald took Lee's first-draft manuscript, a critique of the British suspense writer, and rewrote it from start to finish. It remains one of the weakest books in the Milford Series, consisting primarily of loosely strung-together plot summaries.
   CONTENTS: Introduction, by Robert A. Lee; The War Novels; The Secret Agents; Transitions; Renaissance; The Search for Something New; Conclusion; Biography and Bibliography.

SECONDARY SOURCES AND REVIEWS

1. Broberg, Jan. "Smått Och Gott om Brott," in *Jury* no. 3 (1980): 18.

A7.   *Ancient Hauntings*, edited by Douglas Menville and R. Reginald. Supernatural & Occult Fiction: 63 Books. New York: Arno Press, December 1976, [383] p., cloth (ISBN 0-405-08163-4). LC 75-46303. [anthology]

An anthology of nineteenth-century weird and supernatural fiction, reproduced facsimile from the original sources, mostly single-author book collections. Most of the authors are European.

CONTENTS: "The Ensouled Violin," by H. P. Blavatsky; "The Green Staircase," by Gilbert Campbell; "The Haunted Hansom," by Howell Davies; "The Vial-Genie and Mad Farthing," by Frédéric de La Motte-Fouqué; "The Metempsychosis," by Robert McNish; "Fioraccio," by Giovanni Magherini-Graziani; "A Mystery of the Campagna," by Von Degen [Ann C. Rabe]; "The Green Hands: A Story About a Duet," by George Augustus Sala; and "Ghosts," by Ivan Turgenev.

A8.   *Phantasmagoria*, edited by Douglas Menville and R. Reginald. Supernatural & Occult Fiction: 63 books. New York: Arno Press, December 1976, [357] p., cloth (ISBN 0-405-08152-9). LC 75-46292. [anthology]

  b.   *Phantasmagoria: Classic Tales of the Supernatural.* Mercer Island, WA: Starmont House, 1992, [160] p., cloth. An abridged version of the original.
  bb. *Phantasmagoria: Classic Tales of the Supernatural.* Mercer Island, WA: Starmont House, 1992, [160] p., paper. An abridged version of the original.
  c.   *Phantasmagoria: Classic Tales of the Supernatural.* San Bernardino, CA: The Borgo Press, 1992, [160] p., cloth. An abridged version of the original, with the Borgo Press label stickered over the Starmont imprint on the title page.

An anthology of twentieth-century weird and supernatural fiction, reproduced facsimile from the original sources, usually single-author book collections.
    CONTENTS: "The Closed Cabinet" (anonymous); "The Sanctuary," by E. F. Benson; "The Terror on Tobit," by Charles Lloyd Birkin; "Couching at the Door," by D. K. Broster; "An Amateur Ghost," by James Branch Cabell; "The Demon Pope," by Richard Garnett; "Arria Marcella," by Théophile Gautier; "The Witch Doctor," by Manly P. Hall; "The Seeker of Souls," by Jasper Johns; "The Shadow on the Moor," by the Duke of Northumberland; "The Moon-Slave," by Barry Pain; and "A Porta Inferi," by Roger Pater.

A9.   *R.I.P.: Five Stories of the Supernatural*, edited by R. Reginald and Douglas Menville. Supernatural & Occult Fiction: 63 Books. New York: Arno Press, December 1976, [278] p., cloth (ISBN 0-405-08425-0). LC 76-1539. [anthology]

An anthology of twentieth-century weird and supernatural novellas, reproduced in facsimile from the original sources, including separately-published books and author collections.

CONTENTS: "Souls on Fifth," by Granville Barker; "An Egyptian Love Spell," by Maris Herrington Billings; "Thirty Pieces of Silver," by Clarence B. Kelland; "The Sale of an Appetite," by Paul Lafargue; and "The Cedar Box," by John Oxenham.

A10.   *The Spectre Bridegroom, and Other Horrors*, edited by R. Reginald and Douglas Menville. Supernatural & Occult Fiction: 63 Books. New York: Arno Press, December 1976, [308] p., cloth (ISBN 0-405-08165-0). LC 75-46305. [anthology]

An anthology of nineteenth-century weird and supernatural novellas, reproduced in facsimile from the original sources, including separately-published books and single-author collections.
        CONTENTS: "The Demon Hunter; or, The White Wolf of the Hartz Mountains" (anonymous); "Midnight Horrors; or, The Bandit's Daughter, an Original Romance" (anonymous); "The Spectre Bridegroom, a Terrific and Interesting Tale," by Alexa; "A Noctural Expedition Round My Room," by Xavier de Maistre; "The Pixy; or, The Unbaptized Child, a Story for Christmas," by George W. M. Reynolds; "The Spectre Mother; or, The Haunted Tower" (anonymous); and "The Last of the Vampires, a Tale," by Smyth Upton.

A11.   *Up Your Asteroid! A Science Fiction Farce*, by "C. Everett Cooper." San Bernardino, CA: The Borgo Press, April 1977, 47 p., paper (ISBN 0-89370-206-4). LC 77-866. [novella]

  ab.   San Bernardino, CA: The Borgo Press, February 1979, 47 p., cloth (ISBN 0-89370-106-8).

A science-fiction spoof adapted from the unpublished manuscript, *Star Drek*, which was originally intended to be a parody of the *Star Trek* series. Covers for the original version were printed and later scrapped on the advice of counsel. The penname was *not* taken from Dr. C. Everett Koop, but had been previously used by Reginald early in his writing career, before the other Koop became visible in the public eye.
        The plot of the book—if one exists—is indescribable.

SECONDARY SOURCES AND REVIEWS:

1.   Adlerberth, Roland. "Nya Böcker," in *Jules Verne-Magasinet* no. 376 (1979): 128. [Swedish]

A12. *John D. MacDonald and the Colorful World of Travis McGee*, by Frank D. Campbell, Jr., anonymously edited by R. Reginald. The Milford Series: Popular Writers of Today, Volume Five. San Bernardino, CA: The Borgo Press, April 1977, 63 p., paper (ISBN 0-89370-208-0). LC 77-773. [literary critique]

   ab. San Bernardino, CA: The Borgo Press, February 1979, 63 p., cloth (ISBN 0-89370-108-4).

   Reginald extensively reworked this critique of the modern American mystery and suspense writer and his best-known literary creation.
      CONTENTS: Foreword; Blue; Pink; Purple; Red; Gold; Orange; Amber; Yellow; Gray; Brown; Indigo; Lavender; Tan; Scarlet; Turquoise; Lemon; Biography and Bibliography.

A13. *Things to Come: An Illustrated History of the Science Fiction Film*, by Douglas Menville and R. Reginald, introduction by Ray Bradbury. New York: Times Books, November 1977, xii, 212 p., cloth (ISBN 0-8129-0710-8). LC 77-79033. [film critique]

   ab. New York: Times Books, November 1977, xii, 212 p., trade paper (ISBN 0-8129-6287-7).
   b. San Bernardino, CA: The Borgo Press, 1983, xii, 212 p., cloth (ISBN 0-89370-019-3). The Borgo edition consists of remaindered copies of the original book with a Borgo imprint label placed over the original Times Books imprint on the title page.

   Reginald was approached by Times Books in the Spring of 1977 to do a "coffee-table" history of the science fiction film for the Christmas season, to capitalize on the popularity of the then newly-released film, *Star Wars*. Menville, who had written the first history of the genre in 1959, consented to do half of the work; he contributed the first two chapters. Reginald wrote the last three chapters (covering the period 1950-1977), typeset the text, and completely designed the layout. The book was written in July and August, assembled in August and September of 1977, and rushed into production. A proof cover exists which transposes the names of the authors beneath their respective photographs. The book was remaindered by Times Books in 1983, at which point the remaining cloth copies were purchased by Borgo Press. See also the companion volume, *Futurevisions* (A34).
      CONTENTS: Introduction, by Ray Bradbury. Foreword, by Douglas Menville and R. Reginald (dated August 10, 1977). Chapter 1: Moon Voyages and Metal Maidens (1895-1929). Chapter 2: Serials and Scientists (1930-1949). Chapter 3: Monsters and Menaces (1950-1959). Chap-

ter 4: Monoliths and Monkeys (1960-1969). Chapter 5: Wars and Wizards (1970-1977). Selected Bibliography. Index of Titles.

SECONDARY SOURCES AND REVIEWS:

1. Annas, P. *Science-Fiction Studies* 7 (November, 1980): 323-329.
2. Barron, Neil. "Film and Television," in *Anatomy of Wonder: A Critical Guide to Science Fiction, Third Edition*, edited by Neil Barron. New York & London: R. R. Bowker Co., 1987, cloth, p. 681.
3. Barron, Neil. "Science Fiction on Film and Television," in *Anatomy of Wonder: A Critical Guide to Science Fiction, Second Edition*, edited by Neil Barron. New York & London: R. R. Bowker Co., 1981, cloth, p. 569.
4. Geis, Richard E. *Science Fiction Review* no. 25 (May, 1978): 31.
5. *Magazine of Fantasy & Science Fiction* 54 (May, 1978): 104.
6. *Penthouse* (May, 1978): 49.
7. Tymn, Marshall B. and Roger C. Schlobin. *The Year's Scholarship in Science Fiction and Fantasy: 1976-1979*. Kent, OH: Kent State University Press, 1982, cloth, p. 181.

A14. *Dreamers of Dreams: An Anthology of Fantasy*, edited by Douglas Menville and R. Reginald. Lost Race and Adult Fantasy Fiction: 69 Books. New York: Arno Press, June 1978, [478] p., cloth (ISBN 0-405-11017-0). LC 77-84280. [anthology]

  b. *Dreamers of Dreams: Classic Tales of Fantasy*. Mercer Island, WA: Starmont House, 1992, [160] p., cloth. An abridged version of the original.
  bb. *Dreamers of Dreams: Classic Tales of Fantasy*. Mercer Island, WA: Starmont House, 1991, [160] p., paper. An abridged version of the original.
  c. *Dreamers of Dreams: Classic Tales of Fantasy*. San Bernardino, CA: The Borgo Press, 1992, [160] p., cloth. An abridged version of the original, with the Borgo Press label stickered over the Starmont imprint on the title page.

An anthology of late nineteenth- and twentieth-century fantasy stories, reproduced facsimile from the original sources, mostly single-author story collections.

CONTENTS: "The Affliction of the Plum Pudding," by John Kendrick Bangs; "The Blind God," by Laurence Housman; "The Gray Wolf," by George MacDonald; "The Invisible Giant," by Bram Stoker; "A Professor of Egyptology," by Guy Boothby; "The End of Phaeacia," by

Andrew Lang; "The Last Adventure of Don Quixote," by Kenneth Morris; "Same Time, Same Place," by Mervyn Peake; "That First Affair," by J. A. Mitchell; "The Queen of California," by Edward Everett Hale; "Rutherford the Twice-Born," by Edwin Lester Arnold; "The Journey of the King," by Lord Dunsany; and "The Seekers," by H. E. Bates.

SECONDARY SOURCES AND REVIEWS:

1. Schlobin, Roger C. *The Literature of Fantasy: A Comprehensive, Annotated Bibliography of Modern Fantasy Fiction.* New York & London: Garland Publishing, 1979, cloth, p. 298-299.
2. Tymn, Marshall B., Kenneth J. Zahorski, and Robert H. Boyer. *Fantasy Literature: A Core Collection and Reference Guide.* New York & London: R. R. Bowker Co., 1979, cloth, p. 195.
3. Yoke, Carl. *Science Fiction & Fantasy Book Review* 1 (November, 1979): 140.

A15. *King Solomon's Children: Some Parodies of H. Rider Haggard*, edited by R. Reginald and Douglas A. Menville. Lost Race and Adult Fantasy Fiction: 69 Books. New York: Times Books, June 1978, [564] p., cloth (ISBN 0-405-11018-9). LC 77-84281. [anthology]

Three parodies of the work of Sir Henry Rider Haggard, reproduced facsimile from the original books.
CONTENTS: *King Solomon's Wives; or, The Phantom Mines*, by "Hyder Ragged" (Henry Chartres Biron); *King Solomon's Treasures*, by the Author of "He," "It," "Pa," "Ma," etc. (John De Morgan); and *"Bess," a Companion to "Jess"*, by the Author of "King Solomon's Wives," "King Solomon's Treasures," "He," "It," etc., etc. (John De Morgan). The third selection was originally supposed to have been John De Morgan's *King Solomon's Wives*, a different book from the title listed above, but Arno was unable to locate a copy suitable for reproduction in time to meet the printing deadline.

A16. *They: Three Parodies of H. Rider Haggard's She*, edited by R. Reginald and Douglas Menville. Lost Race and Adult Fantasy Fiction: 69 Books. New York: Times Books, June 1978, [592] p., cloth (ISBN 0-405-11015-4). LC 77-84277. [anthology]

Three parodies of Sir Henry Rider Haggard's famous novel, *She*, reproduced facsimile from the original book versions.
CONTENTS: Introduction, by R. Reginald; *He*, by the Author of "It," "King Solomon's Wives," "Bess," "Much Darker Days," "Mr. Mor-

ton's Subtler," and Other Romances (Andrew Lang and Walter Herries Pollock); *He, a Companion to She, Being a History of the Adventures of J. Theodosius Aristophano on the Island of Rapa Nui in Search of His Immortal Ancestor* (by John De Morgan); and *"It," a Wild, Weird History of Marvelous, Miraculous, Phantasmagorical Adventures in Search of He, She, and Jess, and Leading to the Finding of "It," a Haggard Conclusion* (by John De Morgan). The two-page introduction by Reginald explains the bibliographical mysteries surrounding the nine known contemporaneous book-length Haggard parodies and pastiches.

SECONDARY SOURCES AND REVIEWS:

1.   Schlobin, Roger C.   *The Literature of Fantasy: A Comprehensive, Annotated Bibliography of Modern Fantasy Fiction.*   New York & London: Garland Publishing, 1979, cloth, p. 299.

A17.   *Worlds of Never: Three Fantastic Novels*, edited by Douglas Menville and R. Reginald.   Lost Race and Adult Fantasy Fiction: 69 Books.   New York: Arno Press, June 1978, [430] p., cloth (ISBN 0-405-11016-2).   LC 77-84278. [anthology]

Three short novels of fantasy, reproduced facsimile from their original book publications.
    CONTENTS: *Alice in Blunderland, an Iridescent Dream*, by John Kendrick Bangs; *The Adventures of the Six Princesses of Babylon, in Their Travels to the Temple of Virtue, an Allegory* [by Lucy Peacock]; and *The Log of the Water Wagon; or, The Cruise of the Good Ship "Lithia"*, by Bert Leston Taylor and W. C. Gibson.

SECONDARY SOURCES AND REVIEWS:

1.   Schlobin, Roger C.   *The Literature of Fantasy: A Comprehensive, Annotated Bibliography of Modern Fantasy Fiction.*   New York & London: Garland Publishing, 1979, cloth, p. 299.

A18.   *Science Fiction and Fantasy Literature, a Checklist, 1700-1974; with, Contemporary Science Fiction Authors II*, by R. Reginald; Editorial Associates: Douglas Menville, Mary A. Burgess; Assistants: George Locke, Gordon Johnson, Doris Illes, Barry R. Levin, Michael Grainey.   Detroit: Gale Research Co., October 1979 (but officially released December 7, 1979), xii, vi, 1141, 32 p. of plates, in two volumes, cloth (ISBN 0-8141-1051-1).   LC 76-46130. [bio-bibliography]

This six-year project was a vast expansion and restructuring of *Stella Nova* (see A1).

CONTENTS: The main section is a comprehensive bibliography of fantastic literature from 1700 through the end of 1974, consisting of 15,884 unique titles, with alternate titles, plus complete names and dates of the authors, publishing data, series information, and notes. Also included in Volume 1 are: Title Index, Series Index, Awards Index, and an Ace and Belmont Doubles Index.

Volume 2 includes *Contemporary Science Fiction Authors II*, with biographies of 1443 authors active in the field in recent times, and a 32-page pictorial history of science fiction and fantasy publishing. A lengthy Afterword, describing how the book was compiled, completes the volume. *SFFL* was nominated for the Hugo Award for Best Nonfiction Book of 1979, and was named by *Choice* magazine as one of a hundred noteworthy reference books of the year. It has generally been accepted as the standard bibliography of the field.

SECONDARY SOURCES AND REVIEWS:

1. *Age of the Unicorn* (February, 1980): .
2. *American Notes & Queries* 19 (October, 1980): 31.
3. *American Reference Books Annual* 11 (1980): 552.
4. Barkham, John. *John Barkham Reviews* (February, 1980): .
5. Barron, Neil. "Annotated Bibliography," in *Survey of Modern Fantasy Literature*, edited by Frank N. Magill. Englewood Cliffs, NJ: Salem Press, 1983, cloth, Vol. 5, p. 2520.
6. Barron, Neil. "Bibliographies, Indexes, and Teaching Aids," in *Anatomy of Wonder: Science Fiction*, edited by Neil Barron. New York & London: R. R. Bowker Co., 1976, paper, p. 362-363.
7. Barron, Neil. "General Reference Works," in *Anatomy of Wonder: A Critical Guide to Science Fiction, Third Edition*, edited by Neil Barron. New York & London: R. R. Bowker Co., 1987, cloth, p. 593-594.
8. Barron, Neil. "Indexes and Bibliographies," in *Anatomy of Wonder: A Critical Guide to Science Fiction, Second Edition*, edited by Neil Barron. New York & London: R. R. Bowker Co., 1981, cloth, p. 527.
9. Barron, Neil. *Science Fiction & Fantasy Book Review* 2 (February, 1980): 26.
10. Baumgartner, Kurt O. *Reference Services Review* 11 (Winter, 1983): 87.
11. *Bifrost* (December, 1983): .
12. Bleiler, E. F. *Book World* 10 (December 28, 1980): 4.
13. *Bookdealer* (June 19, 1980): .
14. *Booklist* 77 (June 15, 1981): 1367.

15. Brooks, Ned. *Skiffy Thyme* (Spring, 1980):   .
16. Bunge, C. A. *Wilson Library Bulletin* 54 (April, 1980): 527-528.
17. Charters, Lawrence I. *Locus* no. 231 (March, 1980): 15.
18. *Choice* 17 (June, 1980): 524.
19. Clareson, Thomas D. *Extrapolation* 21 (Spring, 1980): 90-91.
20. Coulson, Robert. *Yandro* (January, 1980):   .
21. Currey, L. W., and Marshall B. Tymn. "Reference Sources for Science Fiction," in *AB Bookman's Weekly* 76 (October 28, 1985): 3086.
22. Elkins, Charles. *Science-Fiction Studies* 7 (November, 1980): 339-341.
23. *Fantasy Media* (December, 1979/January, 1980):   .
24. *Fantasy Newsletter* (January, 1980):   .
25. *Fantasy Newsletter* (March, 1980):   .
26. Feder, Moshe. *Science Fiction Chronicle* (June, 1980):   .
27. Griffin, Brian. *New Library World* 81 (August, 1980): 156-159.
28. Hall, H. W. *RQ Journal* 19 (Summer, 1980): 397.
29. Hall, H. W. *SFBRI: Science Fiction Book Review Index, Volume 10*, by H. W. Hall. College Station, TX: SFBRI, 1979, paper, p. R5.
30. Hedman-Morelius, Iwan. *Dast Magazin* 13 (nr. 2, 1980):   . [Swedish]
31. Justice, Keith L. *Science Fiction, Fantasy, and Horror Reference: An Annotated Bibliography of Works About Literature and Film.* Jefferson, NC & London: McFarland & Co., 1989, cloth, p. 99.
32. Lamens, J. *Prisma* (1980): #80-3313.
33. *Library Journal* 105 (May 15, 1980): 1147.
34. Loomis, Koert C. Jr. *American Reference Books Annual* 11 (1980): 552.
35. Nickerson, Susan L. *Library Journal* 105 (April 1, 1980): 844.
36. Phillips, R. *American Book Collector* n.s. 1 (July/August, 1980): 57-61.
37. "Reference Books of the Trade" *Literary Market Place* (1978): 425.
38. "Reference Books of the Trade." *Literary Market Place* (1982):   .
39. Renard, Jean-Bruno. *Justificate* no. 49 (1970):   . [French]
40. Schlobin, Roger. *Science Fiction & Fantasy Book Review* 2 (February, 1980): 25-26.
41. Schweitzer, Darrell. *Science Fiction Review* 9 (May, 1980): 22.
42. *Science Fiction Chronicle* (January, 1980):   .
43. Searles, Baird. *Isaac Asimov's Science Fiction Magazine* 4 (June, 1980): 18-19.
44. *SFRA Newsletter* (June/July, 1982):   .
45. *SFWA Bulletin* 14 (Winter, 1979): 22-23.
46. Skene, Fran. *Emergency Librarian* 7 (July/August, 1980): 14.
47. *Solaris* (Février, 1980):   . [French]

48. Spiegel, Barry. *Los Angeles Times Book Review* (January 27, 1980): 2. Follow-up letter by Ian Myles Slater appeared in the February 10th issue (p. 2).
49. Spivack, Charlotte. *Literary Research Newsletter* (Summer, 1981): .
50. Staicar, Tom. *Amazing Stories* 27 (August, 1980): 6.
51. Steele, Colin. *Antiquarian Book Monthly Review* (undated): .
52. Stewart, Christina Duff. *Victorian Periodicals Review* (Winter, 1980): .
53. Thiessen, Grant. *Megavore* no. 9 (June, 1980): 47.
54. *Top of the News* 39 (Fall, 1982): 99.
55. Tymn, Marshall B. "Bibliographic Control in Fantastic Literature: An Evaluation of Works Published 1941-1981," in *Special Collections* 2 (Numbers 1/2, 1983): 134-135.
56. Tymn, Marshall B. "Critical Studies and Reference Works," in *The Science Fiction Reference Book: A Comprehensive Handbook and Guide to the History, Literature, Scholarship, and Related Activities of the Science Fiction and Fantasy Fields*, edited by Marshall B. Tymn. Mercer Island, WA: Starmont House, 1981, cloth, p. 65. Published simultaneously in trade paperback.
57. Tymn, Marshall B. and Roger C. Schlobin. *The Year's Scholarship in Science Fiction and Fantasy: 1976-1979*. Kent, OH: Kent State University Press, 1982, cloth, p. 52.
58. Whibley, Vaughan. "Bibliographies." *Library Association Record* (January, 1982): .
59. Woodress, James. "General Reference Works." *American Literary Scholarship* (1979): 537.

A19. *Science Fiction & Fantasy Book Review, Nos. 1-13, February 1979-February 1980.* Publisher: R. Reginald; Assoc. Publisher: Mary A. Burgess; Editor: Neil Barron; Business Manager: Louise Rogers. San Bernardino, CA: The Borgo Press, February 1980, 164, 32 p., cloth (ISBN 0-89370-624-8). [literary criticism]

When *SF&FBR* ceased publication in February of 1980, Borgo bound together many of the remaining stock into cloth form for the library market, listing it in *Books in Print* and its own catalogs. Reginald reworked much of the material in the magazine as he prepared each issue for publication, in essence acting as an uncredited co-editor with Barron, and uncredited co-author with many of the reviewers.

SECONDARY SOURCES AND REVIEWS:

1. Hall, Hal W. "Magazines." *Library Journal* 105 (February 15, 1980): 493.

2.   Lareau, Chris. *Sense of Wonder* (August, 1979): .

A20.   *The Paperback Price Guide, First Edition*, by Kevin B. Hancer, adapted
without credit from *Cumulative Paperback Index, 1939-1959*, by R.
Reginald and M. R. Burgess. Cleveland, TN: Overstreet Publications,
September 1980, xviii, 430 p., cloth (ISBN 0-517-54225-0). LC 80-
150049. [price guide]

   ab.   Cleveland, TN: Overstreet Publications, September 1980, xviii, 419 p.,
trade paper.
   b.   San Bernardino, CA: The Borgo Press, 1982, xviii, 419 p., cloth (ISBN
0-89370-049-5). The original edition with a Borgo Press imprint label
pasted over the Overstreet imprint.

The bibliographic data which constitute the heart of this book were copied
wholesale from A2, including a hundred check entries, typographical mistakes, and other errors. In an ensuing action, the author's right to the material was confirmed, resulting in the addition of Reginald's name as co-
author to all future editions of the book. See also: A2, A25, and A52.
   CONTENTS: Introduction. The rest of the book consists of paperbacks published through 1959, arranged by publisher (in alphabetical order), then chronologically by stock number. Each entry includes stock
number, title, author, market price, and subject category.

SECONDARY SOURCES AND REVIEWS:

1.   Bates, D. & S. *SF & F Journal* no. 92 (September, 1981): R2.

A21.   *Science Fiction & Fantasy Awards, Including Complete Checklists of the
Hugo Awards, Nebula Awards, Locus Awards, Jupiter Awards, Pilgrim
Awards, International Fantasy Awards, Ditmar Awards, August Derleth
Awards, World Fantasy Awards, Eaton Awards, Gandalf Awards,
British Fantasy Awards, John W. Campbell Memorial Awards, Milford
Awards, Prometheus Awards, and Selected Foreign Awards, with a
Complete Index to Winners, a List of Officers of the Science Fiction
Writers of America from the Beginning of That Organization, a Check-
list of World Science Fiction Conventions and Their Guests of Honor,
and Detailed Statistical Tables*, by R. Reginald. Borgo Reference Li-
brary, Vol. II. San Bernardino, CA: The Borgo Press, December 1981,
64 p., cloth (ISBN 0-89370-806-2). LC 80-10788. [index]

   ab.   San Bernardino, CA: The Borgo Press, December 1981, 64 p., trade paper
(ISBN 0-89370-906-9).

The first comprehensive listing of the annual awards presented to and by the writers, editors, and fans of the science fiction, fantasy, and horror genres.

CONTENTS: Includes chronological lists of winners, by award name (listed alphabetically) and year the award was given; a name index to the winners; a listing of the officers of the Science Fiction Writers of America from the beginning of that organization in 1965 through 1980; a list of World Science Fiction conventions and their guests of honor, from 1939; and statistical tables showing who has won the most awards. See also the second edition (A58).

SECONDARY SOURCES AND REVIEWS:

1. Barron, Neil. *Science Fiction & Fantasy Book Review* n.s. no. 4 (May, 1982): 13.
2. Coulson, Robert. *Amazing Stories* 56 (March, 1983): 15.
3. Green, Roland. *Booklist* 78 (June 15, 1982): 1350.
4. *Vertical File Index* (April, 1982): 13.

A22. *The Holy Grail Revealed: The Real Secret of Rennes-Le-Château*, by Patricia and Lionel Fanthorpe, edited and with an introduction by R. Reginald. North Hollywood, CA: Newcastle Publishing Co., April 1982, 144 p., paper (ISBN 0-87877-060-7). LC 82-6315. [occult]

b. San Bernardino, CA: The Borgo Press, April 1982, 144 p, cloth (ISBN 0-89730-660-4). LC 82-4303. This is a rebinding of the Newcastle edition, with a Borgo Press label placed over the original Newcastle imprint on the title page.

c. San Bernardino, CA: The Borgo Press, November 1986, 144 p., cloth (ISBN 0-89370-660-4). A true second printing with the Borgo imprint and date, printed with blank paper covers, and rebound in cloth.

cb. San Bernardino, CA: The Borgo Press, September 1989, 154 p., cloth (ISBN 0-89370-660-4). A third printing which includes a new ten-page index prepared by Mary A. Burgess and Reginald. The book was printed with blank paper covers, and rebound in cloth.

The publication of Baigent, Leigh, and Lincoln's 1982 book, *Holy Blood, Holy Grail* aroused a storm of controversy over its allegations of Christ's supposed non-death on the cross, and subsequent merging of the Savior's bloodline with that of the royal houses of Europe. R. Lionel Fanthorpe, a well-known British author, had previously submitted to Newcastle a manuscript entitled, *The Mysterious Treasure of Rennes-Le-Château*, which dealt with one facet of the subject.

With the authors' permission, Reginald took the manuscript, and re-worked it as a response to Baigent, Leigh, and Lincoln, rearranging the chapters and arguments, inserting bridge passages, substantially editing the text, and contributing a lengthy introduction which systematically refuted Baigent's so-called "proofs." Reginald also designed and typeset the book.

CONTENTS: Foreword; Introduction: Once Upon a Time, by R. Reginald; 1. The Man; 2. The Place; 3. Treasures of Jerusalem and Rome; 4. Franks, Merovingians, and Carolingians; 5. The Cathars, or Albigensians; 6. The Templars; 7. The Priory of Sion; 8. The Broken Tombstone; 9. The Scrolls Behind the Altar; 10. Rennes-le-Château and the Tarot; 11. Poussin and Teniers; 12. Sir Francis Bacon's Cipher; 13. The Shugborough Hall Mystery; 14. Victor Hugo; 15. The Habsburg Dimension; 16. Henri Buthion's Story; 17. Theories Old and New; 18. The Grail Trail of Baigent, Leigh, and Lincoln; 19. The Holy Grail Revealed: An Answer.

A23.   *If J.F.K. Had Lived: A Political Scenario*, by R. Reginald and Jeffrey M. Elliot. Borgo Political Scenarios, Number 1. San Bernardino, CA: The Borgo Press, April 1982, 64 p., cloth (ISBN 0-89370-155-6). LC 81-19516. [novella]

    ab.   San Bernardino, CA: The Borgo Press, April 1982, 64 p., trade paper (ISBN 0-89370-255-2).

A rewritten version of A5, which postulates a world in which the monarchical systems of the Old World never died, and in which Kennedy was never assassinated. Reginald contributed a new section running from pages 18-30, plus new paragraphs scattered throughout the text, some editing of the original material, a new afterword, and study questions. Elliot contributed a new introduction, and some editing of the overall work. This new edition was designed specifically for classroom use.

A24.   *Candle for Poland: 469 Days of Solidarity*, by Dr. Leszek Szymanski, edited by R. Reginald. San Bernardino, CA: The Borgo Press, June 1982, 128 p., cloth (ISBN 0-89370-166-1). LC 82-1231. [current affairs]

    ab.   San Bernardino, CA: The Borgo Press, June 1982, 128 p., trade paper (ISBN 0-89370-266-8).

A history of the Solidarity movement in Poland. The original manuscript, written by a Polish emigré with only partial fluency in English, required extensive editing and rewriting by Reginald to make it publishable.

CONTENTS: Introduction; 1. Struggle for Bread and Freedom: The Magna Carta in the Soviet Empire; 2. Triumph: More Freedom Than Bread; 3. What Is To Be Done? The Burden of the Past and the Threat of the Future; Appendices: A. "On the Present Methods of Prosecution of Illegal Anti-Socialist Activities; B. An Open Letter to Shipyard Workers and All Costal Workers, by Jacek Kuron; C. The Gdansk Accord; D. The Constitution of the Independent, Self-Governing Trade Union Solidarity [excerpts]; E. Government's Report on the Economy and a Program of Reform, August, 1981; F. Who Are the Anti-Socialists?; G. The Program of ISTU Solidarity; H. The Radom Declaration; I. Members of the Presidium of the National Commission of Solidarity; Bibliography; Biographical Notes; Glossary; Index. The book was dedicated by Szymanski to Reginald.

SECONDARY SOURCES AND REVIEWS:

1. Bouscaren, Anthony T. *American Political Science Review* 77 (September, 1983): 794-795.
2. *Choice* 20 (July/August, 1983): 1648.
3. *Jahrbücher für Geschichte Osteuropas* 31 (1983): 41.
4. Kirschbaum, Stanislav. *Canadian Slavonic Papers* 25 (December, 1983): 606-607.
5. Reuben, Ben. "Paper Weight." *Los Angeles Times Book Review* (September 5, 1982): 4.
6. Stern, Fritz. *Foreign Affairs* 61 (Winter, 1982/83): 475.

A25. *The Paperback Price Guide No. 2*, by Kevin B. Hancer with R. Reginald. Cleveland, TN: Overstreet Publications, September 1982, xvii, 390 p., trade paper (ISBN 0-517-54453-9). LC 82-11790. [price guide]

b. San Bernardino, CA: The Borgo Press, October 1982, xvii, 390 p., cloth (ISBN 0-89370-745-7). The Borgo edition consists of rebound copies of the original, with a Borgo imprint label placed over the original title page imprint of Overstreet.

bb. San Bernardino, CA: The Borgo Press, October 1982, xvii, 390 p., trade paper (ISBN 0-89370-899-2). The Borgo edition consists of rebound copies of the original, with a Borgo imprint label placed over the original title page imprint of Overstreet.

A revision and expansion of A20. The bibliographical data were taken with permission from *Cumulative Paperback Index, 1939-1959* (see A2), although Reginald contributed nothing new to this particular version. In the Summer of 1984, Borgo acquired all remaining unsold copies of the paperback edition, eventually declaring this version out of print in 1987, and selling cloth copies only thereafter.

CONTENTS: Introduction; Main Listings; Author Cross-Index. The data is arranged alphabetically by publishing company, then chronologically by book stock number. Each entry typically includes: stock number, title, author, valuations, and category.

SECONDARY SOURCES AND REVIEWS:

1. Budrys, Algis. *The Magazine of Fantasy & Science Fiction* 64 (April, 1983): 47-48.

A26.   *The House of the Burgesses, Being a Genealogical History of Edward Burges of King George and Stafford Counties, Virginia, with His Sons—Garner Burges of Fauquier Co., Virginia; William Burgess of Stafford Co., Virginia; Moses Burgess of Orange Co., Virginia; Reuben Burgess of Rowan Co., North Carolina—and His Grandsons—Edward Burgess of Culpeper Co., Virginia; John Burgess of Harrison Co., Kentucky; Henry Burgess of Fleming Co., Kentucky; Edward Burgess of Scott Co., Kentucky; John P. B. Burgess of Halifax Co., Virginia; Edward Burgess of Kanawha Co., West Virginia; William Burgess of Davie Co., North Carolina; Reuben Burgess of Davie Co., North Carolina; and Thomas Burgess of White Co., Tennessee—Together with Their Known Descendants Named Burgess*, by M. R. Burgess. Borgo Family Histories, Number 1. San Bernardino, CA: The Borgo Press, February 1983, xii, 156 p., cloth (ISBN 0-89370-801-1). LC 80-10759. [genealogy]

ab.   San Bernardino, CA: The Borgo Press, February 1983, xii, 156 p., trade paper (ISBN 0-89370-901-8).

A genealogical history of the author's family, listing some 2,400 descendants in the male line of Edward Burges of King George and Stafford Cos., Virginia (who died in 1759). Includes chart, indices, and illustrations. A second edition is underway (see A75).

SECONDARY SOURCES AND REVIEWS:

1. Everton, Louise M. "New on the Bookshelf." *Genealogical Helper* 37 (July/August, 1983): 168.
2. M., E. S. *Kansas City Genealogist* 24 (1983?): 96.

A27.   *The Wickizer Annals: Wickizer, Wickiser, Wickkiser, Wickkizer, Wick-heiser,* by Mary Wickizer Burgess, with M. R. Burgess. Borgo Family Histories, Number 2. San Bernardino, CA: The Borgo Press, February 1983, xviii, 126 p., cloth (ISBN 0-89370-802-X). LC 80-11075. [genealogy]

   ab.   San Bernardino, CA: The Borgo Press, February 1983, xviii, 126 p., trade paper (ISBN 0-89370-902-6).

   A genealogical history of the author's wife's family, listing some 1,700 descendants in the male line of Conrad Wickizer of Luzerne Co., Pennsylvania. Includes chart, indices, and illustrations.

   SECONDARY SOURCES AND REVIEWS:

   1.   Everton, Louise M. "New on the Bookshelf." *Genealogical Helper* 37 (July/August, 1983): 176.

A28.   *Tempest in a Teapot: The Falkland Islands War,* by R. Reginald and Jeffrey M. Elliot. Stokvis Studies in Historical Chronology and Thought, Number 3. San Bernardino, CA: The Borgo Press, August 1983, 176 p., cloth (ISBN 0-89370-167-X). LC 83-8807. [political science]

   ab.   San Bernardino, CA: The Borgo Press, August 1983, 176 p., trade paper (ISBN 0-89370-267-6).
   b.   *Congressional Record* 131 (April 22, 1985): E1623-E1626. A reproduction of the concluding Chapter V (by Reginald), as inserted by U.S. Representative Mervyn M. Dymally (D-Calif.).

   The first objective history of the Falklands conflict. Reginald wrote all of the material except for Chapter IV, the interviews with the two officials, which Elliot obtained on a trip to New York. Both authors edited each others' sections. Reginald also designed the book.
   CONTENTS: Introduction; Chronology. I. Invitation to a Tea Party: 1. The Falkland Islands/Las Islas Malvinas; 2. Colonial Land Claims; 3. The British Occupation of the Islands. II. A Simmering Brew: 1. The Argentine Government; 2. A Period of Negotiations; 3. Impasse. III. The Pot Boils Over: 1. Ominous Mutterings; 2. The Argentine Invasion; 3. War! IV. Pekoe and Pekoe: Two Views on the Falklands: 1. Background to the Interviews; 2. The Official British Position; 3. The Official Argentine Position. V. Reading the Tea Leaves: 1. Claims and Blames; 2. To the Last Dregs; 3. Prognostications. Appendices: A. Governors of the Falkland Islands; B. Chart of Forces and Losses; C. Selected Documents. Notes; Bibliography; Index; Maps.

SECONDARY SOURCES AND REVIEWS:

1. *Choice* 21 (February, 1984): 876.
2. Johnson, Wayne E. *Texas Journal of Political Studies* 6 (Spring/ Summer, 1984): 77-78.
3. *Latin America and Caribbean Contemporary Record, Volume III, 1983-1984*, edited by Jack W. Hopkins. New York & London: Holmes & Meier, 1984, cloth, p. 1265.
4. *Raleigh News & Observer* (October 3, 1983): .
5. Scheck, George, Mary Ann Varoutsos, and Jane Viti. "Recent Books." *Naval War College Review* 37 (November/December, 1984): 128.
6. W., T. L. *Latin America in Books* (July, 1983): 23.
7. Witherspoon, David. "History of Falkland Islands Provides Objective Look of 'Bizarre Little War'." *Durham Morning Herald* 90 (October 2, 1983): .

A29.   *A Guide to Science Fiction and Fantasy in the Library of Congress Classification Scheme*, by Michael Burgess. The Borgo Reference Library, Vol. VIII. San Bernardino, CA: The Borgo Press, August 1984, 86 p., cloth (ISBN 0-89370-807-0). LC 80-11418. [cataloging manual]

ab.   San Bernardino, CA: The Borgo Press, August 1984, 86 p., spiral-bound paper (ISBN 0-89370-907-7).

A comprehensive guide to the cataloging of science fiction and fantasy in the Library of Congress (LC) classification system. See also the second edition (A40).
CONTENTS: Introduction, Subject Headings, Author Main Entries and Literature and Bibliography Numbers, Artist Main Entries and Artist Numbers, Motion Picture and Television Main Entries and Classification Numbers, Subject Classification Numbers, Index to Subject Classification Numbers.

SECONDARY SOURCES AND REVIEWS:

1. *AB Bookman's Weekly* 74 (October 1, 1984): 2155.
2. *AB Bookman's Weekly* 76 (October 28, 1985): 3128.
3. *American Reference Book Annual* 16 (1985): 379.
4. Barron, Neil. "General Reference Works," in *Anatomy of Wonder: A Critical Guide to Science Fiction, Third Edition*, edited by Neil Barron. New York & London: R. R. Bowker Co., 1987, cloth, p. 603.
5. Clareson, Thomas D. *Extrapolation* 25 (December, 1984): 374-375.

6. Elkins, Charles. *Science-Fiction Studies* 12 (March, 1985): 103.
7. *Extrapolation* 25 (Winter, 1985): 374-375.
8. Galbreath, R. *Fantasy Review* 8 (February, 1985): 29.

A30. **The Work of Jeffrey M. Elliot: An Annotated Bibliography & Guide**, by Boden Clarke. Bibliographies of Modern Authors, Number 2. San Bernardino, CA: The Borgo Press, December 1984, 50 p., cloth (ISBN 0-89370-381-8). LC 84-21745. [bibliography]

ab. San Bernardino, CA: The Borgo Press, December 1984, 50 p., trade paper (ISBN 0-89370-481-4).

An annotated bibliography of the works of Dr. Jeffrey M. Elliot, well-known American political scientist, interviewer, commentator, scholar, and specialist on minority studies. This was the first *published* volume in the Bibliographies of Modern Authors series, and set the pattern for all the rest.

CONTENTS: Introduction; Section A. Books; Section B. Articles; Section C. Book Reviews; Section D. Letters to the Editor; Section E. Speeches and Papers; Section F. Television Productions and Appearances; Section G. Radio Appearances; Section H. Other Media; Section J. Honors and Awards; Section K. About the Author; Section L. Unpublished Works; Quoth the Critics; Title Index.

SECONDARY SOURCES & REVIEWS:

1. Brown, Charles N. and William G. Contento. *Science Fiction in Print: 1985: A Comprehensive Bibliography of Books and Short Fiction Published in the English Language*. Oakland, CA: Locus Press, 1986, cloth, p. 18.
2. Palen, Roberta R. *American Reference Books Annual* 17 (1986): 260.

A31. **The Work of R. Reginald: An Annotated Bibliography & Guide**, by Michael Burgess with Jeffrey M. Elliot. Bibliographies of Modern Authors, Number 5. San Bernardino, CA: The Borgo Press, January 1985, 48 p., cloth (ISBN 0-89370-384-2). LC 84-21672. [bibliography]

ab. San Bernardino, CA: The Borgo Press, January 1985, 48 p., trade paper (ISBN 0-89370-484-9).

An annotated bibliography of the works of R. Reginald, well-known American publisher, librarian, author, and editor. See also the Second Edition (A60).

CONTENTS: "I Fear the Greeks...": An Introduction, by Jeffrey M. Elliot; Section A: Books; B: Articles and Reviews; Section C: Periodicals, Serials, and Publishing Companies; Section D: Juvenilia; Section E: Radio and Television Appearances; Section F: About the Author; Section G: Honors and Awards; Section H: Unpublished Works; Section J: Miscellanea; Index.

SECONDARY SOURCES AND REVIEWS:

1. Brown, Charles N. and William G. Contento. *Science Fiction in Print: 1985: A Comprehensive Bibliography of Books and Short Fiction Published in the English Language.* Oakland, CA: Locus Press, 1986, cloth, p. 16.

A32. *The Work of Julian May: An Annotated Bibliography & Guide*, by Thaddeus Dikty and R. Reginald. Bibliographies of Modern Authors, Number 3. San Bernardino, CA: The Borgo Press, March 1985, 66 p., cloth (ISBN 0-89370-382-6). LC 84-21705. [bibliography]

ab. San Bernardino, CA: The Borgo Press, March 1985, 66 p., trade paper (ISBN 0-89370-482-2).

A bibliography of the works of this well-known American children's writer and science fiction novelist, co-authored with her husband, T. E. Dikty, well-known SF anthologist and publisher of Starmont House.

CONTENTS: Introduction, by Ted Dikty; Section A. Books; Section B. Articles; Section C. Short Fiction; Section D. Study Prints; Section E. Lesson Plans; Section F. Kits; Section G. Audio Cassettes; Section H. Audio Recordings; Section I. Music; Section J. Maps; Section K. Media Productions; Section L. About the Author; Section M. Unpublished Works; Section N. Miscellanea; Title Index.

SECONDARY SOURCES AND REVIEWS:

1. Barron, Neil. "Author Studies," in *Anatomy of Wonder: A Critical Guide to Science Fiction, Third Edition*, edited by Neil Barron. New York & London: R. R. Bowker Co., 1987, cloth, p. 654-655.
2. Brake, Laurel, ed. *The Year's Work in English Studies, Volume 66, 1985*. London: Published for The English Association by John Murray, 1988, cloth, p. 629-630.

3. Brown, Charles N. and William G. Contento. *Science Fiction in Print: 1985: A Comprehensive Bibliography of Books and Short Fiction Published in the English Language.* Oakland, CA: Locus Press, 1986, cloth, p. 22.
4. Clareson, Thomas D. *Extrapolation* 26 (1985): 262.
5. D'Ammassa, Don. *Science Fiction Chronicle* 7 (October, 1985): 43.
6. Fratz, D. *Thrust* no. 24 (Summer, 1986): 25.
7. Kelly, Richard J. *American Reference Books Annual* 17 (1986): 446.

A33. *Lords Temporal and Lords Spiritual: A Chronological Checklist of the Popes, Patriarchs, Katholikoi, and Independent Archbishops and Metropolitans of the Monarchical Autocephalous Churches of the Christian East and West,* by Boden Clarke. Stokvis Studies in Historical Chronology and Thought, Number 1. San Bernardino, CA: The Borgo Press, May 1985, 136 p., cloth (ISBN 0-89370-800-3). LC 80-10979. [history]

ab. San Bernardino, CA: The Borgo Press, May 1985, 136 p., trade paper (ISBN 0-89370-900-X).

A history and chronology of the Eastern Orthodox churches, as reflected in their elected primates. Reginald spent twenty years researching this book, transliterating the names of the church leaders from sources in the original languages of each ecclesiastical body.

CONTENTS: Introduction, Abbreviations, Aght'amar, Albania, Albania (Caucasian), Alexandria (Coptic), Alexandria (Coptic Catholic), Alexandria (Greek), America (Various Churches), Antioch (Greek), Antioch (Greek Melkite), Antioch (Maronite), Antioch (Syrian Catholic), Antioch (Syrian Jacobite), Armenia, Assyria, Babylon and Assyria (Chaldean), Belorussia, Bulgaria, Cilicia (Armenian Apostolic), Cilicia (Armenian Catholic), Constantinople (Armenian), Constantinople (Greek), Cyprus, Czechoslovakia, Estonia, Ethiopia, Georgia, Greece, Jerusalem (Armenian), Jerusalem (Greek), Latvia, Macedonia and Ohrid, Malabar and Malankara, Poland, Romania, Rome, Russia, Serbia and Pec, Sinai, Turkey, Ukraine, Selected Bibliography, Comparative Name Tables, Index. Each chapter includes a brief history of the church, focusing particularly on its claims of apostolic succession, plus a chronological checklist of its primates.

See also the second edition (A64).

SECONDARY SOURCES AND REVIEWS:

1. Russell, Norman. *Sobornost* 8 (no. 1, 1986): 68-69.
2. Youdell, Basil. *Orthodox News* 2 (July, 1985): 4.

A34.   *Futurevisions: The New Golden Age of the Science Fiction Film*, by Douglas Menville and R. Reginald, with Mary A. Burgess. North Hollywood, CA: A Greenbriar Book, Newcastle Publishing Co., October 1985, 192 p., trade paper (ISBN 0-87877-081-X). LC 85-20098. [film critique]

   b.   San Bernardino, CA: The Borgo Press, October 1985, 192 p., cloth (ISBN 0-89730-681-7). This is a rebinding of the Newcastle edition, with a Borgo Press label placed over the original Newcastle imprint on the title page.

   A copiously-illustrated sequel to *Things to Come* (see A13). Menville contributed the first three chapters, Reginald and Burgess the last two chapters, and Reginald the Foreword; Reginald also edited the first three chapters, and designed the layout of the book. Includes over a hundred illustrations from the original motion pictures, including a number of full-page spreads.
   CONTENTS: Introduction, by William F. Nolan; Foreword, by Douglas Menville and R. Reginald (but written by Reginald); Chapter 1. Futures Past (1897-1976); Chapter 2. Starships and Superheroes (1977-1979); Telepaths and Time Travelers (1980-1981); Horrors and Holocausts (1982-1983); Dreams and Dimensions (1984-1985); Selected Bibliography; Title Index.
   The book was a featured alternate selection of the Movie Book Club (which redistributed copies of the Newcastle printing).

SECONDARY SOURCES AND REVIEWS:

   1.   Barron, Neil. "Film and Television," in *Anatomy of Wonder: A Critical Guide to Science Fiction, Third Edition*, edited by Neil Barron. New York & London: R. R. Bowker Co., 1987, cloth, p. 681.
   2.   Brown, Charles N. and William G. Contento. *Science Fiction in Print: 1985: A Comprehensive Bibliography of Books and Short Fiction Published in the English Language*. Oakland, CA: Locus Press, 1986, cloth, p. 44.
   3.   Fratz, D. *Thrust* no. 24 (Summer, 1986): 25.
   4.   Searles, Baird. *Isaac Asimov's Science Fiction Magazine* 10 (December, 1986): 189-190.
   5.   Zebrowski, George. *The Bulletin of the Science Fiction Writers of America* 20 (Winter, 1986): 17.

A35.   *The Work of Bruce McAllister: An Annotated Bibliography & Guide*, by David Ray Bourquin, anonymously edited by R. Reginald. Bibliographies of Modern Authors, Number 10. San Bernardino, CA: The Borgo Press, December 1985, 30 p., cloth (ISBN 0-89370-389-3). LC 85-22400. [bibliography]

ab.   San Bernardino, CA: The Borgo Press, December 1985, 30 p., trade paper (ISBN 0-89370-489-X).

Reginald edited the manuscript to fit the series format, added some new data, and rewrote the introduction. See also the revised edition (A38).
    CONTENTS: Introduction; A. Books; B. Short Fiction; C. Non-Fiction; D. Poetry; E. Graphic/Experimental Work; F. Papers; G. Editorial Posts; H. Media Appearances; I. Awards and Prizes; J. About the Author; Critical Comments; Title Index.

A36.   *The Work of Charles Beaumont: An Annotated Bibliography & Guide*, by William F. Nolan, edited by R. Reginald. Bibliographies of Modern Authors, Number 6. San Bernardino, CA: The Borgo Press, May 1986, 48 p., cloth (ISBN 0-89370-385-0). LC 85-460. [bibliography]

ab.   San Bernardino, CA: The Borgo Press, May 1986, 48 p., trade paper (ISBN 0-89370-485-7).
ac.   San Bernardino, CA: The Borgo Press, January 1988, 48 p., cloth (ISBN 0-89370-385-0). Identical to the first edition except for "Second Printing" notice.
ad.   San Bernardino, CA: The Borgo Press, January 1988, 48 p., trade paper (ISBN 0-89370-485-7). Identical to the first edition except for "Second Printing" notice.

Reginald took Nolan's manuscript, originally prepared as a supplement to Harold Lee Prosser's *Running from the Hunter: The Life and Works of Charles Beaumont*, and adapted it to the series format, with further assistance from Nolan. This volume represented the first major overhaul in the series format.
    CONTENTS: Introduction; A. Books; B. Fiction; C. Non-Fiction; D. Screenplays; E. Teleplays; F. Comics; G. Letters; H. Unpublished Stories; I. Awards; J. Artwork; K. Editorial Posts; L. About the Author; Title Index.
    See also the second edition (A55).

SECONDARY SOURCES AND REVIEWS:

1.   Brown, Charles N., and William G. Contento. *Science Fiction, Fantasy, & Horror 1988: A Comprehensive Bibliography of Books and*

Short Fiction Published in the English Language. Oakland, CA: Locus Press, 1989, cloth, p. 59.
2. Prosser, H. L. *Fantasy Review* 9 (November, 1986): 37.

A37. *The Work of George Zebrowski: An Annotated Bibliography & Guide*, by Jeffrey M. Elliot & R. Reginald. Bibliographies of Modern Authors, Number 4. San Bernardino, CA: The Borgo Press, May 1986, 54 p., cloth (ISBN 0-89370-383-4). LC 84-24239. [bibliography]

ab. San Bernardino, CA: The Borgo Press, May 1986, 54 p., trade paper (ISBN 0-89370-483-0).

A comprehensive bibliography of the novels, anthologies, stories, and essays of a well known Polish-American writer. Some of the material is based on information supplied from Zebrowski's own files and personal collection of his works.
CONTENTS: Introduction, by Dr. Jeffrey M. Elliot; A. Books; B. Short Fiction; C. Translations; D. Articles and Reviews; E. Journals and Publishing Series; F. Juvenilia; G. About the Author; H. Honors and Awards; I. Public Appearances; J. Unpublished Works; K. Miscellanea; Quoth the Critics; Title Index.
See also the second edition (A53).

SECONDARY SOURCES AND REVIEWS:

1. *Analog Science Fiction/Science Fact* 107 (May, 1987): 179.
2. *Vertical File Index* (December, 1987): 29.

A38. *The Work of Bruce McAllister: An Annotated Bibliography & Guide*, [Revised Edition], by David Ray Bourquin, edited and anonymously co-authored by R. Reginald. Bibliographies of Modern Authors, Number 10. San Bernardino, CA: The Borgo Press, May 1986, 32 p., cloth (ISBN 0-89370-389-3). LC 85-22400. [bibliography]

ab. San Bernardino, CA: The Borgo Press, May 1986, 32 p., trade paper (ISBN 0-89370-489-X).

Reginald edited the manuscript to fit the series format, added some new data, and rewrote the introduction. This edition was completely reset into the new series format, and updated with new material. See also the original edition (A35).
CONTENTS: Introduction; A. Books; B. Short Fiction; C. Non-Fiction; D. Poetry; E. Graphic/Experimental Work; F. Papers; G. Edito-

rial Posts; H. Media Appearances; I. Awards and Prizes; J. About the Author; Critical Comments; Title Index.

A39.   *Mystery and Detective Fiction in the Library of Congress Classification Scheme*, by Michael Burgess. Borgo Cataloging Guides, Number Two. San Bernardino, CA: The Borgo Press, December 1987, 184 p., cloth (ISBN 0-89370-818-6). LC 84-12344. [cataloging manual]

ab.   San Bernardino, CA: The Borgo Press, December 1987, 184 p., trade paper (ISBN 0-89370-918-2).

A comprehensive guide to LC cataloging practice in the field of mystery and detective fiction, organized similarly to the previous volume on science fiction and fantasy (see A29 and A40).
   CONTENTS: Introduction; I. Subject Headings; II. Classification Numbers; Index to Classification Numbers; III. Author Main Entries and Literature Numbers; LC Literature Tables; IV. Motion Picture Main Entries and Classification Numbers; V. Television Program Main Entries and Classification Numbers; VI. Comic Strip Main Entries and Classification Numbers.

SECONDARY SOURCES AND REVIEWS:

1.   Breen, Jon L. *The Armchair Detective* 23 (Spring, 1990): 214.
2.   D'Ammassa, Don. *Science Fiction Chronicle* 10 (February, 1989): 37.
3.   Osborn, Jeanne. *Library and Information Science Annual* Vol. 5 (1989): 85-86.

A40.   *A Guide to Science Fiction and Fantasy in the Library of Congress Classification Scheme, Second Edition, Revised and Expanded*, by Michael Burgess. Borgo Cataloging Guides, Number One. San Bernardino, CA: The Borgo Press, February 1988, 168 p., cloth (ISBN 0-89370-827-5). LC 87-6308. [cataloging manual]

ab.   San Bernardino, CA: The Borgo Press, February 1988, 168 p., trade paper (ISBN 0-89370-927-1).

An extensive revision and updating of the author's 1984 book (see A29), virtually doubling its size, adding several new sections, and reworking and rechecking all old material.
   CONTENTS: Introduction; I. Subject Headings; II. Classification Numbers; Index to Classification Numbers; III. Author Main Entries and

Literature Numbers; LC Literature Tables; IV. Artist Main Entries and Artist Numbers; V. Motion Picture Main Entries and Classification Numbers; VI. Television and Radio Program Main Entries and Classification Numbers; VII. Comic Strip Main Entries and Classification Numbers; About the Author.

SECONDARY SOURCES AND REVIEWS:

1. Barron, Neil. "Library Guide Revisited," in *The SFRA Newsletter* no. 162 (November, 1988): 28.
2. Brown, Charles N., and William G. Contento. *Science Fiction, Fantasy, & Horror 1988: A Comprehensive Bibliography of Books and Short Fiction Published in the English Language.* Oakland, CA: Locus Press, 1989, cloth, p. 16.
3. D'Ammassa, Don. *Science Fiction Chronicle* 10 (February, 1989): 37.
4. "1988 Research Index," by Hal W. Hall, in *Science Fiction, Fantasy, & Horror 1988: A Comprehensive Bibliography of Books and Short Fiction Published in the English Language*, edited by Charles N. Brown, and William G. Contento. Oakland, CA: Locus Press, 1989, cloth, p. 399.
5. Osborn, Jeanne. *Library and Information Science Annual* Vol. 5 (1989): 85.

A41. *Western Fiction in the Library of Congress Classification Scheme*, by Michael Burgess and Beverly A. Ryan. Borgo Cataloging Guides, Number Three. San Bernardino, CA: The Borgo Press, October 1988, 48 p., cloth (ISBN 0-89370-822-4). LC 87-6309. [cataloging manual]

ab. San Bernardino, CA: The Borgo Press, October 1988, 48 p., trade paper (ISBN 0-89370-922-0).

A comprehensive guide to Library of Congress cataloging practices for Western fiction and literature. Burgess prepared the original format and authors' list, and searched about a third of the entries through OCLC; Ryan added additional names to the original list, and searched all remaining entries. Burgess then took the raw data, resolved any conflicts, and completed the book.

CONTENTS: Introduction; I. Subject Headings; II. Classification Numbers; Index to Classification Numbers; III. Author Main Entries and Literature Numbers; LC Literature Tables; IV. Motion Picture Main Entries and Classification Numbers; V. Television Program Main Entries and Classification Numbers; VI. Radio Program Main Entries and Classification Numbers.

SECONDARY SOURCES AND REVIEWS:

1. Osborn, Jeanne. *American Reference Books Annual* 21 (1990): 248.

A42. *California Ranchos: Patented Private Land Grants Listed by County*, by
Burgess McK. Shumway, edited by Michael and Mary Burgess. Stokvis
Studies in Historical Chronology and Thought, Number 11.   San
Bernardino, CA: The Borgo Press; Glendale, CA: The Sidewinder
Press, October 1988, 144 p., cloth (ISBN 0-89370-835-6).   LC 87-
11696. [history]

  ab. San Bernardino, CA: The Borgo Press; Glendale, CA: The Sidewinder
Press, October 1988, 144 p., trade paper (ISBN 0-89370-935-2).

A complete reworking of Burgess McK. Shumway's *Ranchos of California: Patented Private Land Grants Listed by County*, originally compiled
and published by the Federal Writers' Project in 1941-42.   Shumway attempted to list every land grant patented in California prior to its takeover
by the U.S. government in 1848. The material was reset, checked, veri-
fied, and thoroughly indexed.

CONTENTS: Introduction: The Ranchos of California, by Burgess;
Preface: California's Land Grants, by Robert G. Cowan; Note, by Burgess
based on Cowan; Alameda County; Amador County; Butte County; Calav-
eras County; Colusa County; Contra Costa County; Fresno County; Glenn
County; Kern County; Kings County; Lake County; Los Angeles County;
Marin County; Mariposa County; Mendocino County; Merced County;
Monterey County; Napa County; Orange County; Riverside County;
Sacramento County; San Benito County; San Bernardino County; San
Diego County; San Francisco County; San Joaquin County; San Luis
Obispo County; San Mateo County; Santa Barbara County; Santa Clara
County; Santa Cruz County; Shasta County; Solano County; Sonoma
County; Stanislaus County; Sutter County; Tehama County; Ventura
County; Yolo County; Yuba County; Governors of Spanish and Mexican
California; Index of Governors and Other Grantors; Index of Ranchos; In-
dex of Grantees.

A43. *The Work of William F. Nolan: An Annotated Bibliography & Guide*, by
Boden Clarke and James Hopkins [*i.e.*, William F. Nolan].   Bibliographies of Modern Authors, Number 14. San Bernardino, CA: The
Borgo Press, October 1988, 224 p., cloth (ISBN 0-89370-393-1).   LC
87-6334. [bibliography]

ab.   San Bernardino, CA: The Borgo Press, October 1988, 224 p., trade paper
      (ISBN 0-89370-493-8).

A comprehensive bibliography of the writings, published and unpublished,
of this prolific American author, based upon his own voluminous records
of his 1,400 publications. This book represented the second major re-
design and expansion of the series format.
      CONTENTS: Introduction: "The Multi-Media Man," by Jeffrey M.
Elliot; William F. Nolan: A Chronology; A. Books; B. Short Fiction; C.
Verse; D. Personality Profiles; E. Reviews; F. Other Nonfiction; G.
Screenplays; H. Teleplays; I. Film and Television Outlines; J. Radio; K.
Stage; L. Comics; M. Letters; N. Juvenilia; O. Interviews; P. Speeches
and Public Appearances; Q. Television and Radio Appearances; R. Other
Media; S. Artwork; T. Editorial Posts; U. Honors and Awards; V. About
the Author; W. Unpublished Works; X. Miscellanea; Quoth the Critics;
Index.

SECONDARY SOURCES AND REVIEWS:

1.   "1988 Research Index," by Hal W. Hall, in *Science Fiction, Fantasy,
     & Horror 1988: A Comprehensive Bibliography of Books and Short
     Fiction Published in the English Language*, edited by Charles N.
     Brown, and William G. Contento. Oakland, CA: Locus Press,
     1989, cloth, p. 400.

A44.   *The Arms Control, Disarmament, and Military Security Dictionary*, by
       Jeffrey M. Elliot, Robert Reginald, [with the assistance of Austin J. Lee
       and Mary A. Burgess]. Clio Dictionaries in Political Science. Santa
       Barbara, CA, Oxford, England: ABC-CLIO, June 1989, xvi, 349 p.,
       cloth (ISBN 0-87436-430-2). LC 88-37151. [dictionary]

   ab.   Santa Barbara, CA, Oxford, England: ABC-CLIO, June 1989, xvi, 349
         p., trade paper (ISBN 0-87436-532-5).

A comprehensive guide in dictionary form to the major terms, events,
weapons systems, and personalities of significance to arms control and
military security in the modern era. The introduction and four chapters
were penned by Elliot, two chapters by Reginald, and three chapters jointly
by Reginald and Mary A. Burgess. Each entry, following the series format, is broken into two sections: description, providing an objective definition of the term; and significance, explaining the relation of the term to
the modern world and to other, similar words. Lee assisted Elliot with his
chapters. NOTE: the first printing of both the cloth and paper editions

misspell Elliot's name as "Elliott" three times on the copyright page (but nowhere else).

CONTENTS: A Note on How to Use This Book, by Elliot; Preface, by Elliot; 1. War and Peace, by Elliot; 2. Military Security, by Elliot; 3. The Arms Race, by Reginald and Burgess; 4. Collective Security, by Elliot; 5. Conventional Wars and Weapons, by Reginald and Burgess; 6. Nuclear Weapons, by Elliot; 7. Nuclear Strategy, by Reginald and Burgess; 8. Nuclear Proliferation, by Reginald; 9. Arms Control and Disarmament, by Reginald; Notes; Index, by Reginald and Burgess.

SECONDARY SOURCES AND REVIEWS:

1. *American Libraries* 20 (October, 1989): 901.
2. *American Reference Books Annual* 21 (1990): 280.
3. *Reference & Research Book News* 4 (October, 1989): 18.
4. Scarlott, Jennifer. *Library Journal* 114 (September 1, 1989): 182.
5. Smith, M. J., Jr. *Choice* 27 (December, 1989): 606.
6. Whiteley, Sandy. *Reference Books Bulletin* (September 15, 1989): 202.
7. *Wilson Library Bulletin* 64 (November, 1989): 114.

A45. *The Work of Colin Wilson: An Annotated Bibliography & Guide*, by Colin Stanley, edited by Boden Clarke. Bibliographies of Modern Authors, Number 1. San Bernardino, CA: The Borgo Press, September 1989, 312 p., cloth (ISBN 0-89370-817-8). LC 84-11181. [bibliography]

  ab. San Bernardino, CA: The Borgo Press, September 1989, 312 p., trade paper (ISBN 0-89370-917-4). Half of the run had laminated covers.

A comprehensive, chronological guide to this prolific British philosopher's hundreds of publications, extensively edited and updated from the author's original manuscript and Wilson's own records.

CONTENTS: Acknowledgments and Note; Introduction: "The Quest for Colin Wilson," by Colin Stanley; A Colin Wilson Chronology; A. Books; B. Short Fiction; C. Nonfiction; D. Introductions and Afterwords; E. Book Reviews; F. Other Media; G. Editorial Credits; H. About the Author: Monographs; I. About the Author: Critiques, Profiles, Interviews; J. About the Author: Short Bio-Bibliographies; K. About the Author: Other Materials; L. Miscellanea; Quoth the Critics; Afterword: "Inside Outside: Reflections on Being Bibliographed," by Colin Wilson; About Colin Stanley; Title Index to Colin Wilson's Works; Subject Index with Author/Title Index.

SECONDARY SOURCES AND REVIEWS:

1. Collings, Michael R. *Science Fiction & Fantasy Book Review Annual 1990*, edited by Robert A. Collins and Robert Latham. Westport, CT: Meckler Corp., 1991, cloth, p. 638-639.
2. D'Ammassa, Don. *Science Fiction Chronicle* 11 (July, 1990): 38.

A46.   *The Work of Chad Oliver: An Annotated Bibliography & Guide*, by Hal W. Hall, edited by Boden Clarke. Bibliographies of Modern Authors, Number 12. San Bernardino, CA: The Borgo Press, October 1989, 88 p., cloth (ISBN 0-89370-391-5). LC 86-2288. [bibliography]

ab.   San Bernardino, CA: The Borgo Press, October 1989, 86 p., trade paper (ISBN 0-89370-491-1). Half of the run had laminated covers.

This comprehensive, annotated bibliography of Oliver's publications was adapted from *Chad Oliver: A Preliminary Bibliography* (Bryan, TX: Dellwood Press, 1985), with additional data from the compiler. The editor reworked the material from its original format (alphabetical by section) into the standard chronological arrangement of this series. The lengthy interview with Oliver was also edited to remove anachronisms and redundancies.
   CONTENTS: Acknowledgments; Introduction, by Howard Waldrop; A Chad Oliver Chronology; A. Books; B. Short Fiction; C. Nonfiction; D. Letters; E. Other Media; F. Unpublished Works; G. About the Author: Monographs, Profiles, Critiques; H. About the Author: News Releases; I. Honors and Awards; J. Miscellanea; "An Interview with Chad Oliver," conducted by Hal W. Hall and Richard D. Boldt; Second Thoughts, by Chad Oliver; About Hal W. Hall; Index.

SECONDARY SOURCES AND REVIEWS:

1. D'Ammassa, Don. *Science Fiction Chronicle* 11 (August, 1990): 39.

A47.   *The Work of Ross Rocklynne: An Annotated Bibliography & Guide*, by Douglas Menville, edited by Boden Clarke, Bibliographies of Modern Authors, Number 17. San Bernardino, CA: The Borgo Press, November 1989, 70 p., dark blue cloth (ISBN 0-8095-0511-8). LC 88-34360. [bibliography]

ab.   San Bernardino, CA: The Borgo Press, November 1989, 70 p., trade paper (ISBN 0-8095-1511-3). Dark blue cover. The first printing of this bibliography was scrapped due to printer's errors, twelve examples having been set aside as file copies.

ac.   San Bernardino, CA: The Borgo Press, November 1989 [i.e., January, 1990], 70 p., light blue cloth (ISBN 0-8095-0511-8). This reprint, together with its trade paper companion (see "ad."), was the first edition in general release. The first half of the book was reshot, but the text is identical to the true first printing.

ad.   San Bernardino, CA: The Borgo Press, November 1989 [i.e., January, 1990], 70 p., trade paper (ISBN 0-8095-1511-3). Light blue cover. Half of the run had laminated covers.

Ross Rocklynne (1913-1988) was a leading science-fiction writer of the pulp era, publishing over a hundred stories in the period from 1936-56; this is the first bibliography of and guide to his work. The editor revised Menville's manuscript, and provided some additional material from his own library.

    CONTENTS: Introduction: "A Man for All Magazines," by Arthur Jean Cox; A Ross Rocklynne Chronology; A. Books; B. Short Fiction; C. Nonfiction; D. Fanzine Contributions; E. Radio Productions; F. Juvenilia; G. About the Author; H. Unpublished Works; I. Miscellanea; Quoth the Critics; Index; About Douglas Menville.

SECONDARY SOURCES AND REVIEWS:

1.   D'Ammassa, Don. *Science Fiction Chronicle* 11 (August, 1990): 39.

A48.   *The Work of Ian Watson: An Annotated Bibliography & Guide*, by Douglas A. Mackey, edited by Boden Clarke. San Bernardino, CA: The Borgo Press, December 1989, 148 p., cloth (ISBN 0-8095-0512-6). LC 88-36646. [bibliography]

ab.   San Bernardino, CA: The Borgo Press, December 1989, 148 p., trade paper (ISBN 0-8095-1512-1). Half of the run had laminated covers.

A comprehensive bibliography and literary guide to the writings of this well-known British SF writer. The author provided camera-ready copy (a first for this series), which was reworked in several back-and-forth sessions between editor and compiler.

    CONTENTS: About Douglas A. Mackey; Introduction: "Elementary Watson," by Douglas A. Mackey; An Ian Watson Chronology; A. Books; B. Short Fiction; C. Nonfiction; D. Letters; E. Poetry; F. Campaign Literature; G. Other Media; H. Unpublished Manuscripts; I. Awards; J. Editorial Posts; K. Public Appearances; L. Interviews; M. About the Author; N.

Miscellanea; Quoth the Critics; Afterword: "Dancing on a Tightrope," by Ian Watson; Index.

SECONDARY SOURCES AND REVIEWS:

1.　D'Ammassa, Don. *Science Fiction Chronicle* 11 (July, 1990): 36.

A49.　*The Work of Reginald Bretnor: An Annotated Bibliography & Guide*, by Scott Alan Burgess, edited by Boden Clarke. Bibliographies of Modern Authors, Number 8. San Bernardino, CA: The Borgo Press, December 1989 [i.e., January 1990], 122 p., cloth (ISBN 0-89370-387-7). LC 85-31405. [bibliography]

ab.　San Bernardino, CA: The Borgo Press, December 1989 [i.e., January 1990], 122 p., trade paper (ISBN 0-89370-487-3). Half of the run had laminated covers.

A complete guide to the publications of this American science fiction writer and military historian, edited from Burgess's manuscript and Bretnor's own records. Bretnor provided a number of final details to complete the book. This was the maiden publication of Scott Alan Burgess, the editor's youngest brother.

CONTENTS: Introduction: "The Ghosts We Share," by Judith Merril; A Reginald Bretnor Chronology; A. Books; B. Short Fiction; C. Nonfiction; D. Feghoots; E. Verse; F. Editorial Credits; G. Unpublished Works; H. Honors and Awards; I. About the Author; J. Miscellanea; Quoth the Critics; About Scott Alan Burgess; "Through Time and Space with Ferdinand Feghoot #118," by Bretnor; "On the Proper Perpetration of Feghoots," by Bretnor; "Through Time and Space with Ferdinand Feghoot #119," by Bretnor; Afterword: "Debts and Acknowledgments," by Bretnor; Index.

SECONDARY SOURCES AND REVIEWS:

1.　D'Ammassa, Don. *Science Fiction Chronicle* 11 (August, 1990): 39.

A50.　*The Work of Pamela Sargent: An Annotated Bibliography & Guide*, by Jeffrey M. Elliot, edited by Boden Clarke. Bibliographies of Modern Authors, Number 13. San Bernardino, CA: The Borgo Press, January 1990, 80 p., cloth (ISBN 0-89370-394-X). LC 88-34361. [bibliography] ab. San Bernardino, CA: The Borgo Press, January 1990, 80 p., trade paper (ISBN 0-89370-494-6). Half of the run had laminated covers.

A comprehensive bibliography to the works of this rising American writer of the fantastic, edited from the original manuscript supplied by Elliot (with Sargent's assistance). The editor reworked the data, and added additional material, particularly in the "About the Author" section.

CONTENTS: Introduction: "Let the Rest Take Care of Itself," by Jeffrey M. Elliot; A Pamela Sargent Chronology; A. Books; B. Short Fiction; C. Nonfiction; D. Unpublished Works; E. Editorial Credits; F. Other Media; G. Juvenilia; H. Public Appearances; I. Honors and Awards; J. About the Author; K. Miscellanea; Quoth the Critics; Afterword: "Through the Looking Glass," by Pamela Sargent; About Jeffrey M. Elliot; Index.

SECONDARY SOURCES AND REVIEWS:

1. D'Ammassa, Don. *Science Fiction Chronicle* 11 (August, 1990): 39.
2. Mullen, Richard D. *Science-Fiction Studies* 18 (March, 1991): 152-153.
3. Sturgis, Susanna. "Susanna Sturgis on Science Fiction." *Feminist Bookstore News* 14 (May/June, 1991): 49.

A51. *The Work of Jack Dann: An Annotated Bibliography & Guide*, by Jeffrey M. Elliot, edited by Boden Clarke. Bibliographies of Modern Authors, Number 16. San Bernardino, CA: The Borgo Press, April 1990, 128 p., cloth (ISBN 0-8095-0506-1). LC 88-34679. [bibliography]

ab. San Bernardino, CA: The Borgo Press, April 1990, 128 p., trade paper (ISBN 0-8095-1506-7). Laminated covers.

The first published bibliography of this American SF writer and editor was reworked by Reginald from Elliot's original manuscript.

CONTENTS: Introduction: "In Pity and Terror," by Elliot; A Jack Dann Chronology; A. Books; B. Short Fiction; C. Poetry; D. Nonfiction; E. Editorial Credits; F. About the Author; G. Honors and Awards; H. Public Appearances; I. Miscellanea; Quoth the Critics; Afterword: "Advice to Aspiring Writers," by Dann; Postscript: "Echoes of the Future: An Interview with Jack Dann," conducted by Gregory Feeley; Title Index; About Jeffrey M. Elliot.

SECONDARY SOURCES AND REVIEWS:

1. D'Ammassa, Don. *Science Fiction Chronicle* 12 (February, 1991): 46.
2. Mullen, Richard D. *Science-Fiction Studies* 18 (March, 1991): 152-153.

A52. *Hancer's Price Guide to Paperback Books, Third Edition*, by Kevin Hancer, with the assistance of R. Reginald. Radnor, PA: Wallace-Homestead Book Co., June 1990, xlii, 353 p., trade paper (ISBN 0-87069-536-3). LC 89-51552. [price guide]

The third edition of a continuing price guide and bibliography of mass market paperbacks, adapted from the author's *Cumulative Paperback Index, 1939-1959* (see A2).

A53. *The Work of George Zebrowski: An Annotated Bibliography & Guide, Second Edition, Revised and Expanded*, by Jeffrey M. Elliot and Robert Reginald, edited by Boden Clarke. Bibliographies of Modern Authors, Number 4. San Bernardino, CA: The Borgo Press, September 1990, 118 p., cloth (ISBN 0-8095-0514-2). LC 89-7093. [bibliography]

ab. San Bernardino, CA: The Borgo Press, September 1990, 118 p., trade paper (ISBN 0-8095-1514-8).

A much expanded and revised edition of A37, reworked and supplemented by the editor.
CONTENTS: Introduction: "Between Sensitivity and Concern," by Elliot; A George Zebrowski Chronology; A. Books; B. Short Fiction; C. Nonfiction; D. Translations; E. Editorial Credits; F. Juvenilia; G. Unpublished Works; H. Other Media; I. Honors and Awards; J. Public Appearances; K. About the Author; L. Miscellanea; Quoth the Critics; Afterword: "6,250 Bits of Immortality," by Zebrowski; Index; About the Authors.

SECONDARY SOURCES AND REVIEWS:

1. D'Ammassa, Don. *Science Fiction Chronicle* 12 (April, 1991): 29.
2. Mullen, Richard D. *Science-Fiction Studies* 18 (March, 1991): 152-153.

A54. *To Kill or Not to Kill: Thoughts on Capital Punishment*, by Rep. William L. Clay, Sr., edited by Michael and Mary Burgess. Great Issues of the

Day, Number 4. San Bernardino, CA: The Borgo Press, October 1990, 208 p., cloth (ISBN 0-89370-331-1). LC 87-812. [sociology]

ab. San Bernardino, CA: The Borgo Press, October 1990, 208 p., trade paper (ISBN 0-89370-431-8).

A virulent discourse against capital punishment, by a Democratic congressman from St. Louis, extensively reworked by the two editors.
CONTENTS: Introduction: "The Question of Capital Punishment," by Gwen Giles; Foreword: "The Moral Dilemma of State-Sponsored Murder," by Dr. Jeffrey M. Elliot; Preface: "A Few Words from Capitol Hill," by Clay; 1. The Position of America's Religious Leaders; 2. Roman Justice; 3. The Most Infamous Execution in History; 4. The Death Penalty As a Deterrent; 5. Why Not Public Executions? 6. Discrimination and Capital Punishment; Notes; Bibliography; Appendix: Statistic Tables; Index; About the Author.

A55. *The Work of Charles Beaumont: An Annotated Bibliography & Guide, Second Edition, Revised and Expanded*, by William F. Nolan, edited by Boden Clarke. Bibliographies of Modern Authors, Number 6. San Bernardino, CA: The Borgo Press, November 1990, 92 p., cloth (ISBN 0-8095-0517-7). LC 90-15043. [bibliography]

ab. San Bernardino, CA: The Borgo Press, November 1990, 92 p., trade paper (ISBN 0-8095-1517-2).

A greatly enlarged version of A36, edited and expanded by the author and editor.
CONTENTS: Preface to the Second Edition; Introduction to the First Edition; Chronology; A. Books; B. Short Fiction; C. Nonfiction; D. Screenplays; E. Teleplays; F. Comics; G. Letters; H. Unpublished Works; I. Verse; J. Honors and Awards; K. Artwork; L. Editorial Credits; M. About the Author; N. Miscellanea; Quoth the Critics; Afterword: "My Grandmother's Japonicas," by Charles Beaumont; Index; About William F. Nolan.

SECONDARY SOURCES AND REVIEWS:

1. D'Ammassa, Don. *Science Fiction Chronicle* 12 (April, 1991): 29.

A56. *The Work of Dean Ing: An Annotated Bibliography & Guide*, by Scott Alan Burgess, edited by Boden Clarke. Bibliographies of Modern Authors, Number 11. San Bernardino, CA: The Borgo Press, December 1990, 82 p., cloth (ISBN 0-89370-395-8). LC 87-827. [bibliography]

ab.   San Bernardino, CA: The Borgo Press, December 1990, 82 p., trade paper (ISBN 0-89370-495-4).

A comprehensive guide to the works of this Oregon science fiction and suspense writer, revised and expanded by the editor.

CONTENTS: Introduction: "Delphi Must Be Near," by Scott Alan Burgess; A Dean Ing Chronology; A. Books; B. Short Fiction; C. Nonfiction; D. Unpublished Works; E. Editorial Credits; F. Radio and Television Appearances; G. Honors and Awards; H. About the Author; I. Miscellanea; Quoth the Critics; Afterword: "Excuse the Shouting...," by Dean Ing; Index; About Scott Alan Burgess.

SECONDARY SOURCES AND REVIEWS:

1.   Taormina, Angela. *SFRA Newsletter* no. 193 (December, 1991): 16.

A57.   *The Trilemma of World Oil Politics*, by Sheikh R. Ali and Jeffrey M. Elliot, edited by Paul David Seldis and Michael Burgess. Great Issues of the Day, Number 2. San Bernardino, CA: The Borgo Press, October 1991, 152 p., cloth (ISBN 0-89370-168-8). LC 84-275. [current affairs]

ab.   San Bernardino, CA: The Borgo Press, October 1991, 152 p., trade paper (ISBN 0-83970-268-4).

This discussion of petroleum resources examines how long-term fluctuations in the supply of oil affect international geopolitics.

CONTENTS: Introduction; 1. The Politics of Oil; 2. Country—Company—Consumer Relationships; 3. Arab Oil as a Volatile Weapon; 4. American Peace Initiatives; 5. The Impact of OPEC Petrolism; 6. The Myth and Reality of Chinese Oil; 7. Soviet Oil Strategy in the World; 8. Oil Hegemony and the International Crisis; 9. After Oil, What Then? 10. Conclusions; 11. Postscript; Acronyms; Appendix A: The Statute of the Organization of Petroleum Exporting Countries; Appendix B: Resolution of Arab Oil Ministers; Notes; Bibliography; Index; About the Authors.

A58.   *Reginald's Science Fiction and Fantasy Awards: A Comprehensive Guide to the Awards and Their Winners, Second Edition, Revised and Expanded*, by Daryl F. Mallett and Robert Reginald. Borgo Literary

Guides, Number 1. San Bernardino, CA: The Borgo Press, October 1991, 248 p., cloth (ISBN 0-89370-826-7). LC 90-15074. [directory]

ab. San Bernardino, CA: The Borgo Press, October 1991, 248 p., trade paper (ISBN 0-89370-926-3).

A revised edition of A21, expanded some four times over the original, covering over a hundred different awards, with histories of each, chronological checklists of the winners, a comprehensive author index, and statistical tables.
CONTENTS: Introduction; How to Use This Book; Part I. English-Language Awards; Part II. Foreign-Language Awards; Part III. Non-Genre Awards; Appendix 1: Officers of the Science Fiction Research Association; Appendix 2: Officers of the Science Fiction Writers of America, Inc.; Appendix 3: World Fantasy Conventions; Appendix 4: World Science Fiction Conventions; Author Index; Statistical Tables; Index to Award Names; About the Authors.

A59. *The Work of Louis L'Amour: An Annotated Bibliography & Guide*, by Hal W. Hall, edited by Boden Clarke. Bibliographies of Modern Authors, Number 15. San Bernardino, CA: The Borgo Press, October 1991, 192 p., cloth (ISBN 0-8095-0510-X). LC 88-34678. [bibliography]

ab. San Bernardino, CA: The Borgo Press, October 1991, 192 p., trade paper (ISBN 0-8095-1510-5).

A comprehensive, annotated bibliography of this well-known Western writer's works, expanded, revised, and supplemented by the editor.
CONTENTS: Introduction: "The Several Literary Careers of Louis L'Amour," by Michael T. Marsden; A Louis L'Amour Chronology; A. Books; B. Short Fiction; C. Nonfiction; D. Poetry; E. Editorial Credits; F. Audio Tapes and Records; G. Motion Picture and Television Adaptations; H. Secondary Sources; I. Honors and Awards; J. Miscellanea; Quoth the Critics; Afterword: "A Conversation with Louis L'Amour," by Michael T. Marsden and Kristine Fredriksson; "Presentation of an Honorary Ph.D. Degree"; Series Index; Title Index; About Hal W. Hall.

A60. *The Work of Robert Reginald: An Annotated Bibliography & Guide, Second Edition, Revised and Expanded*, by Michael Burgess. Bibliographies of Modern Authors, Number 5. San Bernardino, CA: The Borgo Press, February 1992, 176 p., cloth (ISBN 0-8095-0505-3). LC 87-6306. [bibliography]

ab. San Bernardino, CA: The Borgo Press, February 1992, 176 p., trade paper (ISBN 0-8095-1505-9).

A much revised version of A31, expanded almost four times over the
original, being the author's own guide to his prolific career as writer, editor, librarian, researcher, and genealogist. Reginald estimates that he has
been directly or indirectly responsible for the publication of some 1,750
monographic volumes.
CONTENTS: Introduction: "Comets Don't Slow Down," by William
F. Nolan; Preface: "It Was Twenty Years Ago Today," by Dr. Fran J.
Polek; A Robert Reginald Chronology; A. Books; B. Nonfiction; C. Short
Fiction; D. Editorial Credits; E. Documents; F. Catalogs; G. Book Pro-
duction and Design; H. Unpublished Works; I. Juvenilia; J. Public Ap-
pearances; K. Secondary Sources; L. Honors and Awards; M. Miscellanea;
Quoth the Critics; Afterword: "Harvesting the Vineyards of Obscurity," by
Robert Reginald; Afterword: "A Few Words from Our Sponsor," by Jack
Dann; Index.

FORTHCOMING:

A61. *The Work of Brian W. Aldiss: An Annotated Bibliography & Guide*, by
Margaret Aldiss, edited by Boden Clarke. Bibliographies of Modern
Authors, Number 9. San Bernardino, CA: The Borgo Press, Spring
1992, [300] p., cloth (ISBN 0-89370-388-5). LC 87-746. [bibliography]

ab. San Bernardino, CA: The Borgo Press, Spring 1992, [300] p., trade paper
(ISBN 0-89370-488-1).

A guide to this prolific British writer's many publications, extensively re-
worked and edited by Reginald under his Boden Clarke penname.
CONTENTS: Introduction: "Map and Territory," by David
Wingrove; A Brian W. Aldiss Chronology; A. Books (Annotations by
Brian Aldiss); B. Short Fiction; C. Nonfiction; D. Reviews; E. Poetry; F.
Other Media; G. Editorial Credits; H. Papers; I. Unpublished Works; J.
Honors and Awards; K. Secondary Sources; L. Miscellanea; Quoth the
Critics; Afterword, by Brian Aldiss; Index.

A62. *The Work of Katherine Kurtz: An Annotated Bibliography & Guide*, by
Boden Clarke. Bibliographies of Modern Authors, Number 7. San
Bernardino, CA: The Borgo Press, Spring 1992, [80] p., cloth (ISBN 0-
89370-386-9). LC 85-31401. [bibliography]

ab. San Bernardino, CA: The Borgo Press, Spring 1992, [80] p., trade paper
(ISBN 0-89370-486-5).

A guide to the life and works of an American fantasy writer, now living in Ireland.

CONTENTS: Introduction; A Katherine Kurtz Chronology; A. Books; B. Short Fiction; C. Short Nonfiction; D. Songs; E. Editorial Credits; F. Scripts; G. Other Media; H. Unpublished Works; I. Honors and Awards; J. Secondary Sources; K. Miscellanea; Quoth the Critics; Afterword: "Talking with Katherine Kurtz," by Jeffrey M. Elliot and Robert Reginald; Index; About the Author.

A63. *A Reference Guide to Science Fiction, Fantasy, and Horror*, by Michael Burgess. Reference Guides in the Humanities. Littleton, CO: Libraries Unlimited, Spring 1992, [467] p., cloth. [bibliography]

A comprehensive, annotated bibliography of science fiction reference sources, arranged by subject and then alphabetically in each chapter by author. Each entry includes: bibliographical data, a descriptive annotation, and an evaluation of the work.

CONTENTS: Introduction; How to Use This Book; Encyclopedias and Dictionaries; Atlases and Gazetteers; Cataloging Guides; Yearbooks, Annuals, and Almanacs; Annual Directories; Statistical Sources; Awards Lists; Pseudonym Lists; Biographical and Literary Directories; Readers' and Critical Guides; Guides to Secondary Sources; Library Catalogs and Collection Guides; Magazine and Anthology Indexes: Cyclopedias of SF Magazines, General Indexes and Checklists, Indexes to Specific Magazines; General Bibliographies; National Bibliographies; Subject Bibliographies; Publisher Bibliographies: General Works, Bibliographies of Individual Publishers; Author Bibliographies: Bibliography Series, Bibliographies of Individual Authors; Artist Bibliographies: General Works, Bibliographies of Individual Artists; Character Dictionaries: General Works, Dictionaries on Individual Authors; Film and Television Catalogs: General Works, Specific Movies, TV Programs, or Subjects; Calendars and Chronologies; Quotations Dictionaries; Collectors' and Price Guides; Fan Guides; Core Periodicals; Professional Organizations; Core Collections: Academic Libraries, Public Libraries, Personal Research Libraries; Author Index; Title Index; Subject Index.

A64. *Lords Temporal and Lords Spiritual: A Chronological Checklist of the Popes, Patriarchs, Katholikoi, and Independent Archbishops and Metropolitans of the Monarchical Autocephalous Churches of the Christian East and West, Second Edition, Revised and Expanded*, by Boden Clarke. Stokvis Studies in Historical Chronology & Thought, Number 1. San Bernardino, CA: The Borgo Press, 1992, [224] p., cloth (ISBN 0-89370-326-5). LC 87-6319. [history]

ab.   San Bernardino, CA: The Borgo Press, 1992, [224] p., trade paper (ISBN
      0-89370-426-1).

A history and chronology of the Eastern Orthodox churches. The author
has spent more than a quarter century researching this book, transliterating
the names of the church leaders from sources in the original languages of
each ecclesiastical body. A typical entry includes: a political history of
the church, delineating major events (particularly divisions into smaller
churches), with the succession claims of that body, and a chronological
checklist of each church's primates.
      CONTENTS: Introduction; Abbreviations; 1. Aght'amar; 2. Alba-
nia; 3. Albania (Caucasian); 4. Alexandria (Coptic); 5. Alexandria (Coptic
Catholic); 6. Alexandria (Greek); 7. America (Various Churches); 8. Antioch (Greek); 9. Antioch (Greek Melkite); 10. Antioch (Maronite); 11. Antioch (Syrian Catholic); 12. Antioch (Syrian Jacobite); 13. Armenia; 14.
Assyria; The Old Apostolic Catholic Church of the East; 15. Babylon and
Assyria (Chaldean); 16. Belorussia; 17. Bulgaria; 18. Cilicia (Armenian
Apostolic); 19. Cilicia (Armenian Catholic); 20. Constantinople (Arme-
nian); 21. Constantinople (Greek); The Church of Turkey; 22. Crete; 23.
Cyprus; 24. Czechoslovakia; The Slavonic Orthodox Church; 25. Estonia;
26. Ethiopia; 27. Finland; 28. Georgia; The Church of Abkhazia; 29.
Greece; 30. Japan; 31. Jerusalem (Armenian); 32. Jerusalem (Greek); 33.
Latvia; 34. Macedonia and Ohrid; 35. Malabar and Malankara (Various
Churches); 36. Poland; 37. Romania; 38. Rome; 39. Russia; The Russian
Orthodox Church Outside of Russia; 40. Serbia and Pec; The Serbian Or-
thodox Church of Hungary; The Serbian Orthodox Church of Austria; The
Church of Montenegro; 41. Sinai; 42. Ukraine (Various Churches); Se-
lected Bibliography; Comparative Name Tables; Index.
      See also the first edition (A33).

A65.   *Zephyr and Boreas: Winds of Change in the Fiction of Ursula K. Le
       Guin*, edited by Robert Reginald and George Edgar Slusser. Starmont
       Studies in Literary Criticism, Number 7. Mercer Island, WA: Starmont
       House, 1992, [160] p., cloth. [nonfiction anthology]

An anthology of scholarly critical articles by and about well-known writer
Ursula K. Le Guin, most of them previously published in various academic
journals.
      CONTENTS: Introduction: "Le Guin Today," by Slusser; "A Citizen
of Mondath: The Development of a Science Fiction Writer," by Le Guin;
"Saurian Ooze and Ivory Tower: The Early Hainish Novels," by Slusser;
"What Is Human? Ursula K. Le Guin and Science Fiction's Great Theme,"
by Keith N. Hull; "Ursula K. Le Guin and Arthur C. Clarke on Imma-
nence, Transcendence, and Massacres," by Richard D. Erlich; "On a Far
Shore: The Myth of Earthsea," by Brian Attebery; "Conservatism in the

Fantasy of Le Guin," by C. N. Manlove; "The Touching of Love and Death in Ursula K. Le Guin, with Comparisons to Jane Austen," by Donald M. Hassler; "Variations on Newspeak," by T. A. Shippey; "Beyond Negation:: The Critical Utopias of Ursula K. Le Guin and Samuel R. Delany," by Tom Moylan; "Reactionary Utopias," by Gregory Benford; "To Read *The Dispossessed*," by Samuel R. Delany; "The Complementarity of Myth, Magic, and Science," by James W. Bittner; "The Ideal Worlds of Science Fiction," by Slusser; "*Always Coming Home*: The Book As World," by Elizabeth Cummins; "Determinism, Free Will, and Point of View in Le Guin's *Left Hand of Darkness*," by Eric S. Rabkin; "A Guide to Secondary Sources on Ursula K. Le Guin," by Reginald; Index.

A66. *Yesterday or Tomorrow? Questions of Vision in the Fiction of Robert A. Heinlein*, edited by George Edgar Slusser and Robert Reginald. Starmont Studies in Literary Criticism, Number 5. Mercer Island, WA: Starmont House, 1992, [160] p., cloth. [nonfiction anthology]

An anthology of scholarly essays on the work of America's premier science-fiction author, the late Robert A. Heinlein, mostly taken from previously-published sources.
    CONTENTS: Introduction: "The Career of Robert A. Heinlein," by Slusser; "Reading Heinlein Subjectively: An Analysis," by Alexei Panshin and Cory Panshin; "Intrigue and Adventure: Heinlein in the 1950s," by Slusser; "What Is One to Make of Robert A. Heinlein?" by Daniel Dickenson; "Justifying the Ways of Man to God: The Novels of Robert A. Heinlein," by Elizabeth Ann Hull; "Ideology and Narrative: The Cold War and Robert Heinlein," by R. A. MacDermott; "Going Around in Generic Circles," by David Clayton; "*Stranger in a Strange Land* As Modern Myth: Robert A. Heinlein and Carl Jung," by Kenneth L. Golden; "Heinlein's Perpetual Motion Fur Farm," by Slusser; "Robert A. Heinlein: The Novelist As Preacher," by Diane Parkin-Speer; "Lazarus, Come Forth from That Tomb!" by Joe R. Christopher; "Knowing the Unknown: Heinlein, Lem, and the Future," by Bradford Lyau; "*Glory Road*," by Samuel R. Delany; "*Job: A Comedy of Justice*," by Slusser; "A Guide to Secondary Sources on Robert A. Heinlein," by Reginald; Index.

A67. *Space Log: A Chronological Checklist of Manned Space Flights, 1961-1991*, by John Hansen Gurley, edited by Michael Burgess. Borgo Reference Guides, Number 3. San Bernardino, CA: The Borgo Press, 1992, [160] p., cloth (ISBN 0-89370-819-4). LC 87-6313. [directory]

  ab. San Bernardino, CA: The Borgo Press, 1992, [160] p., trade paper (ISBN 0-89370-919-0).

A comprehensive guide to Russian and American manned space flights, arranged chronologically by mission, and provided data on the length of each flight, crew members, designations, and major accomplishments. Complete with index and biographical data on the major astronauts and cosmonauts.

A68.   *The Work of Stephen King: An Annotated Bibliography & Guide*, by Michael R. Collings, edited by Boden Clarke. Bibliographies of Modern Authors, Number 25. San Bernardino, CA: The Borgo Press, 1992, [400] p., cloth (ISBN 0-8095-0520-7). [bibliography]

  ab.   San Bernardino, CA: The Borgo Press, 1992, [400] p., trade paper (ISBN 0-8095-1520-2).

A69.   *Murder Was Bad: Mystery and Detective Fiction in Paperback Publishing, from the Pages of Paperback Quarterly*, edited by R. Reginald and Billy C. Lee. Starmont Popular Culture Studies, Number 5. Mercer Island, WA: Starmont House, 1992, [160] p., cloth. Published simultaneously in trade paperback. [nonfiction anthology]

A70.   *The Stars Were Ours: Science Fiction and Fantasy in Paperback Publishing, from the Pages of Paperback Quarterly*, edited by R. Reginald and Billy C. Lee. Starmont Popular Culture Studies, Number 4. Mercer Island, WA: Starmont House, 1992, [160] p., cloth. Published simultaneously in trade paperback. [nonfiction anthology]

A71.   *PQ-liar Perambulations: Studies in the History of the Mass Market Paperback, from the Pages of Paperback Quarterly*, edited by R. Reginald and Billy C. Lee. Starmont Popular Culture Studies, Number . Mercer Island, WA: Starmont House, 1992, [160] p., cloth. Published simultaneously in trade paperback. [nonfiction anthology]

A72.   *The Work of Julian May: An Annotated Bibliography & Guide, Second Edition*, by Thaddeus Dikty and R. Reginald. Bibliographies of Modern Authors, Number 3. San Bernardino, CA: The Borgo Press, 1992, [140] p., cloth (ISBN 0-8095-0513-4). [bibliography]

  ab.   San Bernardino, CA: The Borgo Press, 1992, [140] p., trade paper (ISBN 0-8095-1513-X).

A73.   *The Work of Jeffrey M. Elliot: An Annotated Bibliography & Guide, Second Edition*, by Bret Adams [*i.e.*, Jeffrey M. Elliot], edited by Boden Clarke. Bibliographies of Modern Authors, Number 2. San Bernardino, CA: The Borgo Press, 1992, [160] p., cloth (ISBN 0-8095-0508-8). [bibliography]

ab. San Bernardino, CA: The Borgo Press, 1992, [140] p., trade paper (ISBN 0-8095-1508-3).

A74. *The State and Province Vital Records Guide*, by Mike and Mary Burgess. Borgo Reference Guides, Number 1. San Bernardino, CA: The Borgo Press, 1992, [96] p., cloth (ISBN 0-89370-815-1). LC 87-6312. [directory]

ab. San Bernardino, CA: The Borgo Press, 1992, [96] p., trade paper (ISBN 0-89370-915-8).

A75. *The House of the Burgesses, Being a Genealogical History of William Burges of Richmond (later King George) Co., Virginia, and His Son Edward Burges of King George Co., Virginia, with the Descendants in the Male Line of Edward's Sons, Garner Burges of Fauquier Co., Virginia, William Burges of Stafford Co., Virginia, Edward Burgess, Jr., of Fauquier Co., Virginia, Moses Burgess of Orange Co., Virginia, and Reuben Burgess, Sr., of Rowan (later Davie) Co., North Carolina, Second Edition*, by Michael Burgess. Borgo Family Histories, Number 1. San Bernardino, CA: The Borgo Press, 1992, [700] p., cloth (ISBN 0-89370-379-6). LC 87-6316. [genealogy]

ab. San Bernardino, CA: The Borgo Press, 1992, [700] p., trade paper (ISBN 0-89370-479-6).

A76. *Science Fiction and Fantasy Literature: A Supplement, 1975-1991, with Contemporary Science Fiction, Fantasy, and Horror Authors III*, by R. Reginald. Detroit: Gale Research Co., 1992, [1200 p. in 2 v.], cloth. [bio-bibliography]

A77. *The Work of Orson Scott Card: An Annotated Bibliography & Guide*, by Michael R. Collings, edited by Boden Clarke. Bibliographies of Modern Authors, Number 19. San Bernardino, CA: The Borgo Press, 1992, [200] p., cloth (ISNB 0-8095-0516-9). [bibliography]

ab. San Bernardino, CA: The Borgo Press, 1992, [200] p., trade paper (ISBN 0-8095-1516-4).

A78. *The Work of Harry Harrison: An Annotated Bibliography & Guide*, by Paul Tomlinson, edited by Boden Clarke. Bibliographies of Modern Authors, Number 20. San Bernardino, CA: The Borgo Press, 1992, [256] p., cloth (ISBN 0-8095-0515-0). [bibliography]

ab. San Bernardino, CA: The Borgo Press, 1992, [256] p., trade paper (ISBN 0-8095-1515-6).

A79. *The Work of William Eastlake: An Annotated Bibliography & Guide*, by W. C. Bamberger, edited by Boden Clarke. Bibliographies of Modern Authors, Number 21. San Bernardino, CA: The Borgo Press, 1992, [80] p., cloth (ISBN 0-89370-398-2). [bibliography]

ab. San Bernardino, CA: The Borgo Press, 1992, [80] p., trade paper (ISBN 0-89370-498-9).

A80. *The Work of Michael R. Collings: An Annotated Bibliography & Guide*, by Willard Reuben, edited by Boden Clarke. Bibliographies of Modern Authors, Number 22. San Bernardino, CA: The Borgo Press, 1992, [160] p., cloth (ISBN 0-8095-0501-0). [bibliography]

ab. San Bernardino, CA: The Borgo Press, 1992, [160] p., trade paper (ISBN 0-8095-1501-6).

A81. *The Work of Gary Brandner: An Annotated Bibliography & Guide*, by Martine Wood Brandner, edited by Boden Clarke. Bibliographies of Modern Authors, Number 23. San Bernardino, CA: The Borgo Press, 1992, [160] p., cloth (ISBN 0-8095-0519-3). [bibliography]

ab. San Bernardino, CA: The Borgo Press, 1992, [160] p., trade paper (ISBN 0-8095-1519-9).

A82. *The Work of Raymond Z. Gallun: An Annotated Bibliography & Guide*, by Jeffrey M. Elliot, edited by Boden Clarke. Bibliographies of Modern Authors, Number 24. San Bernardino, CA: The Borgo Press, 1992, [128] p., cloth (ISBN 0-8095-0503-7). [bibliography]

ab. San Bernardino, CA: The Borgo Press, 1992, [128] p., trade paper (ISBN 0-8095-1503-2).

A83. *The Work of Joseph Payne Brennan: An Annotated Bibliography & Guide*, by Randall D. Larson, edited by Boden Clarke. Bibliographies of Modern Authors, Number 26. San Bernardino, CA: The Borgo Press, 1992, [100] p., cloth (ISBN 0-8095-0521-5). [bibliography]

ab. San Bernardino, CA: The Borgo Press, 1992, [100] p., trade paper (ISBN 0-8095-1521-0).

A84. *The Work of Elizabeth Chater: An Annotated Bibliography & Guide*, by Daryl F. Mallett and Annette Y. Mallett, edited by Boden Clarke. Bibliographies of Modern Authors, Number 27. San Bernardino, CA: The Borgo Press, 1992, [80] p., cloth (ISBN 0-89370-390-7). [bibliography]

ab. San Bernardino, CA: The Borgo Press, 1992, [80] p., trade paper (ISBN 0-89370-490-3).

A85. *The Work of Robert Nathan: An Annotated Bibliography & Guide*, by Michael Burgess, edited by Boden Clarke. Bibliographies of Modern Authors, Number __. San Bernardino, CA: The Borgo Press, 1992, [160] p., cloth. [bibliography]

ab. San Bernardino, CA: The Borgo Press, 1992, [160] p., trade paper.

A86. *Horror Fiction in the Library of Congress Classification Scheme*, by Michael Burgess. Borgo Cataloging Guides, Number 5. San Bernardino, CA: The Borgo Press, 1992, [128] p., cloth (ISBN 0-89370-334-6). [cataloging manual]

ab. San Bernardino, CA: The Borgo Press, 1992, [128] p., trade paper (ISBN 0-89370-434-2).

A87. **The Work of William F. Temple: An Annotated Bibliography & Guide**, by Mike Ashley, edited by Boden Clarke. Bibliographies of Modern Authors, No. 28. San Bernardino, CA: The Borgo Press, 1992, [128] p., cloth (ISBN 0-8095-0507-X). [bibliography]

ab. San Bernardino, CA: The Borgo Press, 1992, [128] p., trade paper (ISBN 0-8095-1507-5).

B.

SHORT NONFICTION

B1.   "Anatomy of a Phenomenon," by R. Reginald, in *Charter, Journal of Liberal Arts* (Spring, 1968): 85-96. [literature]

This critical appraisal of modern science fiction and fantasy is the first appearance of the name "R. Reginald" in print, and is regarded by the author as the start of his professional career as a writer and editor.

B2.   "*The Man Whose Name Wouldn't Fit*, by Theodore Tyler," by "Everett Cooper," in *Pegasus* no. 2 (1969): 12-14. [review]

B3.   "Calibrations: *The Well at the World's End*, by William Morris," by "RR," in *Forgotten Fantasy* 1 (February, 1971): 37-38. [review]

b.   Ann Arbor, MI: University Microfilms, 1973, 35 mm. microfilm, p. 37-38.

B4.   "Calibrations: *Golden Cities, Far*, edited by Lin Carter," by "RR," in *Forgotten Fantasy* 1 (April, 1971): 45-46. [review]

b.   Ann Arbor, MI: University Microfilms, 1973, 35 mm. microfilm, p. 45-46.

B5.   "Calibrations: *The Broken Sword*, by Poul Anderson," by "RR," in *Forgotten Fantasy* 1 (June, 1971): 74-75. [review]

b.   Ann Arbor, MI: University Microfilms, 1973, 35 mm. microfilm, p. 74-75.

B6.   "Introduction to the Newcastle Edition," by Robert Reginald, in *The Book of Dreams and Ghosts*, by Andrew Lang. Hollywood, CA: Newcastle Publishing Co., February 1972, paper, p. xix-xxii. [introduction]

b.   San Bernardino, CA: The Borgo Press, February 1979, cloth, p. xix-xxii. The Borgo edition is a rebinding of the original, with new title page imprint label placed over the original Newcastle imprint.

B7. "Published by Members: Report of the Monitoring Committee," Alan E. Nourse, Chairman, in *The Bulletin of the Science Fiction Writers of America* 9 (Summer, 1973): 34-37. Most of the contributions are by R. Reginald. [bibliography]

B8. "Published by Members: Report of the Monitoring Committee," Alan E. Nourse, Chairman, in *The Bulletin of the Science Fiction Writers of America* 9 (no. 50, 1974): 18-21. Most of the contributions are by R. Reginald ("R.R."). [bibliography]

B9. "Published by Members: Report of the Monitoring Committee," Alan E. Nourse, Chairman, in *The Bulletin of the Science Fiction Writers of America* 9/10 (Summer, 1974): 39-40. Most of the contributions are by R. Reginald. [bibliography]

B10. "Published by Members," in *The Bulletin of the Science Fiction Writers of America* 10 (Winter, 1974/75): 32-35. Most of the contributions are by R. Reginald. [bibliography]

B11. *"The Printed Book Catalogs of the Library of the State Historical Society of Wisconsin,"* by R. Reginald, in *Microform Review* 4 (July, 1975): 231-232. [review]

B12. "Looking Back on Films That Look Far Ahead," by R. Reginald and Douglas Menville, in *Science Digest* 83 (February, 1978): 12-13. [film critique]

   Abridged from *Things To Come: An Illustrated History of the Science Fiction Film.*

B13. "Predictions from Science Fiction," by "R.R.," in *The People's Almanac #2*, edited by David Wallechinsky and Irving Wallace. New York: William Morrow & Co., September 1978, cloth, p. 16-21. [literature]

   b. Toronto, New York: Bantam Books, October 1978, paper, p. 16-21.

B14. "George Orwell's *1984*—How Close Are We," by Robert Reginald and James Natal, in *The People's Almanac #2*, edited by David Wallechinsky and Irving Wallace. New York: William Morrow & Co., September 1978, cloth, p. 52-56. [current affairs]

   b. Toronto, New York: Bantam Books, October 1978, paper, p. 52-56.

B15.   "Utopias in Science Fiction," by "R.R.," in *The People's Almanac #2*, edited by David Wallechinsky and Irving Wallace. New York: William Morrow & Co., September 1978, cloth, p. 1344-1347. [literature]

b.   Toronto, New York: Bantam Books, October 1978, paper, p. 1344-1347.

B16.   "The Borgo Press," in *Paperback Quarterly* 2 (Spring, 1979): 14-22. [publishing]

Includes a bibliography of all Borgo Press titles published through 1979.

B17.   "*Space Lust*, bound with *Mixed Doubles*, by Cynthia Bellmore," by "Miguel Alcalde," in *Science Fiction & Fantasy Book Review* 1 (February, 1979): 4. [review]

B18.   "*The Cylon Death Machine*, by Glen A. Larson and Robert Thurston," by "Miguel Alcalde," in *Science Fiction & Fantasy Book Review* 1 (February, 1979): 5. [book review]

B19.   "*I—Alien*, by J. Michael Reaves, a Second Opinion," by Boden Clarke, in *Science Fiction & Fantasy Book Review* 1 (February, 1979): 6. [review]

This marks the first appearance in print of the name "Boden Clarke," which, like "Lucas Webb," was taken from a marriage announcement in the *San Bernardino Sun*—someone named Boden was marrying someone named Clarke.

B20.   "Commentary," by R. Reginald, in *Science Fiction & Fantasy Book Review* 1 (March, 1979): 13. [editorial]

B21.   "*Golden Scorpion*, by Alan Burt Akers, a Second Opinion," by R. Reginald, in *Science Fiction & Fantasy Book Review* 1 (March, 1979): 18. [review]

B22.   "*The Bibliography of Crime Fiction, 1749-1975*, by Allen J. Hubin," by R. Reginald, in *Science Fiction & Fantasy Book Review* 1 (March, 1979): 19. [review]

B23.   "Awards," by R. Reginald, in *Science Fiction & Fantasy Book Review* 1 (April, 1979): 26. [literary news]

B24.   "*Titans of the Universe*, by Moonchild/James Harvey," by R. Reginald, in *Science Fiction & Fantasy Book Review* 1 (April, 1979): 26. [review]

B25. "Commentary," by R. Reginald, in *Science Fiction & Fantasy Book Review* 1 (May, 1979): 37. [editorial]

B26. "*Between the Planets* [with eleven others], by Kurt Mahr," by "Michael Demotes," in *Science Fiction & Fantasy Book Review* 1 (May, 1979): 40. [review]

B27. "*Satan's Mistress* [with eleven others], by Tabatha Jervis," by "Peter Harding," in *Science Fiction & Fantasy Book Review* 1 (May, 1979): 41. [review]

B28. "*World Without Mercy* [with five others], by William Voltz," by R. Reginald, in *Science Fiction & Fantasy Book Review* 1 (June, 1979): 57. [review]

B29. "*Hell's Bitch* [with three others]," by "Peter Harding," in *Science Fiction & Fantasy Book Review* 1 (June, 1979): 57. [review]

B30. "*Dimension of Horror,* by Jeffrey Lord," by R. H. Blackburn and Boden Clarke, in *Science Fiction & Fantasy Book Review* 1 (June, 1979): 57-58. [review]

B31. "*A Life for Kregen,* by Dray Prescot," by Loay Hall and "Rex Miletus," in *Science Fiction & Fantasy Book Review* 1 (June, 1979): 63. [review]

B32. "Part Two: Directory," by Robert Reginald, in *The Encyclopedia of Alternative Medicine and Self-Help,* devised and edited by Malcolm Hulke. New York: Schocken Books, June 1979, cloth, p. 213-243. [bibliography]

   ab. New York: Schocken Books, June 1979, trade paper, p. 213-243.

B33. "*Bring the Jubilee,* by Ward Moore," by R. Reginald, in *Survey of Science Fiction Literature,* edited by Frank N. Magill. Englewood Cliffs, NJ: Salem Press, July 1979, cloth, p. 260-264. [criticism]

B34. "*Pavane,* by Keith Roberts," by R. Reginald, in *Survey of Science Fiction Literature,* edited by Frank N. Magill. Englewood Cliffs, NJ: Salem Press, July 1979, cloth, p. 1660-1664. [criticism]

B35. "*Conan* [with seven others], by Robert E. Howard, L. Sprague de Camp, and Lin Carter," by Thomas M. Egan and "Rex Miletus," in *Science Fiction & Fantasy Book Review* 1 (August, 1979): 90-91. [review]

B36.   "*The Official Guide to Comic & Science Fiction Books*, by **Michael Resnick**," by "Misha Grazhdanin," in *Science Fiction & Fantasy Book Review* 1 (September, 1979): 110-111. [review]

B37.   "*An Introduction to the J. Lloyd Eaton Collection of Science Fiction and Fantasy*, by **Clifford Wurfel**; *Space Voyages, 1591-1920*, by **Lynn S. Smith**," by R. Reginald, in *Science Fiction & Fantasy Book Review* 1 (September, 1979): 111. [review]

B38.   "*Paralittératures*, by **Yvon Allard**," by R. Reginald, in *Science Fiction & Fantasy Book Review* 1 (October, 1979): 112. [review]

B39.   "Commentary," by R. Reginald, in *Science Fiction & Fantasy Book Review* 1 (October, 1979): 117-118. [editorial]

B40.   "*Spacedust One* [with four others], by **C. C. Coffman**," by "C. Everett Cooper," in *Science Fiction & Fantasy Book Review* 1 (October, 1979): 118-119. [review]

B41.   "*Legend in Blue Steel*, by **Spider Page**," by "Lucas Webb," in *Science Fiction & Fantasy Book Review* 1 (October, 1979): 120. [review]

B42.   "*Devil's Handmaiden* [with four others]," by "Nero Rale," in *Science Fiction & Fantasy Book Review* 1 (October, 1979): 120. [review]

B43.   "*Spacing Dutchman*, by **Eric Vinicoff and Marcia Martin**," by "G. Forbes Durand," in *Science Fiction & Fantasy Book Review* 1 (October, 1979): 124. [review]

B44.   "*Motel of the Mysteries*, by **David Macaulay**," by "Lucretia Sharpe," in *Science Fiction & Fantasy Book Review* 1 (October, 1979): 124. [review]

B45.   "Commentary," by R. Reginald, in *Science Fiction & Fantasy Book Review* 1 (November, 1979): 133. [editorial]

B46.   "*Fantasy Readers Guide, Number One: The John Spencer Publications*, edited by **Michael Ashley**," by R. Reginald, in *Science Fiction & Fantasy Book Review* 1 (November, 1979): 147. [review]

B47.   "Commentary," by R. Reginald, in *Science Fiction & Fantasy Book Review* 1 (December, 1979): 149. [editorial]

B48.   "Commentary," by R. Reginald, in *Science Fiction & Fantasy Book Review* 2 (January, 1980): 1. [editorial]

B49. *"The Adventures of Doctor Who*, by Terrance Dicks," by "Walt Mobley", in *Science Fiction & Fantasy Book Review* 2 (January, 1980): 1. [review]

B50. *"Riddle of Stars: The Riddle-Master of Hed, Heir of Sea and Fire, Harpist in the Wind*, by Patricia McKillip," by "Daniel Painter," in *Science Fiction & Fantasy Book Review* 2 (January, 1980): 1. [review]

B51. *"Alien*, by Alan Dean Foster," by "Jack B. Nimble," in *Science Fiction & Fantasy Book Review* 2 (January, 1980): 1. [review]

B52. *"Science Fiction: A Selected List of Books That Have Appeared in Talking Book Topics and Braille Book Review*," by "Andrew Kapel," in *Science Fiction & Fantasy Book Review* 2 (January, 1980): 1. [review]

B53. *"14 Official Blueprints, Star Trek, The Motion Picture*, rendered by David Kimble," by "Jacob Lawson," in *Science Fiction & Fantasy Book Review* 2 (January, 1980): 1. [review]

B54. **"Index,"** by R. Reginald, in *Science Fiction & Fantasy Book Review* 2 (January, 1980): 2-13. [index]

B55. *"Futura Man, an Orphan in Time*, by R. G. Taylor [with three others]," by "Tertius Spartacus," in *Science Fiction & Fantasy Book Review* 2 (January, 1980): 16. [review]

B56. **"Awards,"** by R. Reginald, in *Science Fiction & Fantasy Book Review* 2 (February, 1980): 17. [article]

B57. *"Modern Science Fiction: Its Meaning and Its Future*, edited by Reginald Bretnor," by Boden Clarke, in *Science Fiction & Fantasy Book Review* 2 (February, 1980): 21. [review]

B58. *"Die Neologismen in der Modernen Franzosischen Science-Fiction*, by Felix Scherwinsky," by R. Reginald, in *Science Fiction & Fantasy Book Review* 2 (February, 1980): 21. [review]

B59. *"The Literature of Fantasy: A Comprehensive, Annotated Bibliography of Modern Fantasy Fiction*, by Roger C. Schlobin, a Second Opinion," by Boden Clarke, in *Science Fiction & Fantasy Book Review* 2 (February, 1980): 28-29. [review]

B60. *"Ivan Efremov's Theory of Soviet Science Fiction*, by G. V. Grebens," by R. Reginald, in *Science Fiction & Fantasy Book Review* 2 (February, 1980): 29. [review]

B61. "Predictions from Science Fiction," by "R.R.," in *The People's Almanac Presents The Book of Predictions*, edited by David Wallechinsky, Amy Wallace, and Irving Wallace. New York: William Morrow & Co., December 1980, cloth, p. 308-323. [literature]

    ab. Toronto, New York: Bantam Books, December 1981, paper, p. 308-323.

B62. "15 Planets Discovered by Science Fiction Writers," by "R.R.," in *The People's Almanac #3*, edited by David Wallechinsky and Irving Wallace. New York: William Morrow & Co., September 1981, cloth, p. 345-353. [literature]

    ab. Toronto, New York: Bantam Books, October 1981, trade paper, p. 345-353.

    ac. Toronto, New York: Bantam Books, August 1982, paper, p. 345-353.

B63. "*Paperbacks, U.S.A.: A Graphic History, 1939-1959*, by Piet Schreuders," by R. Reginald, in *Science Fiction & Fantasy Book Review* n.s. no. 2 (March, 1982): 7. [review]

B64. "Introduction: Once Upon a Time," by R. Reginald, in *The Holy Grail Revealed: The Real Secret of Rennes-le-Château*, by Patricia and Lionel Fanthorpe, edited by R. Reginald. North Hollywood, CA: Newcastle Publishing Co., April 1982, paper, p. 9-16. [introduction]

    ab. San Bernardino, CA: The Borgo Press, April 1982, cloth, p. 9-16. A rebinding of the original in cloth, with a Borgo Press label stickered over the original imprint.

    ac. San Bernardino, CA: The Borgo Press, November 1986, cloth, p. 9-16. A true second printing of twenty copies.

    ad. San Bernardino, CA: The Borgo Press, September 1989, cloth, p. 9-16. A true third printing of one hundred copies.

B65. "*Havoc in Islandia*, by Mark Saxton," by R. Reginald, in *Science Fiction & Fantasy Book Review* n.s. no. 14 (May, 1983): 41-42. [review]

B66. "*Aladore*, by Sir Henry John Newbolt," by Robert Reginald and Mary A. Burgess, in *Survey of Modern Fantasy Literature*, edited by Frank N. Magill. Englewood Cliffs, NJ: Salem Press, November 1983, cloth, p. 4-6. [criticism]

B67. "The Gor Novels, by John Norman," by "Peter Mauzy," in *Survey of Modern Fantasy Literature*, edited by Frank N. Magill. Englewood Cliffs, NJ: Salem Press, November 1983, cloth, p. 631-634. [criticism]

B68. "*Hasan,* by Piers Anthony," by Robert Reginald, in *Survey of Modern Fantasy Literature,* edited by Frank N. Magill. Englewood Cliffs, NJ: Salem Press, November 1983, cloth, p. 695-697. [criticism]

B69. "*A House-Boat on the Styx; and, The Pursuit of the House-Boat,* by John Kendrick Bangs,*" by Robert Reginald and Mary A. Burgess, in *Survey of Modern Fantasy Literature,* edited by Frank N. Magill. Englewood Cliffs, NJ: Salem Press, November 1983, cloth, p. 752-756. [criticism]

B70. "*Melusine; or, Devil Take Her!,* by Charlotte Franken Haldane,*" by Robert Reginald, in *Survey of Modern Fantasy Literature,* edited by Frank N. Magill. Englewood Cliffs, NJ: Salem Press, November 1983, cloth, p. 1004-1006. [criticism]

B71. "*Monk's Magic,* by Alexander de Comeau," by Robert Reginald, in *Survey of Modern Fantasy Literature,* edited by Frank N. Magill. Englewood Cliffs, NJ: Salem Press, November 1983, cloth, p. 1057-1059. [criticism]

B72. "*The Neustrian Cycle,* by Leslie Barringer," by Robert Reginald, in *Survey of Modern Fantasy Literature,* edited by Frank N. Magill. Englewood Cliffs, NJ: Salem Press, November 1983, cloth, p. 1099-1104. [criticism]

B73. "The Short Fiction of Knowles," by Robert Reginald, in *Survey of Modern Fantasy Literature,* edited by Frank N. Magill. Englewood Cliffs, NJ: Salem Press, November 1983, cloth, p. 1589-1591. [criticism]

B74. "*So Love Returns,* by Robert Nathan," by Robert Reginald, in *Survey of Modern Fantasy Literature,* edited by Frank N. Magill. Englewood Cliffs, NJ: Salem Press, November 1983, cloth, p. 1766-1768. [criticism]

B75. "*The Thing from the Lake,* by Eleanor Marie Ingram," by Robert Reginald and Mary A. Burgess, in *Survey of Modern Fantasy Literature,* edited by Frank N. Magill. Englewood Cliffs, NJ: Salem Press, November 1983, cloth, p. 1901-1903. [criticism]

B76. "The University of Cosmopoli Tales," by Robert Reginald, in *Survey of Modern Fantasy Literature,* edited by Frank N. Magill. Englewood Cliffs, NJ: Salem Press, November 1983, cloth, p. 1999-2001. [criticism]

B77.   "*The Wonderful Adventures of Phra the Phoenician*, by Edwin Lester Arnold," by Robert Reginald, in *Survey of Modern Fantasy Literature*, edited by Frank N. Magill. Englewood Cliffs, NJ: Salem Press, November 1983, cloth, p. 2156-2158. [criticism]

B78.   "*You're All Alone*, by Fritz Leiber," by Robert Reginald, in *Survey of Modern Fantasy Literature*, edited by Frank N. Magill. Englewood Cliffs, NJ: Salem Press, November 1983, cloth, p. 2200-2202. [criticism]

B79.   "Leonard Wibberley (1915-1983)," in *Locus, the Newspaper of the Science Fiction Field* 17 (January, 1984): 18. [obituary]

B80.   "10-Millionth-Record Winner Strikes Back," by Michael Burgess, in *American Libraries* 15 (March, 1984): 134, 136. [letter]

B81.   "Peter Fitting on the Borgo Press: Two Reactions and a Note on *SFS*'s Reviewing Policy," by Robert Reginald, in *Science-Fiction Studies* 11 (March, 1984): 102. [letter]

B82.   "Atreides, House, Foundation of," non-bylined, in *The Dune Encyclopedia*, edited by Willis E. McNelly. New York: Berkley Books, June 1984, paper, p. 55-56. Erroneously uncredited. [fictional history]

    ab.   London: Corgi Books, 1985, paper, p. 55-56.
    ac.   [Garden City, NY: Science Fiction Book Club, 1985], cloth, p. 55-56. Title page reads: New York: Berkley Books.
    ad.   as: "Atreides, Haus, Gründung von," in *Der Wüsten-Planet: Die Dune-Enzyklopädie, Band 1*, [edited by] Willis E. McNelly. München: Wilhelm Heyne Verlag, 1985, p. 118-120. Translated by Ronald M. Hahn. [German]

B83.   "Atreides, House, Prominent Members," by "R.R.," in *The Dune Encyclopedia*, edited by Willis E. McNelly. New York: Berkley Books, June 1984, paper, p. 56-58. [fictional history]

    ab.   London: Corgi Books, 1985, paper, p. 56-58.
    ac.   [Garden City, NY: Science Fiction Book Club, 1985], cloth, p. 55-56. Title page reads: New York: Berkley Books.
    ad.   as: "Atreides, Haus, Prominente Mitglieder," in *Der Wüsten-Planet: Die Dune-Enzyklopädie, Band 1*, [edited by] Willis E. McNelly. München: Wilhelm Heyne Verlag, 1985, p. 120-124. Translated by Ronald M. Hahn. [German]

B84. "Atreides, House, and Imperial Rule," by "R.R.," in *The Dune Encyclopedia*, edited by Willis E. McNelly. New York: Berkley Books, June 1984, paper, p. 58-60. [fictional history]

ab. London: Corgi Books, 1985, paper, p. 58-60.
ac. [Garden City, NY: Science Fiction Book Club, 1985], cloth, p. 58-60. Title page reads: New York: Berkley Books.
ad. as: "Atreides, Haus, und Imperiale Herrschaft," in *Der Wüsten-Planet: Die Dune-Enzyklopädie, Band 1*, [edited by] Willis E. McNelly. München: Wilhelm Heyne Verlag, 1985, p. 124-126, 128. Translated by Ronald M. Hahn. [German]

B85. "Siridar-Dukes of Atreides Caladanides and Arrikides," non-bylined, in *The Dune Encyclopedia*, edited by Willis E. McNelly. New York: Berkley Books, June 1984, paper, p. 60. [fictional table]

ab. London: Corgi Books, 1985, paper, p. 60.
ac. [Garden City, NY: Science Fiction Book Club, 1985], cloth, p. 60. Title page reads: New York: Berkley Books.
ad. as: "Siridar-Herzöge Atreides, Caladanides und Arrikides," in *Der Wüsten-Planet: Die Dune-Enzyklopädie, Band 1*, [edited by] Willis E. McNelly. München: Wilhelm Heyne Verlag, 1985, p. 127. Translated by Ronald M. Hahn. [German]

B86. "Atreides, Minotauros (10059-10163)," by "S.G.," in *The Dune Encyclopedia*, edited by Willis E. McNelly. New York: Berkley Books, June 1984, paper, p. 73-75. Erroneously credited to Stephen Goldman. [fictional history]

ab. London: Corgi Books, 1985, paper, p. 73-75.
ac. [Garden City, NY: Science Fiction Book Club, 1985], cloth, p. 73-75. Title page reads: New York: Berkley Books.
ad. as: "Atreides, Minotauros (10054-10163)," in *Der Wüsten-Planet: Die Dune-Enzyklopädie, Band 1*, [edited by] Willis E. McNelly. München: Wilhelm Heyne Verlag, 1985, p. 153-155. Translated by Ronald M. Hahn. [German]

B87. "Emperors of the Known Universe," non-bylined, in *The Dune Encyclopedia*, edited by Willis E. McNelly. New York: Berkley Books, June 1984, paper, p. 200-205. Erroneously uncredited. [fictional table]

ab. London: Corgi Books, 1985, paper, p. 200-205.
ac. [Garden City, NY: Science Fiction Book Club, 1985], cloth, p. 200-205. Title page reads: New York: Berkley Books.

ad.   as: "Imperatoren (Kaiser) des Bekannten Universums," in *Der Wüsten-Planet: Die Dune-Enzyklopädie, Band 2*, [edited by] Willis E. McNelly. München: Wilhelm Heyne Verlag, 1985, p. 703-713. Translated by Ronald M. Hahn. [German]

B88.   "Ginaz, House of," by "R.R.," in *The Dune Encyclopedia*, edited by Willis E. McNelly. New York: Berkley Books, June 1984, paper, p. 266-267. [fictional history]

ab.   London: Corgi Books, 1985, paper, p. 266-267.

ac.   [Garden City, NY: Science Fiction Book Club, 1985], cloth, p. 266-267. Title page reads: New York: Berkley Books.

ad.   as: "Ginaz, Haus," in *Der Wüsten-Planet: Die Dune-Enzyklopädie, Band 2*, [edited by] Willis E. McNelly. München: Wilhelm Heyne Verlag, 1985, p. 561-563. Translated by Ronald M. Hahn. [German]

B89.   "Great Houses, The," by "R.R.," in *The Dune Encyclopedia*, edited by Willis E. McNelly. New York: Berkley Books, June 1984, paper, p. 272-275. [fictional history]

ab.   London: Corgi Books, 1985, paper, p. 272-275.

ac.   [Garden City, NY: Science Fiction Book Club, 1985], cloth, p. 272-275. Title page reads: New York: Berkley Books.

ad.   as: "Hohe Häuser, Die," in *Der Wüsten-Planet: Die Dune-Enzyklopädie, Band 2*, [edited by] Willis E. McNelly. München: Wilhelm Heyne Verlag, 1985, p. 637-643. Translated by Ronald M. Hahn. [German]

B90.   "Harkonnen, House of," by "R.R.," in *The Dune Encyclopedia*, edited by Willis E. McNelly. New York: Berkley Books, June 1984, paper, p. 292-295. [fictional history]

ab.   London: Corgi Books, 1985, paper, p. 292-295.

ac.   [Garden City, NY: Science Fiction Book Club, 1985], cloth, p. 292-295. Title page reads: New York: Berkley Books.

ad.   as: "Harkonnen, Haus," in *Der Wüsten-Planet: Die Dune-Enzyklopädie, Band 2*, [edited by] Willis E. McNelly. München: Wilhelm Heyne Verlag, 1985, p. 605-611. Translated by Ronald M. Hahn. [German]

B91.   "Houses Minor," by "R.R.," in *The Dune Encyclopedia*, edited by Willis E. McNelly. New York: Berkley Books, June 1984, paper, p. 314-315. [fictional history]

ab.   London: Corgi Books, 1985, paper, p. 314-315.

ac.   [Garden City, NY: Science Fiction Book Club, 1985], cloth, p. 314-315. Title page reads: New York: Berkley Books.

ad.   as: "Kleine Häuser, Die," in *Der Wüsten-Planet: Die Dune-Enzyklopädie,
       Band 2*, [edited by] Willis E. McNelly. München: Wilhelm Heyne
       Verlag, 1985, p. 770-773. Translated by Ronald M. Hahn. [German]

B92.   "Index," by R. Reginald and Mary A. Burgess, in *The Presidential-Con-
       gressional Political Dictionary*, by Jeffrey M. Elliot and Sheikh R. Ali.
       Santa Barbara, CA: ABC-CLIO, July 1984, cloth, p. 343-365. Pub-
       lished simultaneously in trade paperback. [index]

B93.   "Extensions of Remarks: New Book on Falklands War Recommended,"
       by R. Reginald and Jeffrey M. Elliot, in *Congressional Record* 131
       (April 22, 1985): E1623-E1626. [current affairs]

       A reproduction of Chapter V of *Tempest in a Teapot* (see A28), as inserted
       by U.S. Representative Mervyn M. Dymally (D-Calif.), with his com-
       ments.

B94.   "Fanthorpe, R(obert) Lionel," by R. Reginald, in *Twentieth-Century Sci-
       ence-Fiction Writers, Second Edition*, edited by Curtis C. Smith.
       Chicago and London: St. James Press, 1986, cloth, p. 237-239. [criti-
       cism]

B95.   "McAllister, Bruce (Hugh)," by R. Reginald, in *Twentieth-Century Sci-
       ence-Fiction Writers, Second Edition*, edited by Curtis C. Smith.
       Chicago and London: St. James Press, 1986, cloth, p. 491-492. [criti-
       cism]

B96.   "Reaves, J. Michael," by R. Reginald, in *Twentieth-Century Science-Fic-
       tion Writers, Second Edition*, edited by Curtis C. Smith. Chicago and
       London: St. James Press, 1986, cloth, p. 598-599. [criticism]

B97.   "Pfau Library Enters the Computer Age, Part One," by Michael
       Burgess, in *The Coyote Chronicle* 21 (Mar. 4, 1987): 5. [library sci-
       ence]

B98.   "Library Enters Computer Age, Part II," by Michael Burgess, in *The
       Coyote Chronicle* 21 (Apr. 15, 1987): 8. [library science]

B99.   "Librarians: Who We Are," by Michael Burgess, in *LTF Newsletter* no. 1
       (Fall, 1987): 1-2. [editorial]

B100. "First Annual LTF Survey of CSU Librarians," by Michael Burgess,
       based on data collected by Henry DuBois and Nancy Emmick, in *LTF
       Newsletter* no. 1 (Fall, 1987): 2-6. [library science and tables]

B101. "Other Survey Results," non-bylined, in *LTF Newsletter* no. 1 (Fall, 1987): 6-8. [library science]

B102. "Edward Burgess of Scott County, Kentucky—His Family and the Family Bible Record," by Michael Burgess, in *Kentucky Ancestors, Quarterly of the Kentucky Historical Society* 24 (Summer, 1988): 2-6. [genealogy]

B103. "Introduction: The Ranchos of California," by Michael Burgess, in *California Ranchos: Patented Private Land Grants Listed by County*, by Burgess McK. Shumway, edited by Michael and Mary Burgess. Stokvis Studies in Historical Chronology and Thought, No. 11. San Bernardino, CA: The Borgo Press, October 1988, cloth, p. 4-5. Published simultaneously in trade paperback. [history]

B104. "Roster of 'First Kentucky Ancestors': Henry Burgess," by Michael Burgess, in *Kentucky Ancestors, Quarterly of the Kentucky Historical Society* 24 (Autumn, 1988): 124. [genealogy]

B105. "Fiddling in Mañanaland," by Michael Burgess, in *LTF Newsletter* no. 2 (Fall, 1988): 1-3. [editorial]

B106. "Second Annual CSU Librarians Survey," by Michael Burgess, in *LTF Newsletter* no. 2 (Fall, 1988): 4-8. Based upon data collected by Henry DuBois. [library science]

B107. "Thinking About Genealogy: Part II, Comments and Further Thoughts," by Michael Burgess, in *NGS Newsletter* 14 (November-December, 1988): 145-146. [genealogy]

B108. "Obituaries: Michael Lewis Cook," by Robert Reginald, in *Locus, the Newspaper of the Science Fiction Field* 22 (April, 1989): 59. [obituary]

B109. "Ann Shadwick to Retire," non-bylined, in *LTF Newsletter* no. 3 (Spring, 1989): 1, 8. Includes the article, "Reflections on Twenty Years," by Ann Shadwick. [library science]

B110. "Third Annual CSU Librarians Survey," by Michael Burgess, in in *LTF Newsletter* no. 3 (Spring, 1989): 3-7. Based upon data collected by Henry DuBois. [library science]

B111. "Introduction: About Susan Wood," by Robert Reginald, in *The Poison Maiden & the Great Bitch: Female Stereotypes in Marvel Superhero Comics*, by Susan Wood. Essays on Fantastic Literature, No. 5. San

Bernardino, CA: The Borgo Press, September 1989, cloth, p. 3-4. [introduction]

ab.   San Bernardino, CA: The Borgo Press, September 1989, trade paper, p. 3-4.

B112.   **"Introduction: A Monumental Work,"** by Michael Burgess, in *The Monumental Inscriptions in the Churches and Churchyards of the Island of Barbados, British West Indies*, by Vere Langford Oliver. Stokvis Studies in Historical Chronology and Thought, No. 13. San Bernardino, CA: The Borgo Press, September 1989, cloth, p. viii. [introduction/history]

ab.   San Bernardino, CA: The Borgo Press, September 1989, trade paper, p. viii.

B113.   **"The Library Enters the Computer Age,"** by Michael Burgess, in *Library Associates Newsletter* 1 (Fall, 1989): 3. [library science]

A revised and updated version of B92-B93; the revision was conducted by Beverly Ryan.

B114.   **"Introduction: The Stafford Connection,"** by Michael Burgess, in *Stafford County, Virginia Tithables: Quit Rents, Personal Property Taxes, and Related Lists and Petitions, 1723-1790, in Two Volumes*, compiled by John Vogt and T. William Kethley, Jr. Athens, GA: Iberian Publishing Company, January 1990, cloth, Vol. One, p. ix-xviii. [history]

ab.   Athens, GA: Iberian Publishing Company, January 1990, trade paper, Vol. One, p. ix-xviii.
ac.   San Bernardino, CA: The Borgo Press, February 1990, cloth, Vol. One, p. ix-xviii. A library rebinding of the original.

B115.   **"Burgess, Harrison and Etta (Enfield),"** in *The Heritage of Blue Earth County, Minnesota*, edited by Julie Hiller Schrader. Dallas, TX: Curtis Media Corporation, September 1990, cloth, p. 620. [genealogy]

B116.   **"Burgess, Jacob L., Jr., and Lena (Morris) and Mayme (Corbin),"** in *The Heritage of Blue Earth County, Minnesota*, edited by Julie Hiller Schrader. Dallas, TX: Curtis Media Corporation, September 1990, cloth, p. 620-621. [genealogy]

B117.   **"Burgess, Jacob L., Sr., and Maranda (Bell),"** in in *The Heritage of Blue Earth County, Minnesota*, edited by Julie Hiller Schrader. Dallas,

TX: Curtis Media Corporation, September 1990, cloth, p. 621. [genea-
logy]

B118. "Burgess, James Sylvester and Martha (Lawson)," in *The Heritage of
Blue Earth County, Minnesota*, edited by Julie Hiller Schrader. Dallas,
TX: Curtis Media Corporation, September 1990, cloth, p. 621. [genea-
logy]

B119. "Burgess, John H. and Martha," in *The Heritage of Blue Earth County,
Minnesota*, edited by Julie Hiller Schrader. Dallas, TX: Curtis Media
Corporation, September 1990, cloth, p. 622. [genealogy]

B120. "Burgess, John M. and Mary (Davis)," in *The Heritage of Blue Earth
County, Minnesota*, edited by Julie Hiller Schrader. Dallas, TX: Curtis
Media Corporation, September 1990, cloth, p. 622. [genealogy]

B121. "Burgess, Thomas F. and Sarah (Harris)," in *The Heritage of Blue Earth
County, Minnesota*, edited by Julie Hiller Schrader. Dallas, TX: Curtis
Media Corporation, September 1990, cloth, p. 622. [genealogy]

B122. "Burgess, Washington and Marietta," in *The Heritage of Blue Earth
County, Minnesota*, edited by Julie Hiller Schrader. Dallas, TX: Curtis
Media Corporation, September 1990, cloth, p. 622-623. [genealogy]

B123. "Burgess, William H. and Eliza (Bettis)," in *The Heritage of Blue Earth
County, Minnesota*, edited by Julie Hiller Schrader. Dallas, TX: Curtis
Media Corporation, September 1990, cloth, p. 623. [genealogy]

B124. "Burgesses in the 1790 Census," by Michael Burgess, in *The Burgess
Bulletin* n.s. no. 2 (Spring, 1991): 2- . [history]

B125. "Reading List," in *Twentieth-Century Science-Fiction Writers, Third Edition*, edited by Noelle Watson and Paul E. Schellinger. Chicago and
London: St James Press, December 1991, cloth, p. ix-xv. [biblio-
graphy]

B126. "Cover, Arthur Byron," by Robert Reginald, in *Twentieth-Century Science-Fiction Writers, Third Edition*, edited by Noelle Watson and Paul E.
Schellinger. Chicago and London: St James Press, December 1991,
cloth, p. 162-163. [criticism]

B127. "Fanthorpe, R(obert) Lionel," by Robert Reginald, in *Twentieth-Century
Science-Fiction Writers, Third Edition*, edited by Noelle Watson and Paul
E. Schellinger. Chicago and London: St James Press, December 1991,
cloth, p. 261-264. A revision of B94. [criticism]

B128. "**Kurtz, Katherine,**" by Robert Reginald, in *Twentieth-Century Science-Fiction Writers, Third Edition*, edited by Noelle Watson and Paul E. Schellinger. Chicago and London: St James Press, December 1991, cloth, p. 458-459. [criticism]

B129. "**McAllister, Bruce (Hugh),**" by Robert Reginald, in *Twentieth-Century Science-Fiction Writers, Third Edition*, edited by Noelle Watson and Paul E. Schellinger. Chicago and London: St James Press, December 1991, cloth, p. 537-538. A revision of B95. [criticism]

B130. "**Nolan, William F(rancis),**" by Robert Reginald, in *Twentieth-Century Science-Fiction Writers, Third Edition*, edited by Noelle Watson and Paul E. Schellinger. Chicago and London: St James Press, December 1991, cloth, p. 593-595. [criticism]

B131. "**Reaves, Michael,**" by Robert Reginald, in *Twentieth-Century Science-Fiction Writers, Third Edition*, edited by Noelle Watson and Paul E. Schellinger. Chicago and London: St James Press, December 1991, cloth, p. 657-658. A revision of B96. [criticism]

B132. "**Zebrowski, George,**" by Robert Reginald, in *Twentieth-Century Science-Fiction Writers, Third Edition*, edited by Noelle Watson and Paul E. Schellinger. Chicago and London: St James Press, December 1991, cloth, p. 904-906. [criticism]

B133. "**Harvesting the Vineyards of Obscurity,**" by Robert Reginald, in *The Work of Robert Reginald: An Annotated Bibliography & Guide, Second Edition, Revised and Expanded*, by Michael Burgess. San Bernardino, CA: The Borgo Press, February 1992, cloth, p. 166-167. [autobiography]

C.

SHORT FICTION

C1.   "A Little Light Reading," by Michael Burgess, in *The San Bernardino Sun* 112 (October 31, 1985): D-1, D-4.

A short horror story set in the Library at California State University, San Bernardino, written for *The Sun*'s (Halloween) Ghost Writer Contest. It won the $50 Second Prize.

Ironically, the story has formed the basis of a local legend at Cal State, San Bernardino, with some students and employees now actually believing that the Pfau Library is haunted, citing this short tale as evidence.

D.

EDITORIAL CREDITS

D1.　Unicorn & Son, Publishers, Los Angeles. Robert Reginald, Publisher. May 1970. Unicorn & Son was the imprint under which Reginald published his first book in an edition of 108 copies. [publishing company]

　1.　*Stella Nova: The Contemporary Science Fiction Authors*, [by R. Reginald], May 1970, [348] p., paper.

D2.　*Forgotten Fantasy, Classics of Science Fiction and Fantasy.* ISSN 0015-7643. Douglas Menville, Editor; R. Reginald, Associate Editor. Hollywood, CA: Nectar Press, October, 1970-June, 1971 (all issues published), paper. [magazine]

　B.　Ann Arbor, MI: University Microfilms, 1973, 1 reel of 35 mm. microfilm.

　　　a.　Vol. I, No. 1—October, 1970. 130 p.
　　　b.　Vol. I, No. 2—December, 1970. 128 p.
　　　c.　Vol. I, No. 3—February, 1971. 130 p.
　　　d.　Vol. I, No. 4—April, 1971. 127 p.
　　　e.　Vol. I, No. 5—June, 1971. 126 p.

D3.　*The Burgess Bulletin.* Number One, undated [February 1, 1971], eight leaves. A photocopied genealogical newsletter distributed gratis to interested members of the Burgess family. This represented the first attempt by the author to delineate in printed form the genealogy of the Burgess family.

D4.　Newcastle Publishing Co., Inc., Hollywood and North Hollywood, CA. R. Reginald and Douglas Menville, Editors, July, 1971-DATE. Reginald was active as an editor for Newcastle for its first decade, from its inception in late 1970 as an adjunct of *Forgotten Fantasy* magazine, through the end of 1980, helping to choose books to be reprinted, and to write catalog and book cover copy. He has continued to be listed as a Newcastle editor after that date, although his role thereafter was confined to maintaining Newcastle's data file in *Books in Print* and *Forthcoming*

Books, assigning new ISBN numbers, and offering general advice about copyright and editorial matters. The books listed below do not include those published in The Newcastle Forgotten Fantasy Library, which are listed separately in D5. [publishing company]

B. San Bernardino, CA: The Borgo Press, February 1979-DATE, cloth. The Borgo Press editions are rebindings of the originals, with Borgo Press imprint labels covering the Newcastle imprints on the title page, although selected Newcastle titles have actually been reprinted by Borgo as Newcastle has let them go out-of-print.

1. *Fortunate Strangers*, by Cornelius Beukenkamp, Jr. July 1971, [xii], 269 p.
2. *Ritual Magic*, by E. M. Butler. July 1971, x, 329 p.
3. *Love, Hate, Fear, Anger, and the Other Lively Emotions*, by June Callwood. July 1971, xxiv, 168 p.
4. *Magic White and Black*, by Franz Hartmann. July 1971, 298 p.
5. *Ghosts I Have Met, and Some Others*, by John Kendrick Bangs. July 1971, [xvi], 190 p.
6. *You Are What You Eat*, by Victor H. Lindlahr. July 1971, 128 p.
7. *The Importance of Feeling Inferior*, by Marie Beynon Ray. July 1971, xiv, 266 p.
8. *Fortune Telling for Fun*, by Paul Showers. July 1971, [xiv], 349 p.
9. *The Devil in Britain and America*, by John Ashton. February 1972, x, 363 p.
10. *The Conquest of Fear*, by Basil King. February 1972, [vi], 270 p.
11. *The Book of Dreams and Ghosts*, by Andrew Lang. February 1972, [xxii], 301 p.
12. *The Lindlahr Vitamin Cookbook*, by Victor H. Lindlahr. February 1972, 319 p.
13. *The Origins of Popular Superstitions and Customs*, by T. Sharper Knowlson. August 1972, x, 242 p.
14. *An Introduction to Astrology*, by William Lilly. August 1972, xiv, 346 p.
15. *Eat—and Reduce!* by Victor H. Lindlahr. August 1972, x, 194 p.
16. *Romany Remedies and Recipes*, by Gipsy Petulengro. August 1972, xii, [94] p.
17. *The Natural Way to Health*, by Victor H. Lindlahr. March 1973, 255 p.
18. *Practical Astrology*, by Comte C. de Saint-Germain. March 1973, 257 p.
19. *The Practice of Palmistry for Professional Purposes*, by Comte C. de Saint-Germain. March 1973, 416 p.
20. *Thought Vibrations*, by A. Victor Segno. March 1973, 208 p.
21. *Numerology Made Plain*, by Ariel Yvon Taylor. September 1973, 147 p.
22. *Viewpoint on Nutrition*, by Arnold Pike. September 1973, x, 72, vi, 149 p.

23. *Marriage Counseling: Fact or Fallacy?* by Jerold R. Kuhn. September 1973, [x], 146 p.
24. *Lost Atlantis*, by James Bramwell. March 1974, 288 p.
25. *Graphoanalyis: Your Handwriting and What It Means*, by William Leslie French. March 1974, xiv, 226 p.
26. *30 Years Among the Dead*, by Carl Wickland. March 1974, 390 p.
27. *The Arcana of Astrology*, by W. J. Simmonite. September 1974, viii, 418 p.
28. *The Kabala of Numbers*, by Sepharial. September 1974, 215 p.
29. *The Quest of the Golden Stairs: A Mystery of Kinghood in Faërie*, by Arthur Edward Waite. September 1974, vi, 176 p.
30. *Secrets of Stage Hypnotism*, by Professor Leonidas. March 1975, 149 p.
31. *Celtic Myth and Legend, Poetry & Romance*, by Charles Squire. March 1975, xii, 450 p.
32. *Astrology and the Tarot*, by A. E. Thierens. March 1975, 159 p.
33. *Enter Dr. Nikola!* by Guy Boothby. September 1975, 256 p.
34. *Your Psychic Powers and How to Develop Them*, by Hereward Carrington. September 1975, xviii, 358 p.
35. *Dr. Nikola Returns*, by Guy Boothby. March 1976, 256 p.
36. *Astrology: Its Techniques & Ethics*, by C. Aq. Libra. March 1976, xii, 259 p.
37. *Your Handwriting and What It Means*, by William Leslie French. March [?] 1976, xiv, 226 p.
38. *The History and Power of Mind*, by Richard Ingalese. September 1976, 284, xlviii p.
39. *The Romance of Chivalry*, by A. R. Hope Moncrieff. September 1976, [viii], 439 p.
40. *Astrology and Its Practical Application*, by Else Parker. April 1977, [vi], 202 p.
41. *Victor Lindlahr's 7-Day Reducing Diet*, by Victor H. Lindlahr. April 1977, 128 p.
42. *Keys to the Occult: Two Guides to Hidden Wisdom*, by Hereward Carrington and Willis F. Whitehead. October 1977, iv, 86, 96 p.
43. *Tales of Atlantis and the Enchanted Islands*, by Thomas Wentworth Higginson. October 1977, xv, 259 p.
44. *Tai-Chi Ch'uan: Its Effects and Practical Applications*, by Y. K. Chen. April 1979, vi, 184 p.
45. *The Law of the Rhythmic Breath*, by Ella Adelia Fletcher. April 1979, 372 p.
46. *Tarot: A New Handbook for the Apprentice*, by Eileen Connolly. October 1979, x, 244 p.
47. *A Manual of Occultism*, by Sepharial. October 1979, xiv, 356 p.
48. *Your Hidden Potential: A Dynamic New System for Discovering the Power Within You*, by Christopher Markert. April 1980, [iv], 172 p.
49. *Occult Philosophy*, by Isabella Ingalese. April 1980, [x], 321 p.

50. *Handwriting Analysis: The Complete Basic Book*, by Karen Amend and Mary S. Ruiz. October 1980, viii, 196 p.

51. *How to Be a Couple and Still Be Free*, by Tina B. Tessina and Riley K. Smith. October 1980, xiv, 189 p.

52. *The Celtic Dragon Myth*, by J. F. Campbell and George Henderson. April 1981, [xlvi], 172 p.

53. *The Old Herb Doctor, His Secrets and Remedies*. April 1981, 200 p.

54. *Numerology: The Complete Guide, Volume One: The Personality Reading*, by Matthew Oliver Goodwin. October 1981, xvii, 380 p.

55. *Numerology: The Complete Guide, Volume Two: Advanced Personality Analysis and Reading the Past, Present, and Future*, by Matthew Oliver Goodwin. October 1981, xvii, 381-794 p.

56. *Kabalistic Astrology*, by Sepharial. October 1981, 96 p.

57. *Growing Straight*, by Maud Smith Williams. October 1981, x, 137 p.

58. *Telling Fortunes by Cards*, by Cicely Kent. April 1982, 192 p.

59. *Direct Healing*, by Paul Ellsworth. April 1982, [iii], 173 p.

60. *The Holy Grail Revealed: The Real Secret of Rennes-le-Château*, by Patricia and Lionel Fanthorpe. April 1982, 143 p.

61. *Past Lives, Future Lives: Accounts of Regressions and Progressions Through Hypnosis*, by Bruce Goldberg. June 1982, vi, 186 p.

62. *The Complete Palmist*, by Niblo. October 1982, [xiv], 184 p.

63. *Your Name, Your Number, Your Destiny: Two Guides to Numerology*, by Juno Jordan and Helen Houston. October 1982, viii, 34, 52 p.

64. *Reaching for the Other Side*, by Dawn Hill. April 1983, 272 p.

65. *What Are You Doing in My Universe?* by Chuck Hillig. April 1983, [224] p.

66. *Energy Ecstasy and Your Seven Vital Chakras*, by Bernard Gunther. April 1983, 120 p.

67. *The Mystic Test Book*, by Olney H. Richmond. October 1983, 340 p.

68. *The Key of Destiny*, by Harriette Augusta Curtiss and F. Homer Curtiss. October 1983, xii, 340 p.

69. *The Key to the Universe*, by Harriette Augusta Curtiss and F. Homer Curtiss. October 1983, 404 p.

70. *Feeling Great! Enhancing Your Health and Well-Being*, by Jeanne Segal. October 1983, 176 p.

71. *Higher Psychical Development*, by Hereward Carrington. October 1983, [x], 294 p.

72. *Symbols of Numerology*, by Julia Seton. April 1984, 297 p.

73. *Movements of Magic: The Spirit of T'ai-Chi-Ch'uan*, by Bob Klein. April 1984, viii, 158 p.

74. *Living Beyond Fear: A Tool for Transformation*, by Jeanne Segal. April 1984, xviii, 100 p.

75. *The Occult Power of Numbers*, by W. Wynn Westcott. October 1984, 127 p.

76. *Earthdance: A Romance of Reincarnation*, by Eileen Connolly. October 1984, x, 246 p.
77. *Tarot for Your Self: A Workbook for Personal Transformation*, by Mary K. Greer. October 1984, xiv, 253 p.
78. *Picture Me Perfect*, by Dennis Marthaler. April 1985, xii, 141 p.
79. *Twenty Days: A Narrative in Text and Pictures of the Assassination of Abraham Lincoln*, by Dorothy Meserve Kunhardt and Philip B. Kundhardt, Jr. April 1985, [viii], 312 p.
80. *Psychic Breathing: Cosmic Vitality from the Air*, by Robert Crookall. April 1985, 95 p.
81. *F-States*, by Steven Starker. August 1985, viii, 215 p.
82. *The Egyptian Gods: A Handbook*, by Alan W. Shorter. September 1985, xviii, 144 p.
83. *Choice Centered Tarot*, by Gail Fairfield. September 1985, [vi], 151 p.
84. *Futurevisions: The New Golden Age of the Science Fiction Film*, by Douglas Menville and R. Reginald, with Mary A. Burgess. October 1985, 192 p.
85. *The Reality Game & How to Win It*, by Brad Steiger. April 1986, viii, 263 p.
86. *The Longevity Lifestyle*, by Ann Tyndall. April 1986, xiv, 127 p.
87. *Love & Be Loved: A How-To Book*, by John A. Tamiazzo. April 1986, [xii], 145 p.
88. *A Guide to Polarity Therapy: The Gentle Art of Hands-On Healing*, by Maruti Seidman. April 1986, xii, 167 p.
89. *The Mystical Lore of Precious Stones, Volume 1: Superstitions, Talismans & Amulets, Crystal Gazing*, by George Frederick Kunz. August 1986, x, 247 p.
90. *The Mystical Lore of Precious Stones, Volume 2: Astrology, Birth Stones, Therapeutic & Religious Uses*, by George Frederick Kunz. August 1986, x, 189 p.
91. *The Science of Numerology*, by Sepharial. September 1986, 128 p.
92. *Sense Relaxation*, by Bernard Gunther. September 1986, [150] p.
93. *Instant Numerology*, by Sandra Kovacs Stein. October 1986, xvi, 112 p.
94. *Light of Light: A Compendium of the Writings of Rabbi Chaim ben Attar*. October 1986, viii, 236 p.
95. *The Authentic I-Ching*, translated by Henry Wei. January 1987, xxviii, 419 p.
96. *Confessions of a Kamikaze Cowboy*, by Dirk Benedict. April 1987, xxviii, 227 p.
97. *Lovestyles: How to Celebrate Your Differences*, by Tina B. Tessina. April 1987, xii, 276 p.
98. *Love Numbers: A Numerological Guide to Compatibility*, by Sandra Kovacs Stein and Carol Ann Schuler. April 1987, 264 p.
99. *Tarot: The Handbook for the Journeyman*, by Eileen Connolly. October 1987, xiv, 193 p.

100. *Your Daily Numerology*, by Sandra Kovacs Stein and Carol Ann Schuler. October 1987, xvi, 223 p.
101. *Rune Magic: The Celtic Runes as a Tool for Personal Transformation*, by Deon Dolphin. October 1987, xiv, 149 p.
102. *Tarot Constellations: Patterns of Personal Destiny*, by Mary K. Greer. October 1987, xviii, 210 p.
103. *The Connolly Book of Numbers, Volume I: The Fundamentals*. April 1988, xvi, 220 p.
104. *The Power of Your Other Hand: A Course in Channeling the Inner Wisdom of the Right Brain*, by Lucia Capacchione. April 1988, xii, 196 p.
105. *Tarot Mirrors: Reflections of Personal Meaning*, by Mary K. Greer. April 1988, xvi, 206 p.
106. *The Power of Gems and Charms*, by Geo. H. Bratley. April 1988, x, 198 p.
107. *The Palm: A Guide to Your Hidden Potential*, by Rita Robinson. April 1988, xxiv, 128 p.
108. *The Newcastle Guide to Healing with Crystals*, by Jonathan Pawlik and Pamela Chase. May 1988, xxii, 152 p.
109. *The Benham Book of Palmistry*, by William G. Benham. September 1988, xlvi, 635 p.
110. *The Connolly Book of Numbers, Volume II: The Consultant's Manual*, by Eileen Connolly. October 1988, xii, 244 p.
111. *Living the Tarot: Applying an Ancient Oracle to the Challenges of Modern Life*, by Amber Jayanti. October 1988, xvi, 311 p.
112. *Karmic Tarot: A New System for Finding and Following Your Life's Path*, by William C. Lammey. October 1988, xx, 147 p.
113. *The Well-Being Journal: Drawing on Your Inner Power to Heal Yourself*, by Lucia Capacchione. February 1989, xii, 155 p.
114. *New Thoughts on Tarot: Transcripts from the First International Newcastle Tarot Symposium*, edited by Mary K. Greer and Rachel Pollack. April 1989, vi, 174 p.
115. *The Newcastle Guide to Healing with Gemstones*, by Pamela Louise Chase and Jonathan Pawlik. April 1989, xviii, 241 p.
116. *The Creative Journal: The Art of Finding Yourself*, by Lucia Capacchione. June 1989, x, 180 p.
117. *Celtic Britain*, by Nora K. Chadwick. August 1989, 238 p.
118. *Karma Without Stress: A Guidebook for the Soul's Journey*, by Eileen Connolly. October 1989, xx, 202 p.
119. *Behind Numerology*, by Shirley Blackwell Lawrence. October 1989, xxii, 263 p.
120. *The Thursday Night Tarot*, by Jason C. Lotterhand. October 1989, xxvi, 357 p.
121. *Lighten Up Your Body—Lighten Up Your Life*, by Lucia Capacchione. February 1990, xii, 177 p.
122. *Live Your Dream!*, by Joyce Chapman. April 1990, xviii, 189 p.

123. *Develop Your Psychic Powers*, by Eileen Connolly. April 1990, xx, 215 p.

124. *Movements of Power: Ancient Secrets of Unleashing Instinctual Vitality*, by Bob Klein. April 1990, xiv, 176 p.

125. *Personality in Handwriting*, by Alfred O. Mendel. September 1990, 375 p.

126. *The 1991 Original Numerology Annual*, by Matthew Oliver Goodwin. October 1990, xx, 300 p.

126. *The Haindl Tarot, Volume I: The Major Arcana*, by Rachel Pollack. October 1990, xvi, 222 p.

127. *The Haindl Tarot, Volume II: The Minor Arcana*, by Rachel Pollack. October 1990, xvi, 228 p.

128. *Tarot: A New Handbook for the Apprentice, New Revised Edition*, by Eileen Connolly. October 1990, xvi, 7-244 p.

129. *50 and Starting Over*, by Karen Kerkstra Harty. April 1991, xxii, 195 p.

130. *Your Personal Fitness Survey*, by David Gamon and Kathleen O'Brien. April 1991, xvi, 287 p.

131. *Trees for Healing: Harmonizing with Nature for Personal Growth and Planetary Balance*, by Pamela Louise Chase and Jonathan Pawlik. April 1991, xii, 257 p.

132. *Instant People-Reading Through Handwriting*, by Anne Conway. April 1991, 224 p.

133. *Trust: A New Vision of Human Relationships for Business, Education, Family, and Personal Living*, by Jack Gibb. August 1991, xxx, 313 p.

134. *Rainbow Stress Reduction: Play Your Stress Away with Colorful Healing Art and Stress Reducing Games*, by Venu. September 1991, x, 73 p.

135. *Journaling for Joy: Writing Your Way to Personal Growth and Freedom*, by Joyce Chapman. October 1991, 224 p.

136. *Blueprint for Success: The Complete Guide to Starting a Business After 50*, by Albert Myers. October 1991, 192 p.

137. *Living Well: Answers to Life's Practical Mysteries*, by Teresa Herring. October 1991, 224 p.

D5.　**The Newcastle Forgotten Fantasy Library**, edited by R. Reginald and Douglas Menville. ISSN 0163-6251. Hollywood and North Hollywood, CA: Newcastle Publishing Co., Inc., September, 1973-October, 1980, 24 volumes, paper. [book series]

B.　San Bernardino, CA: The Borgo Press, February 1979-October, 1980 (24 volumes), cloth. Rebindings of the original editions in library cloth. A twenty-fifth volume providing a history of the series and a bibliography of Newcastle's publications is proposed for 1992.

1. *The Story of the Glittering Plain*, by William Morris. September 1973, xvi, 173 p., $2.45. Later reprinted with the same cover at $2.95. Cover designed by Douglas Menville.
2. *Eric Brighteyes*, by H. Rider Haggard. March 1974, xiv, 319 p., $2.95. New introduction by Douglas Menville. Later reprinted with the same cover at $3.95, and then with a new cover by George Barr at $3.95.
3. *The Food of Death: Fifty-One Tales*, by Lord Dunsany. September 1974, 138 p., $2.45. Cover by Sidney Sime.
4. *The Haunted Woman*, by David Lindsay. March 1975, 176 p., $2.95.
5. *Aladore*, by Sir Henry Newbolt. September 1975, xiv, 362 p., $3.95.
6. *She and Allan*, by H. Rider Haggard. September 1975, 303 p., $3.45. Later reprinted at $3.95 with a new cover by Tony Yamada and a new introduction by George Edgar Slusser.
7. *Gerfalcon*, by Leslie Barringer. The Neustrian Cycle, Book One. March 1976, iv, 310 p., $3.45. With a new introduction by Douglas Menville. Later reprinted at $3.95 with a new cover by George Barr.
8. *Golden Wings, and Other Stories*, by William Morris. March 1976, xvi, 169 p., $2.95. With a new afterword by Richard B. Mathews.
9. *Joris of the Rock*, by Leslie Barringer. The Neustrian Cycle, Book Two. September 1976, 318 p., $3.95. Cover by George Barr.
10. *Heart of the World*, by H. Rider Haggard. September 1976, 347 p., $3.95. Cover by Tony Yamada.
11. *The Wonderful Adventures of Phra the Phoenician*, by Edwin Lester Arnold. March 1977, xviii, 329 p., $3.95. With a new introduction by Douglas Menville; cover by George Barr.
12. *Child Christopher and Goldilind the Fair*, by William Morris. March 1977, [xviii], 218 p., $3.45. With a new introduction by Richard B. Mathews; cover by Robert Kline.
13. *Shy Leopardess*, by Leslie Barringer. The Neustrian Cycle, Book Three. September 1977, ix, 392 p., $4.95. With a new introduction by Douglas Menville; cover by George Barr.
14. *Ayesha: The Return of She*, by H. Rider Haggard. September 1977, xii, 9-359 p., $3.95. With a new introduction by George Edgar Slusser; cover by Tony Yamada.
15. *The Fates of the Princes of Dyfed*, by Kenneth Morris. April 1978, xix, 362 p., $3.95. With a new introduction by Dainis Bisenieks; cover by George Barr. This was the first book in the series to go permanently out-of-print (after one printing).
16. *A Tale of the House of the Wolfings*, by William Morris. April 1978, x, 199 p., $3.95. With a new introduction by Richard Mathews; cover by Jane Yamada.
17. *Under the Sunset*, by Bram Stoker. October 1978, ix, 190 p., $3.95. With a new introduction by Douglas Menville; cover by Paul Stinson.

18. *Allan Quatermain*, by H. Rider Haggard. October 1978, xii, 278 p., $3.95. With a new introduction by George Edgar Slusser; cover by C. Lee Healy.
19. *The Roots of the Mountains*, by William Morris. April 1979, 423 p., $4.95. Cover by Riley K. Smith. The Richard Mathews introduction mentioned on the cover was not received in time to be used in the book.
20. *Nada the Lily*, by H. Rider Haggard. April 1979, xvii, 295 p., $3.95. With a new introduction by George Edgar Slusser; cover by George Barr.
21. *Jaufry the Knight and the Fair Brunissende*. October 1979, 156 p., $3.95. Cover by George Barr.
22. *The Spirit of Bambatse*, by H. Rider Haggard. October 1979, [xii], 329 p., $4.95. With a new introduction by Alvin F. Germeshausen; cover by Mary Sherman.
23. *When the Birds Fly South*, by Stanton A. Coblentz. April 1980, 223 p., $4.95. With a new introduction by Stanton A. Coblentz; cover by Mary Sherman.
24. *Allan's Wife, with Hunter Quatermain's Story, A Tale of Three Lions, and Long Odds*, by H. Rider Haggard. October 1980, 240 p., $4.95. With a new introduction by Douglas Menville; cover by Tony Gleeson.

D6. **Science Fiction: 62 Books.** Advisory Editors: R. Reginald, Douglas Menville. New York: Arno Press, April 1975, 63 volumes, cloth. Advertising brochure: 24 p., paper. The original series was bound in uniform violet cloth; however, several of the books, particularly the nonfiction titles, were later reprinted in blue-green cloth during the period 1977-1979. [book series]

1. *The Man With the Broken Ear*, by Edmond About. 254 p.
2. *The British Barbarians: A Hill-Top Novel*, by Grant Allen. xxiii, 202 p.
3. *Lieut. Gullivar Jones: His Vacation*, by Edwin L. Arnold. 301 p.
4. *A Trip to Mars*, by Fenton Ash. 318 p.
5. *A Queen of Atlantis*, by Frank Aubrey. 391 p.
6. *Useless Hands*, by Claude Farrère. viii, 300 p.
7. *The Secret of the Earth*, by Charles Willing Beale. 256 p.
8. *Before the Dawn*, by John Taine. 247 p.
9. *Lord of the World*, by Robert Hugh Benson. xxv, 352 p.
10. *The Hampdenshire Wonder*, by J. D. Beresford. viii, 295 p.
11. *The Goddess of Atvatabar*, by William R. Bradshaw. 318 p.
12. *Krakatit*, by Karel Capek. 415 p.
13. *The Gay Rebellion*, by Robert W. Chambers. 297 p.
14. *The Great War of 189-*, by P. Colomb *et al.* x, 308 p.
15. *Adrift in the Unknown*, by William Wallace Cook. 305 p.
16. *The Man Who Mastered Time*, by Ray Cummings. 351 p.
17. *A Strange Manuscript Found in a Copper Cylinder*, by James DeMille. viii, 291 p.

18. *The Fall of a Nation*, by Thomas Dixon. 361 p.
19. *The Golden Blight*, by George Allan England. 350 p.
20. *Hartmann the Anarchist*, by E. Douglas Fawcett. viii, 214 p.
21. *Omega: The Last Days of the Earth*, by Camille Flammarion. 287 p.
22. *The King's Men: A Tale of To-morrow*, by Robert Grant *et al.* 270 p.
23. *Banzai!* by Ferdinand Heinrich Grautoff. xi, 320 p.
24. *The War of the Wenuses*, by C. L. Graves & E. V. Lucas. 140 p.
25. *A Modern Daedalus*, by Tom Greer. xvi, 261 p.
26. *A Honeymoon in Space*, by George Griffith. 302 p.
27. *The Conquest of the Moon*, by A. Laurie. 334 p.
28. *When the World Shook*, by H. Rider Haggard. vi, 407 p.
29. *The Polyphemes*, by F. Hernaman-Johnson. 318 p.
30. *Empire of the World*, by C. J. Cutcliffe Hyne. 314 p.
31. *In the Future.* 104 p.
32. *The Violet Flame*, by Fred T. Jane. vi, 245 p.
33. *After London; or, Wild England*, by Richard Jefferies. vii, 442 p.
34. *The Great White Queen*, by William Le Queux. vi, 312 p.
35. *The Scarlet Plague*, by Jack London. 181 p.
36. *Drowsy*, by John Ames Mitchell. vi, 301 p.
37. *A Narrative of the Life and Astonishing Adventures of John Daniel*, by Ralph Morris. 276 p.
38. *His Wisdom the Defender*, by Simon Newcomb. vii, 328 p.
39. *The Great White Way*, by Albert Bigelow Paine. 327 p.
40. *The Earth-Tube*, by Gawain Edwards. 308 p.
41. *Ancestral Voices: An Anthology of Early Science Fiction*, edited by R. Reginald and Douglas Menville. [298] p.
42. *The Frozen Pirate*, by W. Clark Russell. 2 v. in one.
43. *The Lord of the Sea*, by M. P. Shiel. viii, 496 p.
44. *Symzonia*, by Adam Seaborn. 248 p.
45. *The Man Who Rocked the Earth*, by Arthur Train and Robert W. Wood. 228 p.
46. *The Story of Ab*, by Stanley Waterloo. 351 p.
47. *The Mystery*, by Stewart E. White and Samuel H. Adams. vii, 286 p.
48. *To Mars Via the Moon*, by Mark Wicks. 327 p.
49. *Deluge: a Romance; and, Dawn, by S. Fowler Wright. 395, 349 p.
50. *SF Horizons*, edited by Brian W. Aldiss & Harry Harrison. 64, 64 p.
51. *New Maps of Hell*, by Kingsley Amis. 161 p.
52. *Linguistics and Languages in Science Fiction-Fantasy*, by Myra Barnes. vi, 196 p.
53. *Index to the Weird Fiction Magazines*, by T. G. L. Cockcroft. 100 p.
54. *A Checklist of Science-Fiction Anthologies*, by W. R. Cole. xvi, 374 p.
55. *"333": A Bibliography of the Science-Fantasy Novel*, by Joseph H. Crawford *et al.* 80 p. Later withdrawn from the series.
56. *The Checklist of Fantastic Literature in Paperbound Books*, by Bradford M. Day. 128 p.

57. *The Supplemental Checklist of Fantastic Literature*, by Bradford M. Day. ii, 155 p.
58. *The Imaginary Voyage in Prose Fiction*, by Philip B. Gove. xi, 445 p.
59. *Into Other Worlds*, by Roger Lancelyn Green. 190 p.
60. *A Historical and Critical Survey of the Science Fiction Film*, by Douglas Menville. xvii, 185 p.
61. *Contemporary Science Fiction Authors, First Edition*, by R. Reginald. 365 p.
62. *Visions of Tomorrow*, by David Samuelson. 429 p.

D7. **The Borgo Press**, San Bernardino, California. Robert Reginald, Publisher, April 1975-DATE; Mary A. Burgess, Co-Publisher, June 1975-DATE; Michael Burgess, Editorial Director, June 1975-DATE; Richard Rogers, Business Manager, 1990-DATE. Other staff have included: M. Louise Rogers (1980s), Daryl F. Mallett (1989-DATE), Paul David Seldis (1990-DATE), John Hansen Gurley (1990-DATE), Yvonne Pacheco Tevis (1990-1991), and Scott Alan Burgess (1991). Outside editors include: Dr. Jeffrey M. Elliot, Dr. Dale Salwak, Guy M. Townsend, Dr. Hanes Walton Jr., Bishop Karl Prüter, Dr. William L. Slout, and Dr. Nathan Kravetz.

Reginald founded this academic publishing house in 1975; the first two books in the line were published in April, 1976. Lines acquired outright include: Brownstone Books (Jan. 1, 1991), The Starmont Contemporary Writers Series (Jan. 1, 1991), Sidewinder Books (July 1, 1991), St. Willibrord's Press (Sept. 1, 1991), The Starmont Mystery Guides Series (Sept. 1, 1991), and Galactic Central Publications (Oct. 1, 1991). Xenos Books was an associated imprint from 1986-90. Another Borgo Press imprint founded in 1991 is Burgess & Wickizer. The list below also includes the monographic series published by The Borgo Press.

In addition to the proprietary titles owned by Borgo Press (which are individually recorded), Borgo has also distributed and sold some 1300 other publications from thirty-five publishing companies, producing library cloth editions of books previously available only in trade paperback. [publishing company]

SERIES

a. The Autocephalous Orthodox Churches. 1991-DATE. ISSN 1059-1001.
b. Bibliographies of Modern Authors. 1984-DATE. ISSN 0749-470X.
c. Black Literary Studies. 1992-DATE.
d. Black Political Studies. 1992-DATE. ISSN 0891-9631.
e. Borgo Bioviews. 1983-DATE. ISSN 0743-9628.
f. Borgo Cataloging Guides. 1987-DATE. ISSN 0891-9615.
g. Borgo Family Histories. 1983-DATE. ISSN 0733-6764.
h. Borgo Literary Guides. 1991-DATE. ISSN 0891-9623.

i.   Borgo Political Scenarios. 1982-DATE. ISSN 0278-9752.
j.   Borgo Reference Guides. 1991-DATE. ISSN 0891-9607.
k.   Borgo Reference Library. 1981. ISSN 0270-3653. Succeeded by Borgo Reference Guides.
l.   Brownstone Mystery Guides. 1991-DATE. ISSN 1055-6869.
m.   Clipper Studies in the [American] Theater. 1985-DATE. ISSN 0748-237X.
n.   Essays on Fantastic Literature. 1986-DATE. ISSN 0891-9593.
o.   Great Issues of the Day. 1981-DATE. ISSN 0270-7497.
p.   I.O. Evans Studies in the Philosophy and Criticism of Literature. 1982-DATE. ISSN 0271-9061.
q.   The Milford Series: Popular Writers of Today. 1976-DATE. ISSN 0163-2469.
r.   New Religious Movements Series. 1988-DATE. ISSN 1040-0974.
s.   San Bernardino County Studies. 1985. ISSN 0748-0784. Succeeded by West Coast Studies.
t.   Sidewinder Reprints. 1985-DATE. ISSN 8756-5382.
u.   St. Willibrord Studies in Philosophy & Religion. 1991- . ISSN 1059-8375.
v.   Stokvis Studies in Historical Chronology and Thought. 1982-DATE. ISSN 0270-5338.
w.   Studies in Judaica and the Holocaust. 1986-DATE. ISSN 0884-6952.
x.   West Coast Studies. 1989-DATE. ISSN 1041-1037.
y.   The Woodstock Series: Popular Music of Today. 1976-DATE. ISSN 0891-9585.

BORGO PRESS BOOKS

1.   *Robert A. Heinlein: Stranger in His Own Land*, by George Edgar Slusser. The Milford Series: Popular Writers of Today, Volume 1. March 1976, ii, 60 p.
2.   *The Beach Boys: Southern California Pastoral*, by Bruce Golden. The Woodstock Series: Popular Music of Today, [Number 1]. March 1976, 59 p.
3.   *The Attempted Assassination of John F. Kennedy: A Political Fantasy*, by Lucas Webb. September 1976, 47 p.
4.   *The Farthest Shores of Ursula K. Le Guin*, by George Edgar Slusser. The Milford Series: Popular Writers of Today, Volume 2. September 1976, 60 p.
5.   *Alistair MacLean: The Key Is Fear*, by Robert A. Lee. The Milford Series: Popular Writers of Today, Volume 3. October 1976, 60 p.
6.   *Up Your Asteroid! A Science Fiction Farce*, by C. Everett Cooper. April 1977, 47 p.
7.   *The Bradbury Chronicles*, by George Edgar Slusser. The Milford Series: Popular Writers of Today, Volume 4. April 1977, 63 p.

8. *John D. MacDonald and the Colorful World of Travis McGee*, by Frank D. Campbell, Jr. The Milford Series: Popular Writers of Today, Volume 5. April 1977, 63 p.

9. *Harlan Ellison: Unrepentant Harlequin*, by George Edgar Slusser. The Milford Series: Popular Writers of Today, Volume 6. April 1977, 63 p.

10. *Robert A. Heinlein: Stranger in His Own Land, Second Edition*, by George Edgar Slusser. The Milford Series: Popular Writers of Today, Volume 1. July 1977, 64 p.

11. *Kurt Vonnegut: the Gospel from Outer Space; (or, Yes We Have No Nirvanas)*, by Clark Mayo. The Milford Series: Popular Writers of Today, Volume 7. October 1977, 64 p.

12. *Aldiss Unbound: The Science Fiction of Brian W. Aldiss*, by Richard Mathews. The Milford Series: Popular Writers of Today, Volume 9. October 1977, 64 p.

13. *Piers Anthony's Hasan*, by Piers Anthony. October 1977, 190 p.

14. *The Classic Years of Robert A. Heinlein*, by George Edgar Slusser. The Milford Series: Popular Writers of Today, Volume 11. October 1977, 63 p.

15. *The Delany Intersection: Samuel R. Delany Considered As a Writer of Semi-Precious Words*, by George Edgar Slusser. The Milford Series: Popular Writers of Today, Volume 10. December 1977, 64 p.

16. *The Wings of Madness: A Novel of Charles Baudelaire*, by Geoffrey Wagner. April 1978, 224 p.

17. *Worlds Beyond the World: The Fantastic Vision of William Morris*, by Richard Mathews. The Milford Series: Popular Writers of Today, Volume 13. May 1978, 63 p.

18. *The Dream Quest of H. P. Lovecraft*, by Darrell Schweitzer. The Milford Series: Popular Writers of Today, Volume 12. May 1978, 63 p.

19. *The Space Odysseys of Arthur C. Clarke*, by George Edgar Slusser. The Milford Series: Popular Writers of Today, Volume 8. July 1978, 64 p.

20. *Lightning from a Clear Sky: Tolkien, the Trilogy, and the Silmarillion*, by Richard Mathews. The Milford Series: Popular Writers of Today, Volume 15. July 1978, 63 p.

21. *Beware of the Mouse*, by Leonard Wibberley. October 1978, 189, [iii] p.

22. *Conan's World and Robert E. Howard*, by Darrell Schweitzer. The Milford Series: Popular Writers of Today, Volume 17. November 1978, 64 p.

23. *A Usual Lunacy*, by D. G. Compton. November 1978, 191 p.

24. *Against Time's Arrow: The High Crusade of Poul Anderson*, by Sandra Miesel. The Milford Series: Popular Writers of Today, Volume 18. December 1978, 64 p.

25. *The Clockwork Universe of Anthony Burgess*, by Richard Mathews. The Milford Series: Popular Writers of Today, Volume 19. December 1978, 63 p.

26. *Pretender: Science Fiction*, by Piers Anthony and Frances Hall. April 1979, 159 p.
27. *The Quest of Excalibur*, by Leonard Wibberley. April 1979, 190 p.
28. *The Haunted Man: The Strange Genius of David Lindsay*, by Colin Wilson. The Milford Series: Popular Writers of Today, Volume 20. May 1979, 63 p.
29. *Colin Wilson: The Outsider and Beyond*, by Clifford P. Bendau. The Milford Series: Popular Writers of Today, Volume 21. May 1979, 63 p.
30. *A Poetry of Force and Darkness: The Fiction of John Hawkes*, by Eliot Berry. The Milford Series: Popular Writers of Today, Volume 22. May 1979, 64 p.
31. *Science Fiction Voices #1: Interviews with Science Fiction Writers*, by Darrell Schweitzer. The Milford Series: Popular Writers of Today, Volume 23. October 1979, 63 p.
32. *A Clash of Symbols: The Triumph of James Blish*, by Brian M. Stableford. October 1979, 62 p.
33. *Farewell, Earth's Bliss*, by D. G. Compton. October 1979, 188 p.
34. *Sir Henry*, by Robert Nathan. October 1979, 187 p.
35. *Science Fiction Voices #2: Interviews with Science Fiction Writers*, by Jeffrey M. Elliot. The Milford Series: Popular Writers of Today, Volume 25. October 1979, 62 p.
36. *Earth Is the Alien Planet: J. G. Ballard's Four-Dimensional Nightmare*, by David Pringle. The Milford Series: Popular Writers of Today, Volume 26. October 1979, 63 p.
37. *The Rainbow Quest of Thomas Pynchon*, by Douglas A. Mackey. The Milford Series: Popular Writers of Today, Volume 28. June 1980, 63 p.
38. *Still Worlds Collide: Philip Wylie and the End of the American Dream*, by Clifford P. Bendau. The Milford Series: Popular Writers of Today, Volume 30. August 1980, 63 p.
39. *Literary Voices #1*, by Jeffrey M. Elliot. The Milford Series: Popular Writers of Today, Volume 27. October 1980, 64 p.
40. *Science Fiction Voices #3: Interviews with Science Fiction Writers*, by Jeffrey M. Elliot. The Milford Series: Popular Writers of Today, Volume 29. November 1980, 64 p.
41. *Science Fiction & Fantasy Awards*, by R. Reginald. The Borgo Reference Library, Volume II. December 1981, 64 p.
42. *Anti-Sartre, with an Essay on Camus*, by Colin Wilson. The Milford Series: Popular Writers of Today, Volume 34. December 1981, 63 p.
43. *The Future of the Space Program; Large Corporations & Society: Discussions with 22 Science-Fiction Writers*, by Jeffrey M. Elliot. Great Issues of the Day #1. December 1981, 64 p.
44. *Masters of Science Fiction: Essays on Six Science Fiction Authors*, by Brian M. Stableford. The Milford Series: Popular Writers of Today, Volume 32. December 1981, 64 p.

45. *Science Fiction Voices #5: Interviews with American Science Fiction Writers of the Golden Age*, by Darrell Schweitzer. The Milford Series: Popular Writers of Today, Volume 35. December 1981, 64 p.

46. *Fantasy Voices: Interviews with American Fantasy Writers*, by Jeffrey M. Elliot. The Milford Series: Popular Writers of Today, Volume 31. January 1982, 64 p.

47. *Science Fiction Voices #4: Interviews with Modern Science Fiction Authors*, by Jeffrey M. Elliot. The Milford Series: Popular Writers of Today, Volume 33. January 1982, 63 p.

48. *Wilderness Visions: Science Fiction Westerns, Volume One*, by David Mogen. I.O. Evans Studies in the Philosophy & Criticism of Literature, Number 1. February 1982, 64 p.

49. *If J.F.K. Had Lived: A Political Scenario*, by R. Reginald and Jeffrey M. Elliot. Borgo Political Scenarios, Number 1. April 1982, 64 p.

50. *Candle for Poland: 469 Days of Solidarity*, by Dr. Leszek Szymanski, edited by R. Reginald. Stokvis Studies in Historical Chronology and Thought, Number 2. June 1982, 128 p.

51. *From Here to Absurdity: The Moral Battlefields of Joseph Heller*, by Stephen W. Potts. The Milford Series: Popular Writers of Today, Volume 36. September 1982, 64 p.

52. *The House of the Burgesses*, by M. R. Burgess. Borgo Family Histories, Number 1. February 1983, xii, 155 p.

53. *The Wickizer Annals: Wickizer, Wickiser, Wickkiser, Wickkizer, Wickheiser*, by Mary Wickizer Burgess with M. R. Burgess. Borgo Family Histories, Number 2. February 1983, xviii, 126 p.

54. *Pulp Voices; or, Science Fiction Voices #6: Interviews with Pulp Magazine Writers and Editors*, by Jeffrey M. Elliot. The Milford Series: Popular Writers of Today, Volume 37. March 1983, 64 p.

55. *Deathman Pass Me By: Two Years on Death Row*, by Philip Brasfield with Jeffrey M. Elliot. Borgo Bioviews, Number 3. April 1983, 96 p.

56. *The Pulp Western: A Popular History of the sWestern Fiction Magazine in America*, by John A. Dinan. I.O. Evans Studies in the Philosophy & Criticism of Literature, Number 2. August 1983, 128 p.

57. *Tempest in a Teapot: The Falkland Islands War*, by R. Reginald & Jeffrey M. Elliot. Research Assistants: Renata Parrino and Mary A. Burgess. Stokvis Studies in Historical Chronology and Thought, Number 3. August 1983, 176 p.

58. *Interviews with Britain's Angry Young Men: Literary Voices #2*, by Dale Salwak. The Milford Series: Popular Writers of Today, Volume 39. May 1984, 96 p.

59. *Sleepless Nights in the Procrustean Bed: Essays*, by Harlan Ellison, edited by Marty Clark. I.O. Evans Studies in the Philosophy & Criticism of Literature, Number 5. July 1984, 192 p.

60. *A Guide to Science Fiction & Fantasy in the Library of Congress Classification Scheme*, by Michael Burgess. Borgo Cataloging Guides, Number 1. August 1984, 86 p., 8.5 x 11".

61. *The Magic Labyrinth of Philip José Farmer*, by Edgar L. Chapman. The Milford Series: Popular Writers of Today, Volume 38. December 1984, 96 p.

62. *The Work of Jeffrey M. Elliot: An Annotated Bibliography & Guide*, by Boden Clarke. Bibliographies of Modern Authors, Number 2. December 1984, 50 p.

63. *The Work of R. Reginald: An Annotated Bibliography & Guide*, by Michael Burgess with Jeffrey M. Elliot. Bibliographies of Modern Authors, Number 5. January 1985, 48 p.

64. *The Work of Julian May: An Annotated Bibliography & Guide*, by Thaddeus Dikty and R. Reginald. Bibliographies of Modern Authors, Number 3. March 1985, 66 p.

65. *Exploring Fantasy Worlds: Essays on Fantastic Literature*, edited by Darrell Schweitzer. I.O. Evans Studies in the Philosophy & Criticism of Literature, Number 3. April 1985, 112 p.

66. *Lords Temporal & Lords Spiritual: A Chronological Checklist of the Popes, Patriarchs, Katholikoi, and Independent Archbishops and Metropolitans of the Monarchical Autocephalous Churches of the Christian East and West*, by Boden Clarke. Stokvis Studies in Historical Chronology & Thought, Number 1. May 1985, 136 p.

67. *The Work of Bruce McAllister: An Annotated Bibliography & Guide*, by David Ray Bourquin. Bibliographies of Modern Authors, Number 10. December 1985, 30 p.

68. *The Barstow Printer: A Personal Name and Subject Index to the Years 1910-1920*, by Buckley Barry Barrett. San Bernardino County Studies, Number 1. December 1985, 79 p., 8.5 x 11".

69. *Survivors: A Personal Story of the Holocaust*, by Jacob Biber. Studies in Judaica and the Holocaust, Number 2. March 1986, [viii], 200 p.

70. *The Work of Bruce McAllister: An Annotated Bibliography & Guide, [Revised Edition]*, by David Ray Bourquin. Bibliographies of Modern Authors, Number 10. May 1986, 32 p.

71. *The Work of Charles Beaumont: An Annotated Bibliography & Guide*, by William F. Nolan, edited by R. Reginald. Bibliographies of Modern Authors, Number 6. May 1986, 48 p.

72. *The Work of George Zebrowski: An Annotated Bibliography & Guide*, by Jeffrey M. Elliot and R. Reginald. Bibliographies of Modern Authors, Number 4. May 1986, 54 p.

73. *Demon Prince: The Dissonant Worlds of Jack Vance*, by Jack Rawlins. The Milford Series: Popular Writers of Today, Volume 40. June 1986, 104 p.

74. *The Holy Grail Revealed: The Real Secret of Rennes-le-Château*, by Patricia and Lionel Fanthorpe, edited with an Introduction by R. Reginald. November 1986, 144 p.

75. *Blond Barbarians & Noble Savages*, by L. Sprague de Camp. Essays on Fantastic Literature, Number 2. November 1986, 49 p.

76. *It's Down the Slippery Cellar Stairs*, by R. A. Lafferty. Essays on Fantastic Literature, Number 1. November 1986, 54 p.

77. *George Orwell's Guide Through Hell: A Psychological Study of 1984*, by Robert Plank. The Milford Series: Popular Writers of Today, Volume 41. December 1986, 123 p.

78. *Decisive Warfare: A Study in Military Theory*, by Reginald Bretnor. Stokvis Studies in Historical Chronology and Thought, Number 5. December 1986, [xxiv], 9-192 p.

79. *D. H. Lawrence, the Poet Who Was Not Wrong*, by Douglas A. Mackey. The Milford Series: Popular Writers of Today, Volume 42. December 1986, 149 p.

80. *Science Fiction and Fantasy Research Index, Volume 7*, by Hal W. Hall and Jan Swanbeck. [unknown] 1987, [ii], 197 p., 8.5 x 11".

81. *The Sociology of Science Fiction*, by Brian M. Stableford. I.O. Evans Studies in the Philosophy & Criticism of Literature, Number 4. April 1987, 189 p.

82. *Non-Literary Influences on Science Fiction*, by Algis Budrys. Essays on Fantastic Literature, Number 4. December 1987, 30 p.

83. *Mystery and Detective Fiction in the Library of Congress Classification Scheme*, by Michael Burgess. Borgo Cataloging Guides, Number 2. December 1987, 184 p.

84. *Whaling Masters*, compiled by the Federal Writers Project of the Works Progress Administration of Massachusetts. Stokvis Studies in Historical Chronology and Thought, Number 8. December 1987, 314 p.

85. *Science Fiction and Fantasy Research Index, Volume 8*, compiled by Hal W. Hall. 1988, iv, 68 p., 8.5 x 11".

86. *A Guide to Science Fiction and Fantasy in the Library of Congress Classification Scheme, Second Edition*, by Michael Burgess. Borgo Cataloging Guides, Number 1. February 1988, 168 p.

87. *Ah Julian! A Memoir of Julian Brodetsky*, by Leonard Wibberley. Borgo Bioviews, Number 3. February 1988, [vi], 154 p.

88. *Hugo Gernsback, Father of Modern Science Fiction, with Essays on Frank Herbert and Bram Stoker*, by Mark Siegel. The Milford Series: Popular Writers of Today, Volume 45. March 1988, 96 p.

89. *The Work of William F. Nolan: An Annotated Bibliography & Guide*, by Boden Clarke and James Hopkins. Bibliographies of Modern Authors, Number 14. October 1988, 224 p.

90. *Western Fiction in the Library of Congress Classification Scheme*, by Michael Burgess and Beverly A. Ryan. Borgo Cataloging Guides, Number 3. October 1988, 48 p.

91. *Black Paradise: The Rastafarian Movement*, by Peter B. Clarke. New Religious Movements Series, Number [1]. November 1988, 112 p.

92. *My Sweet Lord: The Hare Krishna Movement*, by Kim Knott. New Religious Movements Series, Number [2]. November 1988, 112 p.

93. *The Way of the Heart: The Rajneesh Movement*, by Judith Thompson and Paul Heelas. New Religious Movements Series, Number [3]. November 1988, 142 p.

94. *The Work of Colin Wilson: An Annotated Bibliography & Guide*, by Colin Stanley, edited by Boden Clarke. Bibliographies of Modern Authors, Number 1. September 1989, 312 p.

95. *Existentially Speaking: Essays on the Philosophy of Literature*, by Colin Wilson, introduction by Colin Stanley. I.O. Evans Studies in the Philosophy and Criticism of Literature, Number 7. September 1989, 144 p.

96. *The Monumental Inscriptions in the Churches and Churchyards of the Island of Barbados, British West Indies*, by Vere Landford Oliver. Stokvis Studies in Historical Chronology and Thought, Number 13. San Bernardino, CA: The Borgo Press; Glendale, CA: The Sidewinder Press, September 1989, viii, 224 p.

97. *The Poison Maiden & the Great Bitch: Female Stereotypes in Marvel Superhero Comics*, by Susan Wood. Essays on Fantastic Literature, Number 5. September 1989, 28 p.

98. *Ray Bradbury: Dramatist*, by Ben P. Indick. Essays on Fantastic Literature, Number 3. September 1989, 48 p.

99. *The Work of Chad Oliver: An Annotated Bibliography & Guide*, by Hal W. Hall, edited by Boden Clarke. Bibliographies of Modern Authors, Number 12. October 1989, 88 p.

100. *Pioneer Tales of San Bernardino County*, compiled by the WPA Writers' Program. West Coast Studies, Number 2. Hollywood, CA: Sidewinder, distributed by The Borgo Press, November 1989, 60 p.

101. *The Work of Ian Watson: An Annotated Bibliography & Guide*, by Douglas A. Mackey. Bibliographies of Modern Authors, Number 18. December 1989, 148 p.

102. *The Work of Reginald Bretnor: An Annotated Bibliography & Guide*, by Scott Alan Burgess. Bibliographies of Modern Authors, Number 8. December 1989, 122 p.

103. *Chronology of the Death Valley Region in California, 1849-1949, and Place Names of the Death Valley Region in California and Nevada, 1845-1947: An Index of the Events, Persons, and Publications Connected with Its History*, by T. S. Palmer. West Coast Studies, Number 3. Hollywood, CA: Sidewinder, distributed by The Borgo Press, December 1989, [ii], 22, 5-80 p.

104. *The Work of Ross Rocklynne: An Annotated Bibliography & Guide*, by Douglas Menville. Bibliographies of Modern Authors, Number 17. December 1989, 70 p.

105. *The Work of Pamela Sargent: An Annotated Bibliography & Guide*, by Jeffrey M. Elliot. Bibliographies of Modern Authors, Number 13. January 1990, 80 p.

106. *T'ai-Chi Ch'uan, Its Effects & Practical Application*, by Chen Yen-Lin. January 1990, vi, 184, [xx] p.

107. *You Are What You Eat*, by Victor H. Lindlahr. January 1990, 128 p.

108. *The Work of Jack Dann: An Annotated Bibliography & Guide*, by Jeffrey M. Elliot. Bibliographies of Modern Authors, Number 16. April 1990, 128 p.

109. *Across the Wide Missouri: The Diary of a Journey from Virginia to Missouri in 1819 and Back Again in 1822, with a Description of the City of Cincinnati*, by James Brown Campbell, edited by Mary Wickizer Burgess. Stokvis Studies in Historical Chronology and Thought, Number 4. May 1990, 139 p.

110. *What Are You Doing in My Universe?*, by Chuck Hillig. August 1990, [224] p.

111. *The Work of George Zebrowski: An Annotated Bibliography & Guide, Second Edition, Revised and Expanded*, by Jeffrey M. Elliot and Robert Reginald, edited by Boden Clarke. Bibliographies of Modern Authors, Number 4. October 1990, 118 p.

112. *To Kill or Not To Kill: Thoughts on Capital Punishment*, by Rep. William L. Clay, edited by Michael and Mary Burgess. Great Issues of the Day, Number 4. October 1990, 208 p.

113. *The Work of Charles Beaumont: An Annotated Bibliography & Guide*, by William F. Nolan, edited by Boden Clarke. Bibliographies of Modern Authors, Number 6. November 1990, 92 p.

114. *The Work of Dean Ing: An Annotated Bibliography & Guide*, by Scott Alan Burgess, edited by Boden Clarke. Bibliographies of Modern Authors, Number 11. December 1990, 82 p.

115. *First Century Palestinian Judaism: A Bibliography of Works in English*, by David Ray Bourquin. Studies in Judaica and the Holocaust, Number 6. December 1990, 104 p.

116. *Victorian Criticism of American Writers: A Guide to British Criticism of American Writers in the Leading British Periodicals of the Victorian Period, 1824-1900*, by Arnella K. Turner. Borgo Literary Guides, Number 6. April 1991, 456 p.

117. *The Beach Boys: Southern California Pastoral, Revised [Second] Edition*, by Bruce Golden, updated by Paul David Seldis. The Woodstock Series: Popular Music of Today, Number 1. April 1991, 104 p.

118. *At Wolfe's Door: The Nero Wolfe Novels of Rex Stout*, by J. Kenneth Van Dover. The Milford Series: Popular Writers of Today, Volume 52. April 1991, 120 p.

119. *Jerzy Kosinski: The Literature of Violation*, by Welch D. Everman. The Milford Series: Popular Writers of Today, Volume 47. April 1991, 160 p.

120. *The Second Marxian Invasion: The Fiction of the Strugatsky Brothers*, by Stephen W. Potts. The Milford Series: Popular Writers of Today, Volume 50. April 1991, 104 p.

121. *Starclimber: The Literary Adventures and Autobiography of Raymond Z. Gallun*, by Raymond Z. Gallun with Jeffrey M. Elliot, edited by Paul David Seldis and Mary A. Burgess. Borgo Bioviews, No. 1. May 1991, 168 p.

122. *David Lodge: How Far Can You Go?*, by Merritt Moseley. The Milford Series: Popular Writers of Today, Volume 16. May 1991, viii, 112 p.

123. *The Italian Theatre in San Francisco, Being a History of the Italian-Language Operatic, Dramatic, and Comedic Productions Presented in the San Francisco Bay Area Through the Depression Era, with Reminiscences of the Leading Players and Impresarios of the Times*, by Lawrence Estavan, edited by Mary A. Burgess. Clipper Studies in the American Theatre, Number 3. May 1991, 120 p.

124. *Mystery Voices: Interviews with British Crime Writers*, by Dale Salwak. Brownstone Mystery Guides, Volume 8. July 1991, 112 p. The first of the "new" Brownstone Mystery Guides.

125. *The Jewish Holocaust: An Annotated Guide to Books in English*, by Marty Bloomberg. Studies in Judaica and the Holocaust, Number 1. August 1991, 248 p.

126. *The Trilemma of World Oil Politics*, by Jeffrey M. Elliot and Sheikh R. Ali, edited by Paul David Seldis and Michael Burgess. Great Issues of the Day, Number 2. October 1991, 152 p.

127. *The Work of Louis L'Amour: An Annotated Bibliography & Guide*, by Hal W. Hall, edited by Boden Clarke. Bibliographies of Modern Authors, Number 15. October 1991, 192 p.

128. *The Little Kitchen Cookbook*, by Scottie Kimberlin, [edited by Mary A. Burgess]. November 1991, 160 p.

129. *Reginald's Science Fiction and Fantasy Awards: A Comprehensive Guide to the Awards and Their Winners, Second Edition, Revised and Expanded*, by Daryl F. Mallett & Robert Reginald. Borgo Literary Guides, Number 1. November 1991, 248 p.

130. *One Day with God: A Guide to Retreats and the Contemplative Life, Revised Edition*, by Bishop Karl Prüter. St. Willibrord Studies in Philosophy & Religion, Number 1. December 1991, 56 p.

131. *The Work of Robert Reginald: An Annotated Bibliography & Guide, Second Edition, Revised and Expanded*, by Michael Burgess. Bibliographies of Modern Authors, Number 5. February 1992, 176 p.

132. *Inside Science Fiction: Essays on Fantastic Literature*, by James Gunn. I. O. Evans Studies in the Philosophy & Criticism of Literature, Number 11. March 1992, 184 p.

XENOS BOOKS
(An Associated Imprint, 1986-1990)

1. *Orgy & Other Things*, by Gary Kern. 1986, 216 p.
2. *The Mad Kokoschka: A Play in 3 Acts*, by Gary Kern. 1986, 87 p.
3. *Anti-Posters: Soviet Icons in Reverse*, by Boris Mukhametshin. 1987, 164 p., 8.5 x 11".
4. *Misfortune*, by Gary Kern. 1990, 177 p.
5. *The Poet Is a Little God: Creationist Verse of Vicente Huidobro*, translated by Jorge García-Gómez. 1990, xxxii, 180 p.

BROWNSTONE BOOKS
(Acquired 1/1/1991)

1. *The Armchair Detective, Volume One*, edited by Allen J. Hubin. 1981. viii, 158 p.
2. *The Sound of Detection: Ellery Queen's Adventures in Radio*, by Francis M. Nevins, Jr. & Ray Stanich. 1983. viii, 109 p.
3. *Detective and Mystery Fiction: An International Bibliography of Secondary Sources*, by Walter Albert. 1984. xii, 781 p.
4. *Hardboiled Burlesque: Raymond Chandler's Comic Style*, by Keith Newlin. Brownstone Chapbook Series, Vol. 1. 1984. 50 p.
5. *The New Hard-Boiled Dicks: A Personal Checklist*, by Robert E. Skinner. Brownstone Chapbook Series, Vol. 2. 1987. 60 p.
6. *TAD-Schrift: Twenty Years of Mystery Fandom in The Armchair Detective*, edited by J. Randolph Cox. 1987. viii, 111 p.
7. *John Nieminski: Somewhere a Roscoe*, by John Nieminski, edited by Ely Liebow and Art Scott. Brownstone Chapbook Series, Vol. 3. 1987. 61 p.
8. *Frederick Irving Anderson (1877-1947): A Biobibliography*, by Benjamin Franklin Fisher IV. Brownstone Chapbook Series, Vol. 4. 1987. 43 p.
9. *A Detective in Distress: Philip Marlowe's Domestic Dream*, by Gay Brewer. Brownstone Chapbook Series, Vol. 5. 1989. 68 p.

THE STARMONT CONTEMPORARY WRITERS SERIES
(Acquired 1/1/1991)

1. *Roald Dahl*, by Alan Warren. 1988. vi, 105 p. Will become: The Milford Series: Popular Writers of Today, Vol. 71.
2. *Margaret Drabble, Symbolic Moralist*, by Nora Foster Stovel. 1989. vii, 224 p. Will become: The Milford Series: Popular Writers of Today, Vol. 72.

SIDEWINDER PRESS
(Acquired 7/1/1991)

1. *Heroes and Incidents of the Mexican War*, by Isaac George. 1985, 296 p.
2. *The Life and Struggles of Negro Toilers*, by George Padmore. 1985, 126 p.

ST. WILLIBRORD'S PRESS
(Acquired 9/1/1991)

1. *Bishops Extraordinary*, by Karl Prüter. 1985, 58 p.
2. *A Directory of Autocephalous Anglican, Catholic, and Orthodox Bishops, Fifth Edition*, by Karl Prüter. 1989, 65 p.
3. *Episcopi Vagantes and the Anglican Church*, by George Brandreth. 1987, xix, 79 p.
4. *A History of the Old Catholic Church*, by Karl Prüter. 1985, 76 p.
5. *Neo-Congregationalism*, by Karl Prüter. 1985, 90 p.
6. *The People of God*, by Karl Prüter. 1985, v, 162 p.
7. *The Priest's Handbook*, by Karl Prüter. 1991, vi, 43 p.
8. *The Strange Partnership of George Alexander McGuire and Marcus Garvey*, by Karl Prüter. 1986, 50 p.
9. *The Teachings of the Great Mystics*, by Karl Prüter. 1985, 118 p.
10. *The Theology of Congregationalism*, by Karl Prüter. 1985, 100 p.

D8. **Supernatural & Occult Fiction: 63 Books.** Advisory Editors: R. Reginald, Douglas Menville. New York: Arno Press, December 1976, 64 v., cloth. Advertising brochure: 40 p., paper. Bound in dark purple cloth. The series subtitle resulted from the fact that *Fantazius Mallare* and its sequel, *The Kingdom of Evil*, were originally slated for publication in one volume. [book series]

1. *Auriol; or, The Elixir of Life*, by W. Harrison Ainsworth. vi, 246 p.
2. *Ghost Stories*, by Michael Arlen. 181 p.
3. *The Centenarian; or, The Two Beringhelds*, by Honoré de Balzac. vi, 454 p.
4. *The Ninth Vibration, and Other Stories*, by L. Adams Beck. 313 p.
5. *Spook Stories*, by E. F. Benson. ix, 287 p.
6. *The Centaur*, by Algernon Blackwood. 347 p.
7. *Strange Stories*, by Algernon Blackwood. 745 p.
8. *Pharos, the Egyptian*, by Guy Boothby. 376 p.
9. *The Boyhood Days of Guy Fawkes; or, The Conspirators of Old London*. 184 p.
10. *Someone in the Room*, by A. M. Burrage. 285 p.
11. *Suomiria: A Fantasy*, by the Earl of Southesk. 322 p.
12. *The Collected Tales of A. E. Coppard*. viii, 532 p.
13. *With the Immortals*, by F. Marion Crawford. 300 p.

14. *The Gentleman in Black*, by James Dalton. iv, 309 p.
15. *The Return*, by Walter de la Mare. 312 p.
16. *Mirrikh; or, A Woman from Mars*, by Francis W. Doughty. 274 p.
17. *The Man-Wolf, and Other Tales*, by Erckmann-Chatrian. 252 p.
18. *Alraune*, by Hanns Heinz Ewers. vi, 341 p.
19. *A Journey from This World to the Next*, by Henry Fielding. 175 p.
20. *Spirite*, by Théophile Gautier. 293 p.
21. *The Mummy and Miss Nitocris*, by George Griffith. viii, 311 p.
22. *Argal; or, The Silver Devil*, by George Hadley. 2 v. in one.
23. *Allan and the Ice-Gods*, by H. Rider Haggard. 316 p.
24. *Midnight House, and Other Tales*, by W. Fryer Harvey. v, 343 p.
25. *Fantastics, and Other Fancies*, by Lafcadio Hearn. ix, 241 p.
26. *Fantazius Mallare: A Mysterious Oath*, by Ben Hecht. 174 p.
27. *The Kingdom of Evil*, by Ben Hecht. 211 p.
28. *The Strange Papers of Dr Blayre*, by Edward Heron-Allen. 271 p.
29. *Elsie Venner*, by Oliver Wendell Holmes. xvi, 487 p.
30. *The Were-Wolf*, by Clemence Housman. 123 p.
31. *The Thing from the Lake*, by Eleanor M. Ingram. 315 p.
32. *The Five Jars*, by M. R. James. 172 p.
33. *Chrysal; or, The Adventures of a Guinea*, by Charles Johnstone. 2 v. in one.
34. *The Devil and the Doctor*, by David H. Keller. v, 308 p.
35. *The Street of Queer Houses, and Other Tales*, by Vernon Knowles. vii, 225 p.
36. *A Stable for Nightmares; or, Weird Tales*. 256 p.
37. *The Devil on Two Sticks*, by Alain René Le Sage. xxii, 274 p.
38. *The Children of the Pool, and Other Stories*, by Arthur Machen. 255 p.
39. *The Strange Visitation of Josiah McNason*, by Marie Corelli. 118 p.
40. *The Dead Man's Message*, by Florence Marryat. 178 p.
41. *The Beetle*, by Richard Marsh. vii, 338 p.
42. *Ancient Hauntings*, edited by Douglas Menville and R. Reginald. [383] p.
43. *Phantasmagoria*, edited by Douglas Menville & R. Reginald. [357] p.
44. *The Fox Woman and the Blue Pagoda; and, The Black Wheel*, by A. Merritt and Hannes Bok. 109, 115 p.
45. *Uncanny Tales*, by Mrs. Molesworth. 228 p.
46. *The Sorcery Club*, by Elliott O'Donnell. vii, 342 p.
47. *Widdershins*, by Oliver Onions. 315 p.
48. *For Maurice: Five Unlikely Stories*, by Vernon Lee. li, 223 p.
49. *Robinson Crusoe's Return*, by Barry Pain. 168 p.
50. *The Mystery of Evelin Delorme*, by Albert B. Paine. 129 p.
51. *A Deal with the Devil*, by Eden Phillpotts. 190 p.
52. *Morwyn; or, The Vengeance of God*, by John Cowper Powys. 321 p.
53. *The Brother of the Shadow*, by Mrs. Campbell Praed. 158 p.
54. *R.I.P.: Five Stories of the Supernatural*, edited by R. Reginald and Douglas Menville. [278] p.

55. *The Spectre Bridegroom, and Other Horrors,* edited by R. Reginald and Douglas Menville. [308] p.
56. *The Necromancer,* by George W. M. Reynolds. 263 p.
57. *The Death Ship,* by W. Clark Russell. 3 v. in one.
58. *The Ghost,* by Clara Sicard. viii, 267 p.
59. *The House of the Vampire,* by George Sylvester Viereck. 190 p.
60. *Maker of Shadows,* by Jack Mann. 288 p.
61. *Ghost Stories,* by H. Russell Wakefield. 288 p.
62. *Ringstones, and Other Curious Tales,* by Sarban. 283 p.
63. *Grey Face,* by Sax Rohmer. vi, 331 p.
64. *Heliondé; or, Adventures in the Sun,* by Sydney Waiting. xiv, 424 p.

D9. **Lost Race and Adult Fantasy Fiction: 69 Books.** Advisory Editors: R. Reginald, Douglas Menville. New York: Arno Press, June 1978, 69 v., cloth. Advertising brochure: 32 p., paper. Bound in brown cloth. [book series]

1. *The Bladed Barrier,* by Joseph Bushnell Ames. viii, 393 p.
2. *The Treasure Vault of Atlantis,* by Olof W. Anderson. 326 p.
3. *Lepidus the Centurion,* by Edwin Lester Arnold. 305 p.
4. *The Devil-Tree of Eldorado,* by Frank Aubrey. xx, 392 p.
5. *King of the Dead,* by Frank Aubrey. 292 p.
6. *Thyra: A Romance of the Polar Pit,* by Robert A. Bennet. 258 p.
7. *The Heads of Cerberus,* by Francis Stevens. 190 p.
8. *The Fruit Stoners,* by Algernon Blackwood. 286 p.
9. *The Xipéhuz; and, The Death of the Earth,* by J. H. Rosny. xxii, 183 p.
10. *Mukara,* by Muriel Bruce. 278 p.
11. *Miss Carter and the Ifrit,* by Susan Alice Kerby. 160 p.
12. *The Vampires of the Andes,* by Henry Carew. 320 p.
13. *The Slayer of Souls,* by Robert W. Chambers. 301 p.
14. *White Python,* by Mark Channing. 320 p.
15. *The Jingo,* by George Randolph Chester. 393 p.
16. *The Light in the Sky,* by Herbert Clock & Eric Boetzal. 304 p.
17. *When the Birds Fly South,* by Stanton A. Coblentz. 223 p.
18. *The Devil, Poor Devil!,* by Murray Constantine. 255 p.
19. *Cast Away at the Pole,* by William Wallace Cook. 311 p.
20. *Revi-Lona,* by Frank Cowan. 247 p.
21. *Bibliography of Adventure,* by Bradford M. Day. 125 p.
22. *Monk's Magic,* by Alexander de Comeau. vi, 250 p.
23. *The Last Man; or, Omegarus and Syderia,* by Jean de Grainville. 220, 204 p.
24. *The Flower of Fate,* by J. Allan Dunn. 254 p.
25. *Styrbiorn the Strong,* by E. R. Eddison. 256 p.
26. *The Prince of Gravas,* by Alfred C. Fleckenstein. 270 p.
27. *The Land of the Living Dead,* by Neal Fyne. 251 p.

28. *Angel Island*, by Inez Haynes Gillmore. 351 p.
29. *Adventures in Sakaeland*, by Ganpat. 652 p.
30. *Z R Wins*, by Fitzhugh Green. 270 p.
31. *Daughter of the Sun*, by Jackson Gregory. viii, 271 p.
32. *The Romance of Golden Star*, by George Griffith. vii, 284 p.
33. *Humour & Fantasy*, by F. Anstey. x, 1173 p.
34. *The Mahatma and the Hare*, by H. Rider Haggard. 164 p.
35. *Wisdom's Daughter*, by H. Rider Haggard. x, 383 p.
36. *Melusine; or, Devil Take Her!* by Charlotte Haldane. 317 p.
37. *The Princess Thora*, by Harris Burland. 360 p.
38. *Among the Gnomes*, by Franz Hartmann. 272 p.
39. *Daughter of the Dawn*, by William Reginald Hodder. 333 p.
40. *Sapphires*, by Vernon Knowles. 202 p.
41. *Shades of Hades*, by Frederic Arnold Kummer. x, 272, 369 p.
42. *Asleep in the Afternoon*, by E. C. Large. 351 p.
43. *The Eye of Istar*, by William Le Queux. 382 p.
44. *The Bride of the Sun*, by Gaston Leroux. 303 p.
45. *Devil's Tor*, by David Lindsay. 487 p.
46. *A Spell for Old Bones*, by Eric Linklater. 223 p.
47. *Hearts of Three*, by Jack London. ix, 373 p.
48. *The Return of William Shakespeare*, by Hugh Kingsmill. 332 p.
49. *The King of Kor*, by Sidney J. Marshall. 258 p.
50. *I Am Thinking of My Darling*, by Vincent McHugh. 292 p.
51. *Dreamers of Dreams*, edited by Douglas Menville and R. Reginald. [478] p.
52. *Worlds of Never: Three Fantastic Novels*, edited by Douglas Menville and R. Reginald. [430] p.
53. *The Fox Woman, and Other Stories*, by A. Merritt. 205 p.
54. *Book of the Three Dragons*, by Kenneth Morris. xii, 206 p.
55. *Gobi or Shamo*, by G. G. A. Murray. 376 p.
56. *The Purple Sea*, by Frank Owen. 153 p.
57. *Istar of Babylon*, by Margaret Horton Potter. xvi, 494 p.
58. *King Solomon's Children*, edited by R. Reginald and Douglas Menville. [564] p.
59. *They*, edited by R. Reginald and Douglas Menville. [592] p.
60. *Hubert's Arthur*, by Frederick Rolfe and Charles Pirie-Gordon. 453 p.
61. *Beyond the Great South Wall*, by Frank Savile. 322 p.
62. *The Last Lemurian*, by G. Firth Scott. viii, 339 p.
63. *The Power of Ula*, by Miles Sheldon-Williams. 320 p.
64. *Prince Hagen*, by Upton Sinclair. 249 p.
65. *Kai Lung Beneath the Mulberry Tree*, by Ernest Bramah. 320 p.
66. *Over the Mountain*, by Ruthven Todd. 272 p.
67. *Aia: Fields of Sleep; and, People of the Darkness*, by E. Charles Vivian. 576 p.
68. *A King There Was—*, by E. Charles Vivian. 320 p.

69. *The Wonderful Visit*, by H. G. Wells. viii, 251 p.

SECONDARY SOURCES AND REVIEWS:

1. Clareson, Thomas D. "Books." *Extrapolation* 20 (Summer, 1979): 189-191.
2. Tymn, Marshall Benton. *Choice* (December, 1978): 1333-1334.

D10. *Science Fiction & Fantasy Book Review.* ISSN 0163-4348. Publisher and uncredited Co-Editor: R. Reginald; Editor: Neil Barron. San Bernardino, CA: The Borgo Press, Feb. 1979-Feb. 1980, 13 issues, paper. Later bound in cloth form and offered by Borgo as a monograph. Many of the reviews included in this magazine were reworked or rewritten by Reginald. [review magazine]

   a. Vol. I, No. 1—February, 1979.
   b. Vol. I, No. 2—March, 1979.
   c. Vol. I, No. 3—April, 1979.
   d. Vol. I, No. 4—May, 1979.
   e. Vol. I, No. 5—June, 1979.
   f. Vol. I, No. 6—July, 1979.
   g. Vol. I, No. 7—August, 1979.
   h. Vol. I, No. 8—September, 1979.
   i. Vol. I, No. 9—October, 1979.
   j. Vol. I, No. 10—November, 1979.
   k. Vol. I, No. 11—December, 1979.
   l. Vol. II, No. 12—January, 1980.
   m. Vol. II, No. 13—February, 1980.

SECONDARY SOURCES AND REVIEWS:

1. Hall, Hal W. "Magazines." *Library Journal* (February 15, 1980): 493.
2. Lareau, Chris. *Sense of Wonder* (August, 1979): .

D11. *Survey of Modern Fantasy Literature*, edited by Frank N. Magill. Consultant: Robert Reginald. Englewood Cliffs, NJ: Salem Press, November 1983, 2538 p. in 5 v., cloth. Reginald was one of six experts used as Consulting Editors. [literary criticism]

D12. *Fandom Directory, No. 7*, edited by Harry A. Hopkins. Art Contest Judge: R. Reginald. San Bernardino, CA: Fandom Computer Services, April 1985, paper. [directory]

D13. *LTF Newsletter.* ISSN 1040-1470. Editor: Michael Burgess. Los Angeles, CA: Librarians' Task Force, California Faculty Association, Fall, 1987-Spring, 1989, paper. Burgess was Founding Editor of this library publication. [professional newsletter]

    a. No. 1—Fall, 1987. 8 p.
    b. No. 2—Fall, 1988. 8 p.
    c. No. 3—Spring, 1989. 8 p.

D14. *Twentieth-Century Science-Fiction Writers, Third Edition,* edited by Noelle Watson and Paul Schellinger. Advisers: Robert Reginald, etc. Chicago and London: St James Press, December 1991, xxvi, 1016 p., cloth. Reginald served on the board of editorial advisers for this academic publication, and also reworked the basic "Reading List" (i.e., suggested bibliography of secondary sources) on pages ix-xv, in addition to contributing seven critical essays of his own (qq.v.). [bio-bibliography]

E.
DOCUMENTS

NOTE: In the course of his official duties as a member of the library faculty at California State University, San Bernardino, the author has produced hundreds of signed and unsigned documents, including position papers, memoranda, evaluations, etc., but has made no attempt to keep track of any except those regarded as major.

E1.   *California State College, San Bernardino Library Policy Manual,* non-bylined. San Bernardino, CA: State College Library, 1973, 113 p., pam bound. [manual]

This was the first attempt on the CSCSB campus systematically to compile a set of policies and guidelines for one academic department, arranged logically by subject, and numbered, section by section, division by subdivision. Produced as an in-house publication for campus use, in an edition of about fifty copies.

E2.   *CSCSB Periodicals Holdings List 1974,* non-bylined. San Bernardino, CA: California State College Library, 1974, [ca. 300 p.], pam bound. [holdings list]

Burgess was responsible for converting a five-year-old periodi-cals holdings list to machine-readable form in 1974, and for producing the first version of that list organized by subject.

E3.   *CSCSB Periodicals Subject List 1974,* non-bylined. San Bernardino, CA: California State College Library, 1974, [ca. 300 p.], pam bound. [holdings list]

E4.   *CSCSB Periodicals Holdings List 1976,* edited by M. R. Burgess. San Bernardino, CA: California State College Library, 1976, [ca. 300 p.], pam bound. [holdings list]

E5.   *CSCSB Periodicals Subject List 1976,* edited by M. R. Burgess. San Bernardino, CA: California State College Library, 1976, [ca. 300 p.], pam bound. [holdings list]

E6.   *CSCSB Periodicals Holdings List 1977*, edited by M. R. Burgess. San Bernardino, CA: California State College Library, 1977, [ca. 300 p.], pam bound. [holdings list]

E7.   *CSCSB Periodicals Subject List 1977*, edited by M. R. Burgess. San Bernardino, CA: California State College Library, 1977, [ca. 300 p.], pam bound. [holdings list]

E8.   *CSCSB Periodicals Holdings List 1980*, edited by M. R. Burgess. San Bernardino, CA: California State College Library, 1980, [ca. 300 p.], pam bound. [holdings list]

E9.   *CSCSB Periodicals Subject List 1980*, edited by M. R. Burgess. San Bernardino, CA: California State College Library, 1980, [ca. 300 p.], pam bound. [holdings list]

E10.   *CSCSB Periodicals Holdings List 1981-82*, edited by M. R. Burgess. San Bernardino, CA: California State College Library, 1981, [ca. 300 p.], pam bound. [holdings list]

E11.   *CSCSB Periodicals Subject List 1981-82*, edited by M. R. Burgess. San Bernardino, CA: California State College Library, 1981, [ca. 300 p.], pam bound. [holdings list]

E12.   *CSCSB Library Policy Manual, Second Edition*, edited by M. R. Burgess. San Bernardino, CA: California State College, Spring 1981, 105 p., pam bound. [policy manual]

A completely revised edition of A3, produced for in-house use in an edition of about one hundred copies. This manual set the standard for similar documents produced by other departments at California State University, San Bernardino.

E13.   "Reorganization Plan, CSUSB Library, October, 1986," nonbylined. 5 p. Prepared at the request of the Library Director. [position paper]

E14.   "CSUSB Librarians," nonbylined. June 1990, 3 p. An historical list (chronological and alphabetical by surname) of the thirty-four librarians who have worked at the Pfau Library, California State University, San Bernardino, prepared for use in conjunction with the twenty-fifth anniversary celebration of the CSUSB campus during the school year 1990/91. [checklists]

E15.   "CSUSB Library Staff Members," nonbylined. October 1990, 9 p. An historical list (alphabetical, chronological, and by years of employment) of the 209 library and clerical assistants who have worked at the Pfau Library, California State University, San Bernardino, prepared in conjunction with the twenty-fifth anniversary celebration of the CSUSB campus during the school year 1990/91. [checklists]

E16.   "CSUSB Alumni Authors," by Michael Burgess. October 1990, 4 leaves. A bibliography of publications produced by the CSUSB alumni, arranged alphabetically by author, and then by title, with complete bibliographical information. [bibliography]

E17.   "A Bibliography of CSUSB Alumni Authors," by Michael Burgess. October 1990, 3 leaves. A bibliography of publications produced by the CSUSB alumni, arranged alphabetically by author, and then by title, with complete bibliographical information. [bibliography]

E18.   "A Bibliography of CSUSB Alumni Authors, Composers, and Playwrights: February, 1991," by Michael Burgess. February 1991, 8 leaves. A bibliography of publications produced by the CSUSB alumni, prepared for an exhibit at the John Pfau Library, California State University, San Bernardino, of alumni publications. The list is arranged alphabetically by author, and then by title, with complete bibliographical information. Authors covered include: Annette Annechild, Arnold Arias, Michelle Bancroft, Danny Bilson, Mary Wickizer Burgess, Frank D. Campbell Jr., Juan Delgado, Paul De Meo, James D. Elder, Joanne Fluke, Robert Gordon, Susan Sterkel Haugh, Phillip W. Holdaway, Jonni Kincher, Jeff Kopang, Marsha Muscato, and Michael Reaves. [bibliography]

E19.   "CSUSB Library Faculty (June 1991)," nonbylined. June 1991, 3 p. An historical list (by name, by date hired, by years of service) of the forty library faculty who have worked at the Pfau Library, California State University, San Bernardino, prepared for use in conjunction with the twenty-fifth anniversary celebration of the CSUSB campus during the school year 1990/91. [checklists]

E20.   "CSUSB Library Staff (June 1991)," nonbylined. June 1991, 15 p. An historical list (by name, by date hired, and by years of service) of the 212 library and clerical assistants who have worked at the Pfau Library, California State University, San Bernardino, prepared in conjunction with the twenty-fifth anniversary celebration of the CSUSB campus during the school year 1990/91. [checklists]

F.

CATALOGS

NOTE: With Douglas Menville, Reginald wrote all of the catalog and cover copy for Newcastle Publishing Company, Inc., from its inception in 1971 through about 1980, and all the catalog copy for The Borgo Press from February, 1979, when Borgo began selling its books directly for the first time, through 1990. All catalogs listed are 8.5 x 11" in size unless otherwise noted.

F1. **Unicorn & Son.** Medford, OR: Unicorn & Son, 1970, 1 p. An 8.5 x 11" single-sheet flyer advertising this company's one and only publication, *Stella Nova*.

F2. **Herder and Herder Distributes Information Books and Newcastle Publishing: Self-Improvement and Occult Books, Spring 1971.** New York: Herder & Herder, 1971, 4 p., paper. Features, in addition to Information Books titles, the first eight releases from Newcastle Publishing Co., Inc. Red and black ink on white paper.

F3. **Herder and Herder: Fall 1971.** New York: Herder & Herder, 1971, paper, p. 43. The first eight Newcastle books appear on one page of this 50-page catalog. Blue and black ink on white paper.

F4. **Newcastle Publishing** [Spring 1972 Catalog]. Hollywood, CA: Newcastle Publishing Co., Inc., March 1972, 1 p., paper. A complete catalog, featuring the four titles from Newcastle's second list, plus the eight titles published in 1971. Black ink on white paper.

F5. **Books to Pep Up Every Collection: Profit Makers** [Newcastle Catalog, Fall 1972]. Hollywood, CA: Newcastle Publishing Co., August 1972, 1 p., 8½ x 14", paper. A complete stock list, with illustrations and annotations. Black ink on yellow paper.

F6. **Fall Harvest, New and Exciting Books, Now from Newcastle** [Fall 1973 Catalog]. Hollywood, CA: Newcastle Publishing Co., Inc., April 1973, 2 p., 8½ x 14", paper. A complete stock list, with annotations, of all Newcastle books. This catalog announces the first volume in the Forgotten Fantasy Library series. Black ink on white stock.

F7.   **Forgotten Fantasy Lives!** Hollywood, CA: Newcastle Publishing Co., Inc., April 1973, 1 p., paper. An announcement of the impending publication in September 1973 of *The Glittering Plain*, by William Morris, first in the Forgotten Fantasy Library series.

F8.   **Newcastle Publishing Company, Inc.: Books for Spring 1974.** Hollywood, CA: Newcastle Publishing Co., Inc., November 1973, 4 p., paper. A complete stock catalog, with annotations and illustrations, of all Newcastle books. Black ink on yellow stock.

F9.   **Newcastle Books in Print, 1974.** Hollywood, CA: Newcastle Publishing Co., Inc., January (?) 1974, 1 p., paper. A photocopied title list by stock number. Black ink on white paper.

F10.   **Newcastle Publishing Company, Inc.: Books for Fall 1974.** Hollywood, CA: Newcastle Publishing Co., Inc., April 1974, 4 p., paper. A complete stock catalog, with annotations and illustrations, of all Newcastle books. Black ink on blue stock.

F11.   **Science Fiction: 62 Books.** Advisory Editors: R. Reginald, Douglas Menville. New York: Arno Press, October 1974, 24 p., paper. Reginald and Menville wrote all of the copy for this catalog, issued by Arno to promote the series they edited; Reginald penned the introductory essay on p. 3.

   b.   as: *Science Fiction: 61 Books.* New York: Arno Press, August 1978, 6 p., paper. An abridged version, with different cover design and shorter annotations. Purple ink on white stock.

F12.   **Newcastle Publishing Company, Inc.: Spring Previews 75.** Hollywood, CA: Newcastle Publishing Co., Inc., October 1974, 4 p., paper. A complete stock catalog, with annotations, of all Newcastle books. Ochre ink on orange stock.

F13.   **Newcastle: Fall '75.** Van Nuys, CA: Newcastle Publishing Co., Inc., April 1975, 4 p., paper. A complete stock catalog, with annotations, of Newcastle titles. Purple ink on white stock.

F14.   **Newcastle Spring '76.** Van Nuys, CA: Newcastle Publishing Company, Inc., November 1975, 4 p., paper. A complete Newcastle stock list, arranged by series, title, author, price, with annotations. This is the first Newcastle catalog to feature the new Borgo Press line, which announces its first three titles. Green ink on white stock.

F15. **Supernatural & Occult Fiction: 64 Books.** Advisory Editors: R. Reginald, Douglas Menville. New York: Arno Press, 1976, 40 p., paper, slick cover stock. Reginald and Menville wrote all of the copy for this catalog, issued by Arno to promote the series they edited. Reginald penned the introductory essay on p. 4.

    b. A later version, with non-slick covers, in 5 x 8" size, was issued in August, 1978.

F16. **Newcastle: Fall '76.** Van Nuys, CA: Newcastle Publishing Co., Inc., April 1976, 4 p., paper. A complete stock catalog, with annotations, of Newcastle and Borgo Press titles. Brown ink on white stock.

F17. **Newcastle: Spring '77.** Van Nuys, CA: Newcastle Publishing Co., Inc., October 1976, 4 p., paper. A complete stock catalog, with annotations, of Newcastle and Borgo Press titles. Orange ink on white stock.

F18. **Newcastle Publishing Company, Inc.: 1977 Catalog.** Van Nuys, CA: Newcastle Publishing Co., Inc., April 1977, 4 p., paper. An author/title catalog. Blue ink on white stock.

F19. **Newcastle: Fall '77.** Van Nuys, CA: Newcastle Publishing Co., Inc., April 1977, 6 p. (one fold-out sheet), paper. A complete stock catalog, with annotations, of Newcastle and Borgo Press titles. Blue ink on white stock.

F20. **Presenting New Worlds of Science Fiction & Fantasy, Health & Nutrition, Mythology & the Occult, Hobbies & Crafts: A New Vitality in Book Appeal from Newcastle: Spring, 1978.** Van Nuys, CA: Newcastle Publishing Co., Inc., October 1977, 8 p., slick paper. A complete stock catalog, with annotations, including Future Crafts Today, Gayle Mot Publishing, and Borgo Press new releases. Green and black ink on white stock.

F21. **Lost Race and Adult Fantasy Fiction: 69 Books.** Advisory Editors: R. Reginald, Douglas Menville. New York: Arno Press, November 1977, 32 p., paper. "First Announcement." Reginald and Menville wrote all of the copy for this catalog, issued by Arno to promote the series they edited. Reginald penned the introductory essay on p. 3.

    b. A later version, with different covers, but identical internal copy, and marked "Available for Immediate Shipment," was issued in February, 1980.

F22. Presenting New Worlds of Science Fiction & Fantasy, Health & Nutrition, Mythology & the Occult, Hobbies & Crafts: A New Vitality in Book Appeal from Newcastle: Fall, 1978. Van Nuys, CA: Newcastle Publishing Co., Inc., April 1978, 8 p., slick paper. A complete stock catalog, with annotations, including Future Crafts Today, Gayle Mot Publishing, and Borgo Press new releases. Blue and black ink on white stock.

F23. The Borgo Press Newsletter #1. San Bernardino, CA: The Borgo Press, May 1978, 1 p., paper. A one-page flyer on Borgo stationery announcing plans to expand the Borgo Press.

F24. Presenting New Worlds of Science Fiction & Fantasy, Health & Nutrition, Mythology & the Occult, Hobbies & Crafts: A New Vitality in Book Appeal from Newcastle: Spring, 1979. Van Nuys, CA: Newcastle Publishing Co., Inc., October 1978, 8 p., slick paper. A complete stock catalog, with annotations, including Future Crafts Today, Gayle Mot Publishing, and Borgo Press new releases. Red and black ink on white stock.

F25. Introducing a New Magazine for the Discriminating Librarian Who Had Trouble Keeping Track of the 1,000+ Titles of Science Fiction and Fantasy Published During 1978. San Bernardino, CA: The Borgo Press, January (?) 1979, 1 p., paper. A one-page flyer announcing the new magazine, *Science Fiction & Fantasy Book Review*. Printed on purple stock.

   b. A virtually identical flyer, replacing the word "Librarian" with the words "SF Reader," and deleting one line from the description, released simultaneously with the above. Printed on green stock.

F26. Newcastle Publishing, Publishers, Distributors, Importers: Fall 1979. Van Nuys, CA: Newcastle Publishing Co., Inc., April 1979, 32 p., paper, 5 x 8", slick covers. A complete stock catalog, with annotations, including new Borgo Press releases distributed by Newcastle.

F27. The Milford Series: Popular Writers of Today, non-bylined. San Bernardino, CA: The Borgo Press, Summer 1979, 4 p., paper. An annotated catalog listing published and forthcoming Milford Series volumes in order by series number. Printed with green ink on white stock.

F28. The Acclaimed Newcastle Forgotten Fantasy Library, non-bylined. Van Nuys, CA: Newcastle Publishing Co., Summer 1979, 4 p., paper. An annotated catalog listing published and forthcoming titles in the Forgotten Fantasy Library. Printed with blue ink on white stock.

F29.   Borgo Press: Great Science Fiction & Fantasy Originals & Reprints, non-bylined. San Bernardino, CA: The Borgo Press, Summer 1979, 2 p., paper. An annotated catalog listing all the Borgo Press fiction titles, published and forthcoming. Printed with brown ink on white stock.

F30.   Newcastle Publishing, Publishers, Distributors, Importers: Spring 1980 Supplement. Van Nuys, CA: Newcastle Publishing Co., Inc., October 1979, 16 p., paper, 5 x 8", no cover stock. A supplement to the Fall 1979 catalog, with new releases (including annotations). The new Borgo Press releases listed in this catalog are the last Borgo Press titles featured by Newcastle before distribution was terminated in the Spring of 1980.

F31.   The Borgo Press: [Order Form Spring 1980], non-bylined. San Bernardino, CA: The Borgo Press, [1980], 2 p., paper. An order form arranged by series, title, binding, and price. Printed with black ink on white stock.

F32.   Newcastle Publishing, Publishers, Distributors, Importers: Fall 1980. Van Nuys, CA: Newcastle Publishing Co., Inc., April 1980, 32 p., paper, 5 x 8", slick covers. A complete stock catalog, with annotations. Past Borgo Press releases distributed by Newcastle are included in this catalog, but no new titles. This list also includes the last volume in the Newcastle Forgotten Fantasy Library.

F33.   The Borgo Press: Fall 1980 Library Catalog, non-bylined. San Bernardino, CA: The Borgo Press, June 1980, 20 p., paper. A complete catalog of Borgo Press publications, the first to be fully annotated and the first to include distributed and rebound titles from other companies, arranged by series, subject, and title. No indexes. Printed on beige stock. Inserted in *Publishers Trade List Annual*, and distributed via direct mail to 9000 libraries in the United States.

F34.   The Borgo Press: Order Form [Fall 1980], non-bylined. San Bernardino, CA: The Borgo Press, [1980], 4 p., paper. An order form arranged by title, binding, and price, and the first order form to include distributed titles and rebindings. Printed with black ink on beige stock.

F35.   Now...Two Great New SF Interview Collections by the Award-Winning SF Interviewer, Jeffrey Elliot, non-bylined. San Bernardino, CA: The Borgo Press, [1980], 1 8.5 x 11" sheet, paper. A one-page flyer for Elliot's two books, *Science Fiction Voices #2* and *Science Fiction Voices #3*.

F36.   The Borgo Press: Order Form [1981], non-bylined. San Bernardino, CA: The Borgo Press, [1981], 4 p., paper. An order form arranged by title, binding, and price. Printed with beige ink on beige stock.

F37.   The Borgo Press: Spring/Summer 1982 Library Catalog, non-bylined. San Bernardino, CA: The Borgo Press, June 1982, 20 p., paper. A complete catalog of Borgo Press publications, the last to be fully annotated until 1988, arranged by series, subject, and title. No indexes. Printed on brown stock. Inserted in *Publishers Trade List Annual*, and distributed via direct mail to 9000 libraries in the United States.

F38.   The Borgo Press: Order Form January 1983, non-bylined. San Bernardino, CA: The Borgo Press, January 1983, 4 p., paper. An order form by title, binding, and price. Printed on white paper with maroon ink.

F39.   The Borgo Press: [Stock List 1984], non-bylined. San Bernardino, CA: The Borgo Press, June 1983, [8] p., paper. A complete catalog of Borgo Press publications, arranged by title, with full bibliographical data. Printed on white stock. Inserted in *Publishers Trade List Annual*.

F40.   Announcing Harlan Ellison's first NEW Book in Two Years!, non-bylined. San Bernardino, CA: The Borgo Press, July 1984, 1 sheet, paper. A one-page flyer with Ellison's portrait announcing publication of *Sleepless Nights in the Procrustean Bed: Essays*.

F41.   The Borgo Press: [Stock List 1985], non-bylined. San Bernardino, CA: The Borgo Press, June 1984, 16 p., paper. A complete catalog of Borgo Press publications, arranged by author, with title and series indexes. Printed on brown groundwood stock. Inserted in *Publishers Trade List Annual*.

F42.   The Borgo Press: Order Form 1985, non-bylined. San Bernardino, CA: The Borgo Press, 1985, [4] p., paper. An order form arranged by title, binding, and price. Printed on beige stock.

F43.   The Borgo Press: Stock List 1986, non-bylined. San Bernardino, CA: The Borgo Press, June 1985, [16] p., paper. A complete catalog of Borgo Press publications, arranged by author, with title and series indexes. Printed on brown groundwood stock. Inserted in *Publishers Trade List Annual*.

F44.   Fidel Castro Speaks!, non-bylined. San Bernardino, CA: The Borgo Press, July 1985, [2] p., paper. A single-sheet flyer (black on white) advertising *Fidel by Fidel*, by Jeffrey M. Elliot and Mervyn M. Dymally, and (verso) *Survivors: A Personal Story of the Holocaust*, by Jacob Biber.

F45. **The Borgo Press: Order Form Fall 1986**, non-bylined. San Bernardino, CA: The Borgo Press, 1986, [12] p., paper. An order form arranged by series, subject, and title. Printed on beige stock.

F46. **The Borgo Press: Stock List 1987**, non-bylined. San Bernardino, CA: The Borgo Press, June 1986, 23 p., paper. A complete catalog of Borgo Press publications, arranged by author, with series and title indexes. Hereafter, all Borgo catalogs are printed on white 20-pound stock. Inserted in *Publishers Trade List Annual*.

F47. **The Borgo Press: Stock List 1988**, non-bylined. San Bernardino, CA: The Borgo Press, June 1987, 24 p., paper. A complete catalog of Borgo Press publications, arranged by author, with series and title indexes. Inserted in *Publishers Trade List Annual*.

F48. **Coming Soon! The Moving Sequel**, non-bylined. San Bernardino, CA: The Borgo Press, March 1988, [2] p., paper. A single-sheet flyer (black on white) advertising Jacob Biber's *Risen from the Ashes*, and (verso) *Survivors*.

   b. *A Story from Yesterday's Headlines That's As Gripping as Any Adventure Novel!* San Bernardino, CA: The Borgo Press, October 1989, [2] p., paper. Black ink on beige paper.

F49. **The Borgo Press: Fall Catalog 1988**, non-bylined. San Bernar-dino, CA: The Borgo Press, July 1988, 32 p., paper. A com-plete catalog of Borgo Press publications, arranged by subject and then by title, with author, ti-tle, date, pagination, LC number, OCLC number, annotation, ISBN, binding, and price. Inserted in *Publishers Trade List Annual*, and dis-tributed via direct mail to 10,000 libraries worldwide.

F50. **The Borgo Press: 1989 Catalog Supplement.** San Bernardino, CA: The Borgo Press, June 1989, 8 p., paper. A supplement to Borgo's 1988 cat-alog, listing about 200 new or refeatured titles, arranged by subject, with similar data as above, but no annotations. Inserted in *Publishers Trade List Annual*.

F51. **Now Available: The Flagship Volume of the Series.** San Bernardino, CA: The Borgo Press, October 1989, [2] p., paper. A one-sheet, 8½ x 11" flyer (black ink on gray paper) featuring *The Work of Colin Wilson*, by Colin Stanley, *The Work of Chad Oliver*, by Hal W. Hall, *The Work of Ross Rocklynne*, by Douglas Menville, *The Work of William F. Nolan*, by Boden Clarke and James Hopkins, and a complete listing of the Bibliographies of Modern Authors Series.

F52. **A New Triumph from a Literary Master!** San Bernardino, CA: The Borgo Press, October 1989, [2] p., paper. A one-sheet, 7 x 10" flyer (black ink on light green paper) featuring *Existentially Speaking*, by Colin Wilson on one side, and *The Work of Colin Wilson*, by Colin Stanley, on the other, with a complete listing of the eight other titles relating to Colin Wilson sold by The Borgo Press.

F53. **The Borgo Press: Summer 1990 Catalog.** San Bernardino, CA: The Borgo Press, May 1990, 48 p., paper. An 8.5 x 11" catalog (black ink on beige paper), side-stitched, providing a completely annotated stock list of roughly 1,000 Borgo Press publications, arranged by subject category and then by title. This was the first Borgo Press catalog to be typeset in house.

F54. **The Borgo Press: 1990/91 Catalog.** San Bernardino, CA: The Borgo Press, July 1990, 48 p., paper. An 8.5 x 11" catalog (black ink on white paper), side-stitched, providing a completely annotated stock list of roughly 1,000 Borgo Press publications, arranged by subject category and then by title. This was produced simultaneously with C52, and is identical to it save for title page (p. 1) and running heads. 6,000 of these catalogs were inserted into *Publishers Trade List Annual* (*PTLA*), published by R. R. Bowker Co. in October, 1990; and 2,500 were distributed directly to the major public and academic libraries throughout the country.

F55. **Available Winter 1990/91: The House of the Burgesses, Second Edition.** San Bernardino, CA: The Borgo Press, July 1990, [2] p., paper. A one-sheet, 5 x 8" flyer (black ink on green paper), featuring *The House of the Burgesses, Second Edition*, by Michael Burgess.

F56. **Now Available! To Kill or Not to Kill: Thoughts on Capital Punishment** (with Paul David Seldis). San Bernardino, CA: The Borgo Press, July 1991, [2] p., paper. A one-sheet, 8.5 x 11" flyer (black ink on variously-colored paper), featuring the book by Congressman William L. Clay, Sr.

F57. **A Modern Story of Guilt and Innocence—And the American Justice System** (with Paul David Seldis). San Bernardino, CA: The Borgo Press, July 1991, [2] p., paper. A one-sheet, 8.5 x 11" flyer (black ink on variously-colored paper), featuring *Deathman Pass Me By: Two Years on Death Row*, by Philip Brasfield with Dr. Jeffrey M. Elliot.

F58. Revised and Expanded Second Edition: The Beach Boys, Southern California Pastoral (with Paul David Seldis). San Bernardino, CA: The Borgo Press, July 1991, [2] p., paper. A one-sheet, 8.5 x 11" flyer (black ink on variously-colored paper), featuring the book by Bruce Golden.

F59. One of America's Most Popular Writers! (with Paul David Seldis). San Bernardino, CA: The Borgo Press, July 1991, [2] p., paper. A one-sheet, 8.5 x 11" flyer (black ink on variously-colored paper), featuring *Jerzy Kosinski: The Literature of Violation*, by Welch D. Everman.

F60. An Invaluable Research Tool for Student and Professor Alike! (with Paul David Seldis). San Bernardino, CA: The Borgo Press, July 1991, [2] p., paper. A one-sheet, 8.5 x 11" flyer (black ink on variously-colored paper), featuring *Victorian Criticism of American Writers: A Guide to British Criticism of American Writers in the Leading British Periodicals of the Victorian Period, 1824-1900*, by Arnella K. Turner.

F61. The Russians Are Coming! The Russians Are Coming...Again! (with Paul David Seldis). San Bernardino, CA: The Borgo Press, July 1991, [2] p., paper. A one-sheet, 8.5 x 11" flyer (black ink on variously-colored paper), featuring *The Second Marxian Invasion: The Fiction of the Strugatsky Brothers*, by Stephen W. Potts.

F62. From One of America's Greatest Pulpsters! Now Available for the First Time! (with Paul David Seldis). San Bernardino, CA: The Borgo Press, July 1991, [2] p., paper. A one-sheet, 8.5 x 11" flyer (black ink on variously-colored paper), featuring *Starclimber: The Literary Adventures and Autobiography of Raymond Z. Gallun*, by Raymond Z. Gallun with Dr. Jeffrey M. Elliot.

F63. A New Literary Guide to the Thinking Man's Detective! (with Paul David Seldis). San Bernardino, CA: The Borgo Press, July 1991, [2] p., paper. A one-sheet, 8.5 x 11" flyer (black ink on variously-colored paper), featuring *At Wolfe's Door: The Nero Wolfe Novels of Rex Stout*, by J. Kenneth Van Dover.

F64. At Last, the Much Expanded SECOND EDITION! (with Daryl F. Mallett). San Bernardino, CA: The Borgo Press, July 1991, [2] p., paper. A one-sheet, 8.5 x 11" flyer (black ink on variously-colored paper), featuring *The Work of Charles Beaumont: An Annotated Bibliography & Guide, Second Edition*, by William F. Nolan.

F65. One of England's Most Versatile Authors! (with Paul David Seldis). San Bernardino, CA: The Borgo Press, July 1991, [2] p., paper. A one-sheet, 8.5 x 11" flyer (black ink on variously-colored paper), featuring *David Lodge: How Far Can You Go?* by Merritt Moseley.

F66. **Number Six — Studies in Judaica and the Holocaust** (with Paul David Seldis). San Bernardino, CA: The Borgo Press, July 1991, [2] p., paper. A one-sheet, 8.5 x 11" flyer (black ink on variously-colored paper), featuring *First Century Palestinian Judaism: A Bibliography of Works in English*, by David Ray Bourquin.

F67. **A New Guide to the Work of a Rising Literary Star** (with Paul David Seldis). San Bernardino, CA: The Borgo Press, July 1991, [2] p., paper. A one-sheet, 8.5 x 11" flyer (black ink on variously-colored paper), featuring *The Work of Dean Ing: An Annotated Bibliography & Guide*, by Scott Alan Burgess.

F68. **New Second Edition!** (with Paul David Seldis). San Bernardino, CA: The Borgo Press, July 1991, [2] p., paper. A one-sheet, 8.5 x 11" flyer (black ink on variously-colored paper), featuring *The Work of George Zebrowski: An Annotated Bibliography & Guide, Second Edition*, by Jeffrey M. Elliot and Robert Reginald.

F69. **Chuck Hillig's Primer for the New Age** (with Paul David Seldis). San Bernardino, CA: The Borgo Press, July 1991, [2] p., paper. A one-sheet, 8.5 x 11" flyer (black ink on variously-colored paper), featuring *What Are You Doing in My Universe?*, by Chuck Hillig.

F70. **Now Available in Paper!** (with Paul David Seldis). San Bernardino, CA: The Borgo Press, July 1991, [2] p., paper. A one-sheet, 8.5 x 11" flyer (black ink on variously-colored paper), featuring *Ray Bradbury: Dramatist*, by Ben P. Indick.

F71. **Completely Reset, Re-Edited, and Indexed!** (with Paul David Seldis). San Bernardino, CA: The Borgo Press, July 1991, [2] p., paper. A one-sheet, 8.5 x 11" flyer (black ink on variously-colored paper), featuring *The Italian Theatre in San Francisco*, edited by Lawrence Estavan.

F72. **First Book Publication!** (with Paul David Seldis). San Bernardino, CA: The Borgo Press, July 1991, [2] p., paper. A one-sheet, 8.5 x 11" flyer (black ink on variously-colored paper), featuring *The Theatrical Rambles of Mr. and Mrs. John Greene*, by Charles Durang.

F73. **The First Comprehensive Guide Published!** San Bernardino, CA: The Borgo Press, July 1991, [2] p., paper. A one-sheet, 8.5 x 11" flyer (black ink on variously-colored paper), featuring *The Work of Jack Dann: An Annotated Bibliography & Guide*, by Jeffrey M. Elliot.

F74. **Not Only Who Did It, But Why They Did It!** (with Paul David Seldis). San Bernardino, CA: The Borgo Press, August 1991, [2] p., paper. A one-sheet, 8.5 x 11" flyer (black ink on variously-colored paper), featuring *Mystery Voices: Interviews with British Crime Writers*, conducted by Dale Salwak.

F75. **Who Done It? Now You Can Find Out** (with Paul David Seldis). San Bernardino, CA: The Borgo Press, August 1991, [2] p., paper. A one-sheet, 8.5 x 11" flyer (black ink on variously-colored paper), featuring Brownstone Mystery Guides.

F76. **A Massive and Dynamic Work Which Will Become the Standard of Its Field** (with Paul David Seldis). San Bernardino, CA: The Borgo Press, August 1991, [2] p., paper. A one-sheet, 8.5 x 11" flyer (black ink on variously-colored paper), featuring *The Jewish Holocaust: An Annotated Guide to Books in English*, by Marty Bloomberg.

F77. **Coming November 1991!** San Bernardino, CA: The Borgo Press, September 1991, [2] p., paper. A one-sheet, 8.5 x 11" flyer (black ink on variously-colored paper), featuring *Vultures of the Void: A History of British Science Fiction Publishing, 1946-1956*, by Philip Harbottle and Stephen Holland.

F78. **Coming December 1991!** San Bernardino, CA: The Borgo Press, September 1991, [2] p., paper. A one-sheet, 8.5 x 11" flyer (black ink on variously-colored paper), featuring *British Science Fiction Paperbacks: An Annotated Bibliography of Science Fiction and Fantasy Books Published in Great Britain Between 1946-1956*, by Philip Harbottle and Stephen Holland.

F79. **Greatly Expanded Second Edition!** (with Daryl F. Mallett). San Bernardino, CA: The Borgo Press: September 1991, [2] p., paper. A one-sheet, 8.5 x 11" flyer (black ink on variously-colored paper), featuring *Reginald's Science Fiction and Fantasy Awards, Second Edition*, by Daryl F. Mallett and Robert Reginald.

F80. **One of the Most Relevant and Burning Topics of Our Time!** (with Paul David Seldis). San Bernardino, CA: The Borgo Press, September 1991, [2] p., paper. A one-sheet, 8.5 x 11" flyer (black ink on variously-colored paper), featuring *The Trilemma of World Oil Politics*, by Dr. Sheikh R. Ali and Dr. Jeffrey M. Elliot.

F81. **Scottie's Favorite Recipes!** San Bernardino, CA: The Borgo Press, September 1991, [1] p., paper. An 8.5 x 11" flyer (black ink on colored paper), featuring *The Little Kitchen Cookbook*, by Scottie Kimberlin.

G.

BOOK PRODUCTION AND DESIGN

NOTE: Reginald acted as production superviser or designer on the following books or catalogs published by other companies, often in conjunction with Mary A. Burgess (who typeset many of these books). He also designed all of the Borgo Press publications from 1977 to date (approximately 130 volumes), and prepared about twenty-five order forms and catalogs for Newcastle Publishing Co., Inc., between 1976-1985 (the catalogs themselves are listed in Section F).

G1. *Cumulative Paperback Index, 1939-1959: A Comprehensive Bibliographic Guide to 14,000 Mass-Market Paperback Books of 33 Publishers Under 69 Imprints,* by R. Reginald and M. R. Burgess [joint by-line]. Detroit: Gale Research Co., September 1973, xxiv, 362 p., cloth.

G2. *Things to Come: An Illustrated History of the Science Fiction Film,* by Douglas Menville and R. Reginald. New York: Times Books, November 1977, [xii], 212 p., cloth. Published simultaneously in trade paper.

G3. *Science Fiction and Fantasy Literature, a Checklist, 1700-1974; with, Contemporary Science Fiction Authors II,* by R. Reginald; Editorial Associates: Douglas Menville, Mary A. Burgess; Assistants: George Locke, Gordon Johnson, Doris Illes, Barry R. Levin, Michael Grainey. Detroit: Gale Research Co., October 1979 (but officially released December 7, 1979), xii, vi, 1141, 32 p. of plates, in two volumes, cloth.

G4. *Science Fiction and Fantasy.* Catalog Number Nine. Los Angeles: Barry R. Levin, Science Fiction & Fantasy Literature, [1979], 40 p., paper.

G5. *Science Fiction & Fantasy Proofs and Review Copies.* Catalog Number 10. Los Angeles: Barry R. Levin, Science Fiction & Fantasy Literature, [1980], [16] p., paper.

G6. *Titles from the Back Room; or, A Fine Selection of Science Fiction & Fantasy.* Catalog Number 12. Los Angeles: Barry R. Levin, Science Fiction & Fantasy Literature, Printed at The Borgo Press, 1981, 46 p., paper. Note: Catalog Number 11 was not typeset by Borgo.

G7. *Great Works & Rarities of Science Fiction & Fantasy.* Catalog Number 13. Los Angeles: Barry R. Levin, Science Fiction & Fantasy Literature, with The Borgo Press, 1982, [64] p., paper.

G8. *Hal Clement,* by Donald M. Hassler. Mercer Island, WA: Starmont House, June 1982, 64 p., cloth (also published in trade paperback).

G9. *Philip K. Dick,* by Hazel Pierce. Mercer Island, WA: Starmont House, September 1982, 64 p., cloth (also published in trade paperback).

G10. *H. P. Lovecraft,* by S. T. Joshi. Mercer Island, WA: Starmont House, October 1982, 83 p., cloth (also published in trade paperback).

G11. *Stephen King,* by Douglas E. Winter. Mercer Island, WA: Starmont House, October 1982, 128 p., cloth (also published in trade paperback).

G12. *One Small Step; or, An Eclectic and Random Sample from Our Stock in Honor of Our Tenth Anniversary.* Catalogue [sic] Number 14. Los Angeles: Barry R. Levin, Science Fiction & Fantasy Literature, 1983, [20] p., paper.

G13. *C. S. Lewis,* by Brian Murphy. Mercer Island, WA: Starmont House, April 1983, 95 p., cloth (also published in trade paperback).

G14. *Robert Silverberg,* by Thomas D. Clareson. Mercer Island, WA: Starmont House, May 1983, 96 p., cloth (also published in trade paperback).

G15. *Piers Anthony,* by Michael R. Collings. Mercer Island, WA: Starmont House, November 1983, 96 p., cloth (also published in trade paperback).

G16. *Jack London,* by Gorman Beauchamp. Mercer Island, WA: Starmont House, June 1984, 96 p., cloth (also published in trade paperback).

G17. *Earthdance: A Romance of Reincarnation,* by Eileen Connolly. North Hollywood, CA: Newcastle Publishing Co., Inc., October 1984, x, 246 p., paper.

G18. *The Annotated Guide to Fantastic Adventures,* by Edward J. Gallagher. Mercer Island, WA: Starmont House, January 1985, xxi, 170 p., cloth (also published in trade paperback).

G19. *Discovering Modern Horror Fiction [I],* edited by Darrell Schweitzer. Mercer Island, WA: Starmont House, July 1985, [iv], 156 p., cloth (also published in trade paperback).

G20. *Marion Zimmer Bradley*, by Rosemarie Arbur. Mercer Island, WA: Starmont House, August 1985, 138 p., cloth (also published in trade paperback).

G21. *J. G. Ballard*, by Peter Brigg. Mercer Island, WA: Starmont House, September 1985, 138 p., cloth (also published in trade paperback).

G22. *Futurevisions: The New Golden Age of the Science Fiction Film*, by Douglas Menville and R. Reginald, with Mary A. Burgess. North Hollywood, CA: Newcastle Publishing Co., Inc., October 1985, 192 p., paper.

G23. *H. G. Wells*, by Robert Crossley. Mercer Island, WA: Starmont House, 1986, 79 p., cloth (also published in trade paperback).

G24. *Olaf Stapledon*, by John Kinnaird. Mercer Island, WA: Starmont House, 1986, 107 p., cloth (also published in trade paperback).

G25. *Suzy McKee Charnas; Octavia Butler; Joan D. Vinge*, by Marleen S. Barr, Ruth Salvaggio, and Richard Law. Mercer Island, WA: Starmont House, 1986, 52, 44, 72 p., cloth (also published in trade paperback).

G26. *The Holy Grail Revealed: The Real Secret of Rennes-le-Château*, by Patricia and Lionel Fanthorpe, edited with an Introduction by R. Reginald. North Hollywood, CA: Newcastle Publishing Co., Inc., November 1986, 144 p., paper.

G27. *Mary Shelley*, by Allene Stuart Phy. Mercer Island, WA: Starmont House, 1988, 124 p., cloth (also published in trade paperback).

G28. *Science Fiction and Fantasy Literature: A Supplement, 1975-1991; with, Contemporary Science Fiction, Fantasy, and Horror Authors III*, by Robert Reginald. Detroit: Gale Research Co., 1992, [1000] p., cloth.

H.

UNPUBLISHED WORKS

H1.   "Badger Science Fiction." 1970, 6 p. [bibliography]

H2.   "The Thief." 1973, 1 p. [sonnet]

H3.   "The R. R. Bowker Company." 1974, 4 p. A critique of Bowker's an-
      nual publication statistics in *Publishers Weekly*, sold to *Library* Journal,
      but never published by them. [article]

H4.   *Star Drek.* 1976, 29 p. First draft of the novella, *Up Your Asteroid! A
      Science Fiction Farce.* [novella]

H5.   "Psychologists Who Needed Help Themselves." 1978, 11 p. Sold to *The
      People's Almanac Presents: The Book of Lists #2*, edited by Irving Wal-
      lace *et al.*, but never published by them. [article]

H6.   "Men and Women Who Claimed to Be God." 1979, 17 p. Sold to *The
      People's Almanac Presents: The Book of Lists #2*, edited by Irving Wal-
      lace *et al.*, but never published by them. [article]

H7.   "Bibliography of Brian W. Aldiss." 1979, 18 p. Commissioned by *Star
      Wars* as a supporting document in their lawsuit against *Battlestar Galac-
      tica.* [bibliography]

H8.   "Bibliography of Jerry Pournelle." 1979, 5 p. Commissioned by *Star
      Wars* as a supporting document in their lawsuit against *Battlestar Galac-
      tica.* [bibliography]

H9.   "Bjo Trimble Bibliography." 1979, 1 p. Commissioned by *Star Wars* as
      a supporting document in their lawsuit against *Battlestar Galactica.*
      [bibliography]

H10. "Jeff Rovin Bibliography." 1979, 1 p. Commissioned by *Star Wars* as a
      supporting document in their lawsuit against *Battlestar Galactica.*
      [bibliography]

H11.   "Larry Niven Bibliography." 1979, 5 p. Commissioned by *Star Wars* as a supporting document in their lawsuit against *Battlestar Galactica*. [bibliography]

H12.   "Willis E. McNelly Bibliography." 1979, 2 p. Commissioned by *Star Wars* as a supporting document in their lawsuit against *Battlestar Galactica*. [bibliography]

H13.   "Bibliography of R. Reginald." 1979, 5 p. [bibliography]

H14.   Science Fiction and Fantasy Criticism. Series Editor: R. Reginald. New York: Arno Press, 1980, 50 v., cloth. NY: The Ayer Company, 1982, 20 v., cloth. Sag Harbor, NY: Sagapress, 1984, 20 v., cloth. Millwood, NY: Kraus Reprint Co., 1985, 20 v., cloth. [book series]

Sold originally to Arno Press as a fifty-volume series of reprints and original books of criticism on science fiction and fantasy literature, the series was first postponed, then dropped when Arno Press collapsed in 1980-81, relegating its remaining stock to The Ayer Company. Ayer then reduced the series to the twenty anthologies of short nonfiction pieces slated for the original set, but the arrangement fell through when Arnold Zohn (founder and first Publisher of Arno Press) left the company. Zohn then offered to publish the books himself through his own imprint, Sagapress, but died shortly thereafter. Zohn's partner, Herbert Cohen (Zohn's successor as Publisher at Arno Press), who eventually became Publisher of Kraus Reprint Co., then tentatively considered the series for publication by that company, but nothing came of the discussions. Some of the individual titles may eventually be salvaged for publication by other companies.

1. *Ashes to Ashes, Dust to Dust: Dystopian Images in Modern Fantasy Literature.*
2. *East of the Sun: Russian and Eastern European Science Fiction.*
3. *Flickering Images: Criticism on the Science Fiction Film.*
4. *Horror of Horrors: The Supernatural Story in Literature.*
5. *Just Imagine: Women in Science Fiction and Fantasy.*
6. *The Lion and the Unicorn: Christian Images in Science Fiction and Fantasy.*
7. *Measuring the Stars: Interviews with Science Fiction Critics and Bibliographers.*
8. *A New Heaven and a New Earth: American and British Utopian Literature.*
9. *Notions of Another World: The Theory of Fantasy.*
10. *The Old Guard: The Critics Look at the Golden Age of Science Fiction.*
11. *Once Upon a Time to Come: The Antecedents of Fantastic Literature.*
12. *Parlez-Vous Science Fiction? Studies on European Science Fiction and Fantasy.*

13. *A Place Called Armageddon: Science Fiction at War.*
14. *Quetzalcoatl and Company: Essays on the Latin American Fantasists.*
15. *Quoth the Critic: The Best of The Milford Series: Popular Writers of Today.*
16. *Something Bright and Alien: The Theory of Science Fiction.*
17. *Tripping the Light Fantastic: Essays on Modern Fantasy Writers.*
18. *Voices of Imaginative Literature: Interviews with Science Fiction Authors and Editors.*
19. *West of the Moon: British Science Fiction and Fantasy.*
20. *The Young Turks: Studies on Modern Science Fiction Writers.*

H15. "Neb." Feb. 6, 1983, 3 p. [memorial]

H16. **"A Comparison of the Screen Treatment Housebound with the Motion Picture Version of Poltergeist."** Oct. 18, 1983, 14 p. Commissioned by *Poltergeist* as a supporting document in defense of a lawsuit filed against them by *Housebound*. [critique]

H17. **"Bibliography of R. Reginald 1984."** 1984, 14 p. [bibliogra-phy]

H18. **"Browsing in the Library,"** by Michael Burgess. Written for *The Coyote Chronicle* in Spring of 1987 (2 handwritten pages), but never used by them.

H19. **"The Big Lie,"** by Michael Burgess. 1989, 2 typeset pages. [editorial]

Originally scheduled to run on pages 2-3 of the *LTF Newsletter* no. 3 (Spring, 1989), it was cut without the author's permission.

H20. **"Thaddeus Dikty,"** by Robert Reginald. November 1991, 1 page. Written for *Locus*, but bumped for lack of space. [obituary]

I.
JUVENILIA

NOTE: In addition to the items listed below, Reginald served as an editor/reporter for a seventh- or eighth-grade elementary school mimeographed newletter, and as Features Editor for the newspaper at Gonzaga Preparatory High School, Spokane, WA, during the school year 1963/64, writing a number of articles and miscellanea on which he has no records.

PUBLISHED JUVENILIA

IA1.   "Finis," by M. R. Burgess, in *Esprit* 7 (Fall, 1964): 19. [poem]

Published in the literary magazine of Gonzaga Preparatory High School, Spokane, WA.

IA2.   "The Stairs," by M. R. Burgess, in *Esprit* 7 (Spring, 1965): 5-6. [story]

IA3.   "The Pond," by M. R. Burgess, in *Esprit* 7 (Spring, 1965): 6. [poem]

IA4.   "The Dark Tower," by Everett Cooper, in *Gradient* no. 2 (1969): 7. Written in 1967. [story]

IA5.   "Mir," in *Pegasus* no. [?] (1970): 4. [poem]

Written for Gonzaga University's annual poetry contest in 1968—it lost. There appear to be no surviving specimens of this particular fanzine issue. The contest rules were changed in the following year (see IB2 below) to again reduce the allowable size for entries.

IA6.   "The Dream," by Everett Cooper, in *Gradient* no. 3 (May, 1970): 10-12. [story]

UNPUBLISHED JUVENILIA

IB1. "The Way of Sataphan." 1967, 1 p. [poem]

IB2. "The Vengeance of Káthan Jolárson." March-April, 1967, 62 p. [epic poem]

An 800-line dactylic hexameter epic written for Gonzaga University's annual poetry contest in 1967 (it lost!). The following year, the contest rules were changed to prevent future submissions exceeding two pages in length.

IB3. "The Song of the Tin-Can Man." 1967, 1 p. [poem]

IB4. "Once Atime and Long Ago." 1967, 1 p. [poem]

IB5. *The Booke of the Rede Hand.* Fall-Winter, 1967-1968, 61 p. [unfinished fantasy novel]

Written for Dr. Fran Polek's creative writing class at Gonzaga University.

IB6. "Limericks." 1972?, 1 p. [poems]

J.

PUBLIC APPEARANCES

NOTE: Reginald has kept few records on his public appearances, but is known to have spoken on numerous occasions before librarians' and other groups, beginning about 1975, on a wide variety of topics. He also taught several extension courses in the late 1970s and early 1980s at the University of California, Riverside, University of California, San Diego, and California State University, San Bernardino. He annually presents The Milford Award at the J. Lloyd Eaton Conference on Science Fiction and Fantasy, University of California, Riverside (since 1980).

J1.   Participant, Quarter Million Volume Ceremony, California State College, San Bernardino Library, May 17, 1977. The author recruited the principal guest speaker, Harlan Ellison, arranged for his transportation, and shepherded him through the functions. The coordinator of the function, John M. Tibbals, stated: "I think that the program was a great success, thanks to Mr. Ellison, and we would probably never have persuaded him to come here had you not talked to him. Thank you very much for all of your help."

J2.   Guest Lecturer, "Science Fiction Films," a class taught by Dr. George Edgar Slusser, University of California, Irvine, January 1978.

J3.   Lecturer, "The Science Fiction Marketplace," a two-day seminar, University of California, San Diego, February 1978.

J4.   Participant in the original planning meeting for the first J. Lloyd Eaton Conference on Science Fiction and Fantasy, May 12, 1978.

J5.   Lecturer, "Publish It Yourself," a two-day seminar, University of California, Riverside, May 12-13, 1978.

J6.   Participant on a panel, "Fantasy Lives—in Various Media," conducted by the Popular Culture Association/West as part of its workshop, "Science Fiction and Disco Dancing," California State University, Long Beach, October 14, 1978.

J7. Featured Speaker, Semi-Annual Banquet Meeting, Inland Empire Chapter of the California Library Association, Redlands, California, June 8, 1979.

J8. Participant, Ninth Annual Conference of the Science Fiction Research Association, South Lake Tahoe, California, June 22-24, 1979.

J9. Presenter, 1st Annual Milford Award, at the 2nd Annual J. Lloyd Eaton Conference, Riverside, CA, February 1980.

J10. Presenter, 2nd Annual Milford Award, at the 3rd Annual J. Lloyd Eaton Conference, Riverside, CA, February 1981.

J11. Featured Speaker, CSUC Librarians Chapter Workshop on Publishing, California State University, Long Beach, May 15, 1981. The title of his speech was: "Beware the Jabberwock, My Friends: A Guided Tour Through the Perils of Publishing." Coordinator John Wood later noted: "Several Workshop participants commented on your 'ten commandments' for prospective authors as a valuable guide, and ranked your contributions among those from which they benefitted most. Your presentation was a major factor in the success of the Workshop."

J12. Presenter, 3rd Annual Milford Award, at the 4th Annual J. Lloyd Eaton Conference, Riverside, CA, February 1982.

J13. Presenter, 4th Annual Milford Award, at the 5th Annual J. Lloyd Eaton Conference, Riverside, CA, February 1983.

J14. Presenter, 5th Annual Milford Award, at the 6th Annual J. Lloyd Eaton Conference, Riverside, CA, April 1984.

J15. Special guest (as R. Reginald) on *Hour-25*, August 10, 1984, Radio Station KPFK-FM (90.7 KH), North Hollywood, CA, 10 P.M.-12 Midnight. The interview was conducted by the late Mike Hodel, and focused on publication of Harlan Ellison's book, *Sleepless Nights in the Procrustean Bed: Essays*, which Reginald had just published from Borgo Press.

J16. Presenter, 6th Annual Milford Award, at the 7th Annual J. Lloyd Eaton Conference, Riverside, CA, April 1985.

J17. Presenter, 7th Annual Milford Award, at the 8th Annual J. Lloyd Eaton Conference, Riverside, CA, April 12, 1986.

J18. Invited Guest, "Meet the Author" tea, San Bernardino Public Library, May 4, 1986. Eight local Inland Empire authors were invited to participate by each giving a five-minute talk and displaying copies of their books.

J19. Participant, Library Exhibit of Faculty Publications, Pfau Library, California State University, San Bernardino, March 18-June 15, 1986.

J20. Presenter, 8th Annual Milford Award, at the 9th Annual J. Lloyd Eaton Conference, Riverside, CA, April 1987.

J21. Featured Speaker, Pomona Valley Writers Association, June 13, 1987, on "The Curse of Amateurism."

J21. Participant, "Faculty in Print" exhibition, Norman Feldheym Branch, San Bernardino Public Library, San Bernardino, California, November 1987. An exhibit of publications authored by the California State University, San Bernardino faculty.

J22. Presenter, 9th Annual Milford Award, at the 10th Annual J. Lloyd Eaton Conference, Riverside, CA, April 1988.

J23. Panelist (as Robert Reginald) for the "Special Marketing Hour," 11th Annual Sell What You Write! Writer's Workshop, sponsored by the Community Education Office, American River College, Sacramento, California, Saturday, March 18, 1989, at Raef Hall, on the ARC campus.

J24. Presenter, 10th Annual Milford Award, at the 11th Annual J. Lloyd Eaton Conference, Riverside, CA, April 1989.

J25. Participant, Library Exhibit of Faculty Publications, Pfau Library, California State University, San Bernardino, May-June 1989.

J26. Invited Panelist (as Robert Reginald), on "The Future for Genre Collections," with Dr. George E. Slusser of the University of California, Riverside, Dr. Donald H. Dyal, Texas A&M University, and Professor Halbert W. Hall, Texas A&M University Library, at the conference, "The Fantastic Imagination in New Critical Theories: An Interdisciplinary Literature Conference," held at Texas A&M University Library, College Station, Texas, on March 1, 1990. Also participant in the remainder of the confab, which lasted from February 28-March 4, 1990.

J27. Presenter, 11th Annual Milford Award, at the 12th Annual J. Lloyd Eaton Conference, Riverside, CA, April 21, 1990.

J28. Participant, Library Exhibit of Faculty Publications, Pfau Library, California State University, San Bernardino, May-June, 1990.

J29. Presenter, 12th Annual Milford Award and 13th Annual Eaton Award, at the 13th Annual J. Lloyd Eaton Conference, Riverside, CA, April 20, 1991.

J30. Participant, Library Exhibit of Faculty Publications, Pfau Library, California State University, San Bernardino, May-June, 1991.

K.

SECONDARY SOURCES

NOTE: In addition to the more formal articles and biographies listed below, Reginald has been mentioned many hundreds of times in the weekly staff *Bulletin* and other publications of California State University, San Bernardino, beginning in September, 1970.

K1.   "R. Reginald," in *Stella Nova: The Contemporary Science Fiction Authors*, [by R. Reginald]. Los Angeles: Unicorn & Son, May 1970, paper, p. [226A]. Reginald's biography appears only in the contributors' copies (numbers 0000-0009), and was not included in the 1975 Arno Press version, *Contemporary Science Fiction Authors*. [biography]

K2.   "Reginald, R(obert), 1948- ," in *Contemporary Authors: A Bio-Bibliographical Guide to Current Authors and Their Works, Volumes 57-60*, edited by Cynthia R. Fadool. Detroit: Gale Research Co., 1976, cloth, p. 473-474. [bio-bibliography]

K3.   "He's a Superman of Letters," by John Weeks, in *The San Bernardino Sun* 104 (July 17, 1977): C-1, C-11. [profile and interview]

b.   *Signum* (September/October, 1977): .

K4.   "An Inside Look at the Publishing Business," by John Weeks, in *Inland Empire Magazine* 1 (August, 1977): 11. [profile]

K5.   "Reginald, Robert," in *The International Authors and Writers Who's Who, Eighth Edition*, edited by Adrian Gaster. Cambridge, England: International Biographical Centre, 1977, cloth, p. 849. [bio-bibliography]

K6.   "Reginald, Robert," in *Who's Who in the West, 16th Edition, 1978-1979*. Chicago: Marquis Who's Who, 1978, cloth, p. 596. [bio-bibliography]

K7.   "*Cumulative Paperback Index, 1939-1959*: A Closer Look," by Billy C. Lee, in *Paperback Quarterly* 1 (Spring, 1978): 39-41. Includes a bibliography of the author's works to date. [review article and bibliography]

K8. **"Reginald, Robert,"** in *The Encyclopedia of Science Fiction*, edited by Peter Nicholls and John Clute. London: Granada, 1979, cloth, p. 492. [biography]

b. *The Science Fiction Encyclopedia*, edited by Peter Nicholls and John Clute. Garden City, NY: Doubleday & Co., 1979, cloth, p. 492.

K9. **"R. Reginald,"** in *Science Fiction and Fantasy Literature, a Checklist, 1700-1974; with, Contemporary Science Fiction Authors II*, by R. Reginald. Detroit: Gale Research Co., 1979, cloth, Vol. 1, p. 436, Vol. 2, p. 1044-1045. [bio-bibliography]

K10. **"Burgess, Michael R.,"** in *Gonzaga University Alumni Directory 1980*. White Plains, NY: Bernard C. Harris Publishing Co., 1980, paper, p. 18. [biography]

K11. **"Your Guide for a Tour of Other Worlds,"** by John Weeks, in *The San Bernardino Sun* 108 (Jan. 5, 1981): A-7, A-14. [profile and interview]

K12. **"Interview: Robert Reginald,"** by Jeffrey M. Elliot, in *Fantasy Newsletter* 4 (January, 1981): 18-23, 30. [interview]

K13. **"Burgess, M(ichael) R(oy), 1948- ,"** in *Contemporary Authors: A Bio-Bibliographical Guide to Current Writers in Fiction, General Nonfiction, Poetry, Journalism, Drama, Motion Pictures, Television, and Other Fields, New Revision Series, Volume 6*, edited by Ann Evory. Detroit: Gale Research Co., 1982, cloth, p. 79-80. [bio-bibliography]

K14. **"9,000 Miles Later, They Found Her Roots,"** in *Towanda Daily Review* (June __, 1982): . This newspaper article highlights the visit of Michael and Mary Burgess to Bradford County, Pennsylvania, while doing genealogical research on Mary's Wickizer family. [profile]

K15. **"Reginald, Robert,"** in *The International Authors and Writers Who's Who, Ninth Edition*, edited by Adrian Gaster. Cambridge, England: International Biographical Centre, 1982, cloth, p. 537. [bio-bibliography]

K16. **"Burgess, M. R.,"** in *Who's Who in Kentucky Genealogy, First Edition: A Biographical and Professional Profile of Over 600 Prominent Researchers in Kentucky Genealogy, with Over 7500 Surnames in Which They Are Particularly Interested*, edited by Michael L. Cook, Bettie Anne Cook, Sam McDowell. Utica, KY: McDowell Publications, 1982, cloth, p. 42. [biography]

K17.   "'Luck of the Draw': Cal-State San Bernardino Adds 10,000,000," in *OCLC Pac-News* no. 19 (November, 1983): 1. [profile]

K18.   "Burgess Contributes Milestone Record," in *OCLC Pac-News* no. 19 (November, 1983): 2. [profile]

K19.   "California State College, San Bernardino Inputs Ten Millionth Record to OCLC Database," in *OCLC Newsletter* no. 149 (November, 1983): 13. A photo of Burgess with caption appears on p. 1. [profile]

K20.   "'CSB' Garners 10-Millionth OCLC Record," in *American Libraries* 14 (December, 1983): 698. [profile]

K21.   "R. Reginald: *Science Fiction and Fantasy Literature*," by Richard S. Watts, in *Reference Services Review* 12 (Winter, 1984): 7-8. [profile]

K22.   "Interview with Michael Burgess (aka R. Reginald)," by Pola Patterson, in *California State University Librarians Chapter Newsletter* (March/ April, 1984): 10-12. [interview]

K23.   "Meet the Editor: Robert Reginald of Borgo Press," by Jeffrey M. Elliot, in *The Bulletin of the Science Fiction Writers of America* 18 (Winter, 1984): 6-10. The original title of this piece was: "Polytropic Thoughts on an Editor's Life; or, A Dead Sinner Revised and Edited." [interview]

K24.   "'I Fear the Greeks...': An Introduction to the Life and Work of Robert Reginald," by Jeffrey M. Elliot, in *The Work of R. Reginald: An Annotated Bibliography and Guide*, by Michael Burgess, with Jeffrey M. Elliot. San Bernardino, CA: The Borgo Press, January 1985, cloth, p. 3-10. [interview]

    ab.   San Bernardino, CA: The Borgo Press, January 1985, trade paper, p. 3-10.

K25.   *The Work of R. Reginald: An Annotated Bibliography & Guide*, by Michael Burgess, with Jeffrey M. Elliot. Bibliographies of Modern Authors, No. 5. San Bernardino, CA: The Borgo Press, January 1985, 48 p., cloth. [bibliography]

    ab.   San Bernardino, CA: The Borgo Press, January 1985, 48 p., trade paper.

K26.   "Extensions of Remarks: New Book on Falklands War Recommended," in *Congressional Record* 131 (April 22, 1985): E1623 (comments only). A reproduction of Chapter V of *Tempest in a Teapot* (see A28), with comments by U.S. Representative Mervyn M. Dymally (D-Calif.). [critique]

K27. **"Burgess, Michael,"** in *Who's Who in the West, 20th Edition, 1985-1986*. Chicago: Marquis Who's Who, 1985, cloth, p. 72. [bio-bibliography]

K28. **"Burgess, M. R.,"** in *Who's Who in Kentucky Genealogy, 1985 Edition: A Biographical and Professional Profile of 595 Prominent Researchers in Kentucky Genealogy, with Over 6550 Surnames in Which They Are Particularly Interested*, edited by Michael L. Cook, Bettie Anne Cook, Sam McDowell. Utica, KY: McDowell Publication, 1985, cloth, p. 38. [biography]

K29. **"*Forgotten Fantasy*,"** by Mike Ashley, in *Science Fiction, Fantasy, and Weird Fiction Magazines*, edited by Marshall B. Tymn and Mike Ashley. Westport, CT & London: Greenwood Press, 1985, cloth, p. 275-276. A history of, and guide to, this reprint magazine edited by Douglas Menville and Robert Reginald. [critique]

K30. **"Author's Note,"** in *Hasan*, by Piers Anthony. New York: Tor, A Tom Doherty Associates Book, January 1986, paper, p. 241. [feature]

K31. **"Burgess, Michael,"** in *Who's Who in the World, 8th Edition, 1987-1988*. Wilmette, IL: Marquis Who's Who, 1986, cloth, p. 143. [bio-bibliography]

K32. **"Reginald, Robert,"** in *Who's Who in U.S. Writers, Editors & Poets: A Biographical Directory, 1986-1987*, edited by Curt Johnson. Highland Park, IL: December Press, 1987, cloth, p. 372. [bio-bibliography]

K33. **"Burgess, Michael,"** in *Gonzaga University Alumni Directory 1987*. White Plains, NY: Bernard C. Harris Publishing Co., 1987, cloth, p. 23. [biography]

K34. **"Burgess, Michael,"** in *Who's Who of Emerging Leaders in America, 1st Edition, 1987-1988*. Wilmette, IL: Marquis Who's Who, 1987, cloth, p. 114. [bio-bibliography]

K35. **"Burgess, Michael,"** in *Who's Who in the West, 21st Edition, 1987-1988*. Wilmette, IL: Marquis Who's Who, 1987, cloth, p. 97. [bio-bibliography]

K36. **"Gale Outside Editors: Full-Time Librarians Explore the Realm of Science Fiction and Fantasy,"** by Amy Marcaccio, in *Gale Gazette* 15 (Fall, 1987): 27-29. Includes photos of Reginald. [profile]

K37.   "Reginald, Robert," in *Who's Who in U.S. Writers, Editors & Poets: A Biographical Directory, 1988,* edited by Curt Johnson and Frank Nipp. Highland Park, IL: December Press, 1988, cloth, p. 463. [bio-bibliography]

K38.   "18 Million Records Input Over 17 Years," compiled by Nita Dean, in *OCLC Newsletter* no. 174 (July/August, 1988): 19-21. A retrospective on the "gold" records input into the OCLC cataloging database, including a photo of Burgess taken from *OCLC Newsletter* no. 149. [profile]

K39.   "Burgess, Michael," in *Who's Who in the World, 9th Edition, 1989-1990.* Wilmette, IL: Marquis Who's Who, 1988, cloth, p. 156. [bio-bibliography]

K40.   "Burgess, Michael," in *Who's Who in California, the Eighteenth Edition, 1989,* edited by Sarah Vitale. [Bainbridge Island, WA]: The Who's Who Historical Society, 1989, cloth, p. 62. [bio-bibliography]

K41.   "Reginald, Robert," in *International Authors and Writers Who's Who, Eleventh Edition,* edited by Ernest Kay. Cambridge: International Biographical Centre, 1989, cloth, p. 714. [bio-bibliography]

K42.   "Burgess, Michael," in *Who's Who in the West, 22nd Edition, 1989-1990.* Wilmette, IL: Marquis Who's Who, 1989, cloth, p. 88. [bio-bibliography]

K43.   "Burgess, Michael," in *Supplement to Who's Who in America, 45th Edition, 1989-1990.* Wilmette, IL: Marquis Who's Who, 1989, cloth, p. 164. [bio-bibliography]

K44.   "Reginald, Robert," in *Who's Who in Writers, Editors & Poets: United States & Canada, 1989-1990,* edited by Curt Johnson and Frank Nipp. Highland Park, IL: December Press, 1989, cloth, p. 435-436. [bio-bibliography]

K45.   "Burgess, Michael," in *Who's Who in California, the Nineteenth Edition, 1990,* edited by Sarah Vitale. [Bainbridge Island, WA]: The Who's Who Historical Society, 1990, cloth, p. 71. [bio-bibliography]

K46.   "Burgess, Michael," in *Who's Who in Genealogy & Heraldry 1990,* edited by Mary Keysor Meyer and P. William Filby. Savage, MD: Who's Who in Genealogy & Heraldry, 1990, trade paper, p. 36. [bio-bibliography]

K47. **"Burgess, Michael,"** in *Who's Who in America, 46th Edition, 1990-91.* Wilmette, IL: Marquis Who's Who, 1990, cloth, Vol. 1, p. 454. [bio-bibliography]

K48. **"Reginald, Robert,"** in *Who's Who in America, 46th Edition, 1990-91.* Wilmette, IL: Marquis Who's Who, 1990, cloth, Vol. 2, p. 2709. [bio-bibliography]

K49. **"Burgess, Michael,"** in *Who's Who in California, the Twentieth Edition, 1991,* edited by Sarah Vitale. [Bainbridge Island, WA]: The Who's Who Historical Society, 1991, cloth, p. 66. [bio-bibliography]

K50. **"Burgess, Michael,"** in *Who's Who of Emerging Leaders in America, 3rd Edition, 1991-1992.* Wilmette, IL: Marquis Who's Who, 1991, cloth, p. 120. [bio-bibliography]

K51. **"Unicorn and Son,"** in *The Science-Fantasy Publishers: A Critical and Bibliographic History, Third Edition,* by Jack L. Chalker and Mark Owings. Baltimore: Mirage Press, December 1991, cloth, p. 614. A history of the publishing house founded by Reginald in 1970, with additional mention of The Borgo Press. [profile and bibliography]

K52. **"Burgess, Michael,"** in *Who's Who in California, the Twenty-First Edition, 1992,* edited by Sarah Vitale. [Bainbridge Island, WA]: The Who's Who Historical Society, January 1992, cloth, p. 48. [bio-bibliography]

K53. *The Work of Robert Reginald: An Annotated Bibliography & Guide, Second Edition,* by Michael Burgess. Bibliographies of Modern Authors, No. 5. San Bernardino, CA: The Borgo Press, February 1992, 176 p., cloth. [bio-bibliography]

   ab. San Bernardino, CA: The Borgo Press, February 1992, 176 p., trade paper.

K54. **"Introduction: Comets Don't Slow Down,"** by William F. Nolan, in *Ibid.,* p. 5-7. [profile]

K55. **"Foreword: It Was Twenty Years Ago Today,"** by Dr. Fran J. Polek, in *Ibid.,* p. 8. [profile]

K56. **"Afterword: Robert Reginald: Force Majeure,"** by Jack Dann, in *Ibid.,* p. 169-171. [profile]

L.

HONORS AND AWARDS

L1.   National Merit Semi-Finalist, Gonzaga Preparatory School, Spokane, Washington, 1964.

L2.   Honors at Entrance, Gonzaga University, Spokane, Washington, 1965.

L3.   Full-Tuition Scholarship, Gonzaga University, Spokane, Washington, 1965-1966.

L4.   Member of Honors Program, Gonzaga University, Spokane, Washington, 1965-1969.

L5.   Graduated Cum laude, Gonzaga University, Spokane, Washington, May, 1969.

L6.   Title II Fellowship, School of Library Science, University of Southern California, Los Angeles, California, 1969-1970.

L7.   Hugo Award nomination, Best Nonfiction Book of the Year, 1979 (1980), for *Science Fiction and Fantasy Literature, a Checklist, 1700-1974; with, Contemporary Science Fiction Authors II*—it didn't win.

L8.   Outstanding Academic Book of the Year, 1980-81 (one of a hundred so named), *Choice* magazine, for *Science Fiction and Fantasy Literature, a Checklist, 1700-1974; with, Contemporary Science Fiction Authors II*.

L9.   Awarded bronze plaque by the On-Line Computer Library Center, Inc. (OCLC) at the annual meeting of the California Library Association, Oakland, California, December, 1983, for inputting the ten millionth bibliographical record into the international OCLC cataloging data base on October 11, 1983.

L10.   Nominated to OCLC Pacific Peer Council, March 1984.

L11.   Nominated for the Board of Trustees, San Bernardino Valley College District, February 1985.

L12. *Sleepless Nights in the Procrustean Bed: Essays*, by Harlan Ellison, edited by Marty Clark, published by Borgo Press in 1984, named Best Nonfiction Book of the Year, *Locus* Awards, 1984 (1985).

L13. Second Prize ($50 and a tee shirt) in *San Bernardino Sun* Ghost Writers Contest, for his short story, "A Little Light Reading," October 31, 1985.

L14. Meritorious Promise and Professional Performance (MPPP) Award ($2500 prize), June 1987, for service to California State University, San Bernardino.

M.

MISCELLANEA

M1.   **LITERARY DERIVATIONS.** In D. G. Compton's novel, *The Mission-aries*, the statement, "May you know your way, and may it be one," is taken verbatim from a letter written by the author to Compton about 1970. New York: Ace Books, 1972, p. 102, lines 12-13, paper. London: Robert Hale & Company, 1975, p. 102, lines 12-13, cloth.

   The author originated the title for Darrell Schweitzer's novel, *We Are All Legends*, which was originally purchased by The Borgo Press when this company was still doing fiction titles. The book was later published by Donning Publishers in 1981, and by Starmont House in 1988.

   Some of the background ideas for Gregory Benford's novel, *Great Sky River*, grew out of a three-hour jam session between the author, Larry Niven, and Benford at the Eighth Annual J. Lloyd Eaton Conference, University of California Riverside, April, 1986. Further discussions took place later, at Benford's home in Laguna Beach, and on the phone. The primary focus of these conversations was the structure of the mech (i.e., robot) civilization, how it might function in practice, and what impact it would have on the surviving remnants of humanity.

   Many of the titles used for books in the Borgo Press line were created by the author, sometimes in consultation with the writers, sometimes before contracts were even signed. This is particularly true of Milford Series volumes, including Colin Wilson's book, *The Haunted Man*.

M2.   **CONFERENCES.** During the course of his work on *Science Fiction and Fantasy Literature*, the author labored extensively in the J. Lloyd Eaton Collection of science fiction at the University of California, Riverside, and met the then University Librarian, Eleanor Montague. While talking with her in 1977, he proposed an annual academic conference on science fiction and fantasy literature, to be sponsored by the University Library. At Montague's request, he wrote and submitted the original prospectus for what later became the annual J. Lloyd Eaton Conference. Dr. George Edgar Slusser, a Borgo author of critical monographs on SF writers, was invited to participate, and later took over the actual organizing of the first conference when Reginald bowed out, in 1978.

M3. **AWARDS.** In his original proposal for the annual J. Lloyd Eaton Conference of Science Fiction and Fantasy, Reginald suggested an annual J. Lloyd Eaton Award, to be sponsored by the Conference, and given to the finest book-length critical work on SF published during the preceding year; he is currently an ongoing member of the Awards Committee, and has presented the Eaton Award at the last few Eaton Conferences.

Reginald originated (and initially sponsored) a second award, the Milford Award, to be given annually for lifetime contributions to the editing and publishing of science fiction and fantasy literature; he later turned the award over to the Conference, but remains Chairman of the Awards Committee, and presents the award annually at the Eaton Conference Banquet. He proposed a third award in 1988, a lifetime Eaton Award, first presented in April of that year to Reginald Bretnor.

M4. **LISTS.** In *The Complete Book of Science Fiction and Fantasy Lists*, by Maxim Jakubowski and Malcolm Edwards, Robert Reginald appears as number 20 in the list, "Twenty-Eight US Writers Born Overseas." London: Granada, 1983, p. 233, paper. Also published as *The SF Book of Lists*: New York: Berkley Books, 1983, p. 233, paper.

M5. **PEN NAMES.** The principal pseudonyms of R. Reginald are: R. Reginald—Robert Reginald—Rob Reginald—RR—R.R. (taken from Saki's fictional character, Reginald); Michael Burgess—M. R. Burgess—Mike Burgess (his legal name); and Boden Clarke (taken from a marriage announcement in the *San Bernardino Sun*).

Pen names he has used on a sometime basis (mostly on one-shot reviews in *Science Fiction & Fantasy Book Review*) include: Miguel Alcalde (his legal name in Spanish), Everett Cooper—C. Everett Cooper (derivation unknown, but not from Dr. C. Everett Koop), Michael Demotes (his legal name in Greek), G. Forbes Durand (taken from the name of a supposed pulp writer mentioned on the television series, *Banyon*), Misha Grazhdanin (his legal name in Russian), Andrew Kapel (his maternal grandfather), Jacob Lawson (his great-great-great-great grandfather), Peter Mauzy (his great-great-great-great-great grandfather), Rex Miletus (his legal name in Latin), Walt Mobley (the name his father used in childhood), Jack B. Nimble (invented), Daniel Painter (taken from Daniel Vasquez, a painter), Nero Rale (invented), Lucretia Sharpe (invented), Tertius Spartacus (derived tongue-in-cheek from a penname of R. Lionel Fanthorpe, Deutero Spartacus), Lucas Webb (taken from a marriage announcement). While publishing *Science Fiction & Fantasy Book Review*, he also used the house name, Peter Harding, originated by critic Neil Barron.

M6. **BOOK DEDICATIONS.** The following books have been dedicated in whole or in part to the author:

1. *A Historical and Critical Survey of the Science-Fiction Film*, by Douglas Menville. New York: Arno Press, April 1975, xvii, 185 p., cloth. "To my Mother and Father, with love, this small return on a large investment, and to Mike Burgess, a true friend, who made it happen."

2. *The Classic Years of Robert A. Heinlein*, by George Edgar Slusser. San Bernardino, CA: The Borgo Press, October 1977, 63 p., paper. "To Mike and Mary."

3. *Candle for Poland: 469 Days of Solidarity*, by Leszek Szymanski. San Bernardino, CA: The Borgo Press, June 1982, 128 p., cloth. Published simultaneously in trade paperback. "For Robert Reginald—in friendship."

4. *Stephen King As Richard Bachman*, by Michael R. Collings. Mercer Island, WA: Starmont House, 1985, 168 p., cloth. Published simultaneously in trade paperback. "...To Ted Dikty of Starmont House and Rob Reginald of Borgo Press for supporting this project...."

5. *Hasan*, by Piers Anthony. New York: Tor SF, A Tom Doherty Associates Book, January 1986, 242 p., paper. "For Richard Delap, Ted White, and Robert Reginald, who believed in *Hasan* before the mundanes did, and without whom this novel might never have been published."

6. *Discovering H. P. Lovecraft*, edited by Darrell Schweitzer. Mercer Island, WA: Starmont House, July 1987, xii, 153 p., cloth. Published simultaneously in trade paperback. "For Robert Reginald, with thanks and gratitude."

7. *The Work of Dean Ing: An Annotated Bibliography & Guide*, by Scott Alan Burgess. San Bernardino, CA: The Borgo Press, December 1990, 82 p., cloth. Published simultaneously in trade paperback. "For my brothers: Mike, Steve, Mark."

8. *Full Frontal Poetry*, edited by Daryl F. Mallett, Chaelyn L. Hakim, and Frances McConnel. Riverside, CA: Full Frontal Poetry Publishing, April 1991, 46 p., paper. "Special thanks go to Robert Reginald and Mary Burgess, and The Borgo Press, San Bernardino, CA," etc.

9. *Inside Science Fiction: Essays on Fantastic Literature*, by James Gunn. San Bernardino, CA: The Borgo Press, March 1992, 184 p., cloth. Published simultaneously in trade paperback. "To Robert and Daryl, with thanks."

10. *New Science Fiction Voices*, by Jeffrey M. Elliot. San Bernardino, CA: The Borgo Press, 1992, p., cloth. Published simultaneously in trade paperback. "To R. Reginald—for his sound judgment, consistent caring, good humor, and steady friendship."

M7. MEMBERSHIPS. Reginald currently is an active member of the following organizations: American Civil Liberties Union; American Library Association; Blue Earth County [Minnesota] Historical Society; California Faculty Association (affiliated with the National Education Association, American Association of University Professors, California

Teachers Association); City of San Bernardino Historical and Pioneer Society; California Library Association; Grant County [Kentucky] Historical Society; Horror Writers of America; International Association for the Fantastic in Arts; International P.E.N., USA Center West; Kentucky Historical Society; Muskingum County Historical Society; National Genealogical Society; Science Fiction Research Association; Science Fiction Writers of America, Inc.; Upper Cumberland Valley Genealogical Association [Putnam County, Tenn.]; Virginia Historical Society; World SF.

M8.   PUBLISHING COMPANIES. Reginald founded two publishing companies, the short-lived Unicorn & Son, Publishers (1970), and The Borgo Press (1975). The latter's name is taken from The Borgo (or Birgau) Pass, the mountain valley nearest Castle Dracula in the book by Bram Stoker (and the later movie adaptations). Il Borgo is also the name of the Vatican Library, and Borgo is a small suburb of Warsawa, Poland. The company name is also a play on the author's real name, Burgess. The Borgo Press was founded in April, 1975, several months before Reginald met his future wife, Mary Wickizer Rogers, on June 3rd of that year. Thus, she was involved in the planning of the company almost from the beginning.

Reginald had received a large royalty check from Gale Research Company earlier in the year, and now proposed to reinvest it into a business venture, a line of books to be distributed by Newcastle Publishing Co., Inc. Alfred Saunders, President of Newcastle, agreed to handle the new line—Newcastle distributed Borgo Press books through February of 1980, and occasionally handled individual titles thereafter. Initially, Borgo's line was a mixture of short critical monographs and science fiction and fantasy novels; the latter titles were dropped when Newcastle ceased distributing BP books to the trade. Since then, Borgo has published only academically-oriented books.

Beginning in February, 1979, Borgo published virtually all of its titles in simultaneous paper and library cloth editions; all earlier titles were now made available in hardcover bindings. At about the same time, Borgo began making available to the library market cloth rebindings of Newcastle paperbacks. This program was later vastly extended to include more than thirty other publishing lines. Borgo's 1992 list includes some 1425 titles in 2000 bindings.

Publishing lines acquired by The Borgo Press include: Brownstone Books (1991), Sidewinder Press (1991), St. Willibrord's Press (1991), the Starmont Contemporary Writers Series (1991), and one book from the Starmont Mystery Guides Series (1991); the first three were maintained as separate imprints, while the third was merged into The Milford Series. An additional imprint developed in 1991 was Burgess & Wickizer.

M9.   ACADEMIC CAREER. Upon receiving his M.S. in L.S. degree from the University of Southern California, in August, 1970, Reginald was offered positions at USC, Occidental College, and at the Pfau Library, California State College (later University), San Bernardino, all three postings in serials. He accepted the latter. He received tenure in 1975, and was promoted to Senior Assistant Librarian in 1978, to Associate Librarian in 1981, and to full Librarian (i.e., full Professor) in 1984, the same year he was awarded his first paid leave. In 1987 he was given a $2500 Meritorious Performance and Professional Promise (MPPP) Award by Cal State. In 1991 he received a sabbatical leave for the Fall term.

From 1970-71, he worked as a reference librarian, from 1971-78 and 1980-81 as Periodicals Librarian, from 1976-80 as Assistant Bibliographer, and from 1980-DATE as Chief Cataloger. His duties in the latter position include monitoring or performing all original cataloging at Cal State, particularly those records input into the OCLC cataloging data base.

Reginald was elected to the Faculty Senate in the mid-1970s, and to various other Senate committees during the same decade. In 1986 he was appointed to the five-member Campus Scholarship Committee, being reappointed in 1988 and 1990. In 1987 he was appointed by the President of the California Faculty Association, of which he is a member, to the new, five-member Librarians' Task Force, and was later named founding editor of the *LTF Newsletter*, the first issue of which appeared in October, 1987. He served for two years with this group.

His suggestions to the Dean of Graduate Education in 1986-87 resulted in the promalgation of the first consistent set of campus-wide production standards for CSUSB's masters' projects and theses.

M10.   10,000,000th OCLC RECORD. On October 11, 1983, the author coordinated the input of the ten millionth bibliographical record into the On-Line Computer Library System (OCLC, Inc.) data base, using three terminals at the Pfau Library, California State University, San Bernardino to transmit the cataloging data for a local master's thesis. The event received more favorable publicity from the library media than any other single occasion in the twenty-five-year history of the Cal State Library. Two months later, at the annual meeting of the California Library Association at Oakland, California, the author was awarded a bronze plaque by OCLC, a duplicate being made for display in the Cal State Library.

M11.   ELLIOT ARCHIVES. The author arranged for the donation of Dr. Jeffrey M. Elliot's manuscripts and papers to the Pfau Library, California State University, San Bernardino, on April 2, 1986. Elliot is a well-known political scientist, interviewer, and specialist in minority studies.

M12. TEACHING. From 1975-1980, Reginald taught about a dozen extension courses at the University of California, Riverside, the University of California, San Diego, and others, on such subjects as "Publish It Yourself," "The Science Fiction Market," "The Science Fiction Film," and related topics. About half of the lectures were taught with George Edgar Slusser. Among the students attending these one-day seminars were neophytes David Brin and Stephen Potts, both of whom became professional writers after taking Reginald's classes.

M13. AGENTING. As agent, Reginald sold *The Second Invasion from Mars*, a short novel by Arkady and Boris Strugatsky, translated by Gary Kern, to Macmillan Publishing Co. The book was published as part of a two-novel collection, *Far Rainbow; The Second Invasion from Mars*, in 1979 (ix, 240 p.), and later reprinted in trade paperback.

Reginald also agented (and edited) *The Holy Grail Revealed: The Real Secret of Rennes-le-Château*, by Patricia and Lionel Fanthorpe to Newcastle Publishing Co. (1982), and translations by George Slusser of *The Centenarian, or, The Two Beringhelds* (by Honoré de Balzac) and *Les Xipéhuz; and, The Death of the Earth* (by J. H. Rosny) to Arno Press (1976 and 1978, respectively).

Reginald also agented *The Ugly Swans*, by Arkady and Boris Strugatsky, translated by George Edgar Slusser, to DAW Books in February 1978. The translation was never published.

Sobel Weber Associates (originally Nat Sobel Associates) of New York have acted as general literary and film agent for The Borgo Press since 1980.

M14. OUTSIDE READER. Reginald was paid as an outsider reader (along with five or six other experts) to survey lists of potential books to be covered in three reference works edited by Neil Barron: *Anatomy of Wonder, Second Edition* (New York: R. R. Bowker Co., 1981); *Fantasy Literature: A Critical Guide* (New York: Garland Publishing Co., 1990); and *Horror Literature: A Critical Guide* (New York: Garland Publishing Co., 1990). Reginald was also an Adviser for the Third Edition of *Twentieth-Century Science-Fiction Authors* (Chicago: St James Press, 1991), and for the *Survey of Modern Fantasy Literature* (Englewood Cliffs, NJ: Salem Press, 1983).

M15. BANTAM BOOKS IMPRINT. At the American Booksellers Association Convention in Anaheim, California, at the end of May, 1988, Reginald met with Lou Aronica, editor of the Bantam Books science fiction line, Spectrum Books, and pointed out to him that the Bantam Books title-page imprint was incorrect, and had been so since October, 1964. The list of cities below the company logo stated "Toronto, New York, etc.," although the main company office was actually located in New York City.

The fact that Toronto was listed first forced librarians cataloging Bantam publications to code them as if they had been issued in Canada—which was not the case. As a result of this conversation, Bantam changed its imprint in March of 1989 to "New York, Toronto," etc.

M16. *THE HARLAN ELLISON HORNBOOK.* The author is mentioned on pages 278-279 of *The Harlan Ellison Hornbook*, by Harlan Ellison (Baltimore: Mirage Press; New York: Penzler Books, 1990): "Mike Burgess of Borgo Press solicited a collection of essays, and did so solely because of the three essays in STALKING THE NIGHTMARE. It took me by surprise, to be honest. Though I'd been writing easily as much non-fiction as stories since I'd begun my career—and had done even more work as journalist, columnist, and magazine article slavey during college and the first years of professionaldom than I had as a fictioneer—I'd always downgraded the importance of the non-fiction in my own mind. Have no idea why that was so. Perhaps because, when I was learning my craft, fiction was more highly considered by the Establishment, magazines published tons of fiction, and those who wrote non-fiction usually did it from some special knowledge.

"But when Burgess asked for the book that became SLEEPLESS NIGHTS IN THE PROCRUSTEAN BED, that new audience appeared; and since that first venture—somehow the two TEAT books seemed out of contention—well, everything I've done in the essay form has found its way into print in hardcover."

M17. *BIO OF AN OGRE.* Reginald is mentioned on pages 195-196 of the cloth edition of *Bio of an Ogre: The Autobiography of Piers Anthony to Age 50* (New York: Ace Books, 1988). In talking of his novel *Hasan*, Anthony states: "Robert Reginald wrote to ask me for biographical and bibliographical information, as he was compiling a book about genre authors. I obliged, not expecting much; these projects come and go and few amount to anything spectacular. But this one *was* spectacular; in 1970 he published *Stella Nova* under the imprint Unicorn & Son and it was a phenomenal production, with information on several hundred genre writers. Later he set up his own publishing house, Borgo Press, devoted mainly to a series of critical booklets on genre authors. He expressed interest in *Hasan*, which he had read in the magazine version. So I signed a contract with him, and the novel had its third sale, and was published in a nice small-press edition in 1977." A similar statement appeared as an Afterword to the Tor edition of *Hasan* (see K30).

M18. MANUSCRIPTS. California State University, San Bernardino, started collecting originals and photocopies of Reginald's manuscripts about 1978, cataloging each item as a separate record in the OCLC cataloging data base, under the author's Library of Congress literature number. The manuscripts are housed in the Rare Book Collection, and are restricted to use at the Pfau Library.

M19. **CATALOGING DATA.** In the Library of Congress classification scheme, each of Reginald's principal pseudonyms is a valid main entry: Reginald, R.; Burgess, Michael, 1948- ; Clarke, Boden, 1948- ; Webb, Lucas; Cooper, C. Everett. Reginald's permanent literature number is PS3568. E4754, and his permanent bibliography number is Z8736.47; books about Reginald as a publisher are classed in Z472.R42.

QUOTH THE CRITICS

STELLA NOVA: THE CONTEMPORARY SCIENCE FICTION AUTHORS (1970)/
CONTEMPORARY SCIENCE FICTION AUTHORS, FIRST EDITION (1975)

"One of the most important recent science fiction checklists. The 1970 edition was not widely advertised, and most copies were sold to public and institutional libraries. The second edition contains some corrections and amendments, but remains essentially the same as the original edition. The work includes 483 bibliographies of authors active during the period 1960-1968. Each entry provides a checklist of the author's science fiction and fantasy books listed in chronological order according to their sequence of publication. A typical book entry contains the following information: identification number, year of publication, publisher, series number (where applicable), book title, and miscellaneous bibliographical information in parentheses, including type and format of each book, and some information regarding reprints. The checklist is arranged alphabetically by author. A title index and list of pseudonyms is also provided. There are biographies of 308 of the authors indexed, which often incorporate comments (sometimes lengthy) by writers responding to the compiler's questionnaire. This work is an absolutely essential tool for access to modern fantasy and science fiction titles."

—Dr. Marshall B. Tymn, Eastern Michigan State University,
Dr. Roger C. Schlobin, Purdue University,
L. W. Currey

"I must make mention of *Stella Nova: The Contemporary Science Fiction Authors*, compiled by Robert Reginald and associates, and published in a limited edition (and doubtless sold out before I even type the words). It is a bibliography with biographical details of most writers alive in the SF field. In a way, it seems like an equalizer; no mention of quality is offered, since its concern is with cataloguing.

"Yet the 483 writers and editors included come bursting out of their dry details in a most individual way. Who wrote *Dr. Who in an Exciting Adventure with the Daleks*? Which writer got out of science fiction, instead of trying to change it, because it was 'too hidebound, too conservative'? Who produced a series of Malaysian fantasy movies such as *Aladin Burok* and *Wily Delilah*? The answers lie among the W's of this ambitious compilation.

"This book provided [one] of the bright spots of the year."

—Brian W. Aldiss, *Best SF: 1970*

CUMULATIVE PAPERBACK INDEX, 1939-1959 (1973)

"Probably the most useful research aid to the paperback collector interested in the 1939 to 1959 period is the *Cumulative Paperback Index, 1939-1959*. Its 362 pages consist of 14,051 book entries alphabetically arranged by author and by title, and giving publisher, book number, date of publication, and price. Pages xiii to xxiv give a rundown of the publisher specifications, including address, stock number spans, book height, book edge color, numbering system, price code, and total books published or recorded. There is a total number of 33 publishers issued under 69 imprints.

"It is interesting to note that R. Reginald and M. R. Burgess are one and the same person. Michael Burgess is a librarian at California State College, San Bernardino, California. When he leaves his librarian job, he assumes the name Robert Reginald for professional use as an editor, publisher, and author. It seems justifiable for Burgess to use pseudonyms when one examines the number of books and magazines he has edited, published, and written in the last eight years in his spare time only.

"R. Reginald is mostly involved in paperbacks or books about paperbacks, of which the *CPI* is a prime example. He began collecting paperbacks in 1964 when he found that the local public library in Spokane, Washington, had very few science fiction and fantasy books to offer. He began buying used science fiction and fantasy paperbacks from local bookstores. That was 14 years ago, and he now has over 16,000 books, all but a few hundred of which are paperbacks. In a recent letter, he says 'Much of my collection consists of science fiction and fantasy material, but I also acquire pbs of historical interest, and have made some effort to pick up unusual items (like the first books in a particular number system)'."

—Billy C. Lee, *Paperback Quarterly*

THE ATTEMPTED ASSASSINATION OF JOHN F. KENNEDY (1976)

"When you see a title like the above, you immediately expect an alternate-universe fantasy. This is one, but the events of 22 November 1963 are by no means the only point of departure from our world.

"This essay is told in the form of a televised press conference with the president-elect on the eve of his inauguration, at the end of this century. This first obvious difference is that this is a truly Imperial presidency, with the monarchical trappings suggested by the more conservative of our Founding Fathers. The president is titled 'Lord President' and addressed in the manner that, say, one would expect our world's British press to address a member of the House of Lords.

"Despite the symbolism, this is basically a democracy as we know it ourselves. The questions are those any newsperson asks any top politician, and the answers are those that any top politican gives for public release. The author writes quite nice dialog and the president comes across as a very charismatic head of state. Kennedy is mentioned because one of the questions is, 'Who's your favorite president, the one among your predecessors whom you most admire?' It was Kennedy, and as Lord President Lister describes the why we see that he embodies many of JFK's personality traits—the intelligence, the sincerity, the warmth, the grasp of international affairs.

"Whenever a work of this sort appears, it's natural to suspect that the author is using his protagonist as a mouthpiece for his own poltical views. I have no idea who Lucas Webb is or what his policies are, but *The Attempted Assassination of John F. Kennedy* is a reasonable policy statement of a pragmatic politician of slightly liberal views. If Webb is making any point, it seems to be that world affairs and cultural evolution are mightier forces than can be changed by individuals or trappings. Also, Webb's view of 2000 A.D. is basically the same as 1976; he ensivions neither space colonies nor ecodisasters in the interim. Much of this could be from a perfectly mundane newscast of our own world—with, every now and then, a tripper:

MR. THOMAS: When will the presidential coin issue be ready?

THE PRESIDENT: I'm told by the Treasurer that the first coins, the five- and ten-dollar pieces, will be issued on February 1st, the others to follow as they're ready. I have a sample planchet stamped on the obverse with the new design, if you're interested. Ah, yes, here it is. *(He hands it over.)*

MR. THOMAS: I wonder if you could hold that up to our cameras, sir, like this. How's that, Jack? Just a little bit closer, Lord President. Yes, right there, please. This is the new obverse of the ten-dollar coin, showing the bust of Lord President Lister. The inscription reads: "James VII, Lord President of the United States." Thank you very much, sir. (p. 37).

"That's a subtle commentary on inflation during the next quarter century, as well as a picture of an America whose coins and stamps show the face of the incumbent president. Other speculations: the eclipse of the Republicans by a new major party. Other differences: Hawaii never joined the U.S.; the rest of the world has evolved democratically in the form of constitutional monarchies rather than as republics; Albert rather than Ford followed Richard I (there being no 25th Amendment to the Constitution).

"This little booklet is not really fiction, but a clever intellectual exercise by someone who knows his political science, and makes reasonable 'what if' speculations. High school and college poli sci majors in particular should find it amusing. It's a nice change of pace from space opera."

—Frederick Patten, *Delap's F&SF Review*

154

THINGS TO COME (1977)

"Speaking of *Things to Come*, a book of that title by Douglas Menville and R. Reginald has been published by *The New York Times*, [as] an "illustrated history of the science fiction film." At this point, there are almost too many such, but this one seems particularly good (perhaps because the authors' opinions and mine agree almost 100%—they admire *Zardoz* immensely, for instance). Illustrated with a fine selection of stills, and carrying their history up to *Star Wars*, it's highly recommended from this corner."

—The Magazine of Fantasy & Science Fiction

LOST RACE AND ADULT FANTASY (1978)
(as Editor)

"I must immediately suggest that Reginald and Menville have reprinted some of the most important titles to be issued in any series in recent years. [The critic then discusses at length the individual titles included in the series.]

"These seem the high points in a series important because it emphasizes the fact that, as Lionel Stevenson once pointed out, during the very period when realism and naturalism seemed to dominate the literary scene, a strong tradition of fantasy was continuing and was sometimes written by the very authors who contributed to the new realism. Moreover, it emphasizes that fantasy and science fiction were in their origins more closely related than some will acknowledge. For the works cited draw upon archaeology, geology, paleontology—sciences that fascinated the literary and popular imaginations late in the nineteenth and early in the twentieth centuries as much as did the machine and the future. In some respects, then, particularly in its emphasis on little known material, this may be the most important series to be published recently."

—Dr. Thomas D. Clareson, College of Wooster

SCIENCE FICTION AND FANTASY LITERATURE (1979)

"If Europe can boast of having Pierre Versins, America in turn has R. Reginald, who has just published a monumental work, fruit of a labor that escapes our understanding of the humanly possible...a work so colossal that it is difficult to find space in the library for the 1141 pages....

"One is agog before such a body of work...This book must be included in all self-respecting public or academic libraries."

—Solaris [translated from the French]

"This work, the most comprehensive general checklist published to date, is an outgrowth of the author's *Stella Nova* (1970). Although no researcher should rely on a single source of bibliographic information, this work comes close to being the *es-*

sential reference volume, as it virtually supersedes all previously published check-lists, including Everett F. Bleiler's *The Checklist of Fantastic Literature* (1948) and its 1978 revision....There is no question that this 2-volume set should be owned by every serious scholar and researcher, and by libraries acquiring core reference collections. It is a remarkable achievement and a major contribution to scholarship in the science fiction and fantasy field."

—*Choice*

"An absolutely indispensable reference work for the science fiction bibliophile. Volume 1 is a massive bibliography of over 15,000 works of fantastic literature, to the end of 1974. The compiler has personally examined almost every work included in this bibliography, unlike many previously compiled works in this field of research. In using this volume, I have found it easy to read, easy to use, and all-encompassing in scope. Other reviewers have taken some exception to the scope of this work, but I find Mr. Reginald more than justified in his scope, by his taking the time to carefully define the *exact* parameters which cause a book to appear or not appear in the listing. To date, I have not come across any exclusions which I take violent exception to, which is a very unusual situation for me when it comes to reference works. I recommend this volume unreservedly."

—Grant Thiessen, *Megavore*

"Volume one of *Science Fiction and Fantasy Literature* lists 15,884 English language first editions of monographs in the fields of science fiction, fantasy, and weird supernatural fiction. Chronologically, the bibliography covers the period 1700-1974. For each entry, the following data are given: Author, pseudonyms, title, publisher, place, date, pages, format, type (novel, anthology, etc.). Cross references are given from pseudonym to author entry. This section is the most comprehensive bibliography of science fiction and fantasy ever assembled. Its sheer bulk commands respect and admiration for 'R. Reginald,' revealed here as M. R. Burgess. A spot check revealed no errors of entry or data (but in a work this size, there must be some!).

"In addition to the author listing, Reginald provides a title index, a series index, an awards index with access by award and by names of winners (covering American awards, for the most part), and an index to Ace and Belmont Doubles.

"This work becomes the standard work of SF and fantasy bibliography. It supersedes—at least for casual use or initial use—Bleiler's *Checklist*, Day 's *Supplement Checklist*, and Day's *Complete Checklst...in Paperback Books*. The completist will still refer to those works, but most users will find Reginald's bibliography all that is required for their use.

"Volume II is the second edition of Reginald's *Contemporary Science Fiction Authors*. This edition presents sketches of 1443 living and dead SF writers and critics. The data in the biographical listings gives full name, birth date and place, parents, wife and children, education, profession, first sale, awards, and 'statement by the author,' when available. The last feature often reveals interesting tidbits, and frequently leads to far more questions than it answers. This is the most com-

156

prehensive work of its type on SF authors, and offers the user some unique features, most notably the 'statement by the author.' Together with Nicholls' *Science Fiction Encyclopedia* a fairly complete view of the author emerges.

"This two-volume work is one of the basic reference works of the field. It is an essential purchase for any large library, and a basic tool for collectors and bibliographers."

—Prof. Hal W. Hall, Texas A&M University

"This is the definitive reference set that SF scholars and collectors have dreamed about for years....There is no doubt that this set is a landmark work which all libraries should have."

—Tom Staicar, *Amazing Stories*

"For those individuals and libraries that can own only one reference work [on science fiction], Reginald's set should be it! It is a masterful job, achieved through dedication and expertise, that everyone connected with science fiction and fantasy will be grateful for now and in the coming years. Recommended without reservation as a necessary core-acquisition."

—Dr. Roger C. Schlobin, Purdue University

"Frankly, I'm overwhelmed by this incredible reference work. According to Reginald, this work was five years in the making and 93% of the books cited were personally seen and evaluated by him. Certainly, this is the most complete bibliography of the fantasy and SF field available. I have spent hours pouring over my copy and have yet to find an error (although I've barely begun to scratch the surface of this massive thing). I have found only a few omissions and they are extremely borderline; Reginald could well have ruled them out. This is an impressive and extremely useful tool that no serious fan, librarian, or researcher should be without."

—*Fantasy Newsletter*

"We just received our two volumes of *Science Fiction and Fantasy Literature* this morning, and five students and I have been fighting over it all day! Thank you, we have needed something like this for a long time. I have yet to show it to the teacher of Science Fiction Literature in this school, but I know she will be delighted and her students will certainly find this work an invaluable aid to their course work."

—Mildred Lee, Librarian, Sonoma Valley High School

"After spending a couple of days with *Science Fiction and Fantasy Literature*, thought I'd like to say how formidable and successful an effort I'm finding it, and that it maintains an astonishing level of accuracy and comprehensiveness—much farther up the asymptote towards that kind of perfection than Peter Nicholls and I and the others involved in our encyclopedia managed, though I'm hoping a second edition [of *The Science Fiction Encyclopedia*] will do something to remove the more embarrassing goofs."

—John Clute

UP YOUR ASTEROID! (1979)

"Och samtidigt kom från samma förlag och till samma pris något som kallar sig 'en SF-fars' av C. Everett Cooper och är betitlat *Up Your Asteroid*. Ytterst entydiga sexsymboler på omslaget, men skall den här krystade humorn vara exempel på sexporr får man förvisst vara tacksam för att det finns så litet av den varan."

—Roland Adlerberth, *Jules Verne-Magasinet*

SCIENCE FICTION & FANTASY BOOK REVIEW (1979/80)
(as Editor/Publisher)

"The genre of science fiction has gone from three excellent reviewing journals in 1977 to none in late 1978. This journal should fill that void. Edited by Neil Barron (*Anatomy of Wonder*) and published by R. Reginald (The Borgo Press, *Stella Nova*) the journal could hardly have more competent hands in control. The review will attempt comprehensive coverage of U.S. science fiction/fantasy book production, with some coverage of foreign titles, and will also review nonbook materials. Occasional short survey articles on SF and fantasy book publishing, both U.S. and foreign, are planned. There are five sections: Fiction; Reprints; Nonfiction; Miscellaneous; Juveniles. Each issue will be 12 pages in length. Reviews range from 100-800 words; the average length is 250 words. Reviews are signed by the reviewer's full name. The quality is quite high, and a number of well-known SF reviewers are featured. A welcome addition to the SF field, this title should be in most academic and public libraries."

—Prof. Hal W. Hall, Texas A&M University, *Library Journal*

SCIENCE FICTION AND FANTASY AWARDS (1981)

"For anyone seeking this sort of information, the Reginald book is relatively inexpensive and easy to consult. Its statistical tables can be used in trivia contests (who's received the most awards in all categories? the most fiction awards? the most Hugo or Nebula awards?). Reginald promises regularly updated and expanded editions."

—Neil Barron

CSCSB PERIODICALS HOLDINGS LIST (1981)

"We've just taken delivery of a copy of your 1981-82 edition of the CSCSB Periodicals Holdings List. No doubt *you're* all too well aware of the 'warts' and frailties of your magnum opus, but from this vantage point *I* detect nothing whatsoever. It is indeed perfection materialized! Simply elegant, informative, adequate, accurate...beautiful!"

—Lawrence Marshburn, Librarian, University of Redlands

CANDLE FOR POLAND (1982)
(as Editor)

"Auch in den USA fördert das tagespolitische Geschehen den Markt für Polen-Bücher. Das äußere des schmalen Bändchens Szymanskis und der Titel sprechen eine ganz bestimmte Käuferschicht an—das Innere hingegen liefert (sieht man von kleineren Fehlern ab) doch einige Erkenntnisse, mit denen die Leser wohl nicht rechnen dürften: Der frühere Herausgeber eines polnischen radikaldemokratischen Blattes, der jetzt in den USA publiziert, schildert den Weg zu den Unruhen von 1970 und 1980—und dann die Geschichte jener 469 Tage zwischen der Unterzeichnung der Gewerkschaftsabkommen und der Ausrufung des Kriegsrechts. Obwohl er gegenüber der 'Solidarnosc' prinzipiell positiv eingestellt ist, versäumt er es nicht, zahlreiche ihrer Ansätze zu kritisieren. Er schreibt, die Forderungen der 'Solidarität' hätten deutlich gegen die Basis des gesamten herrschenden Systems gezielt, äußert sich kritisch über Streiks mit Lohnfortzahlung (die es ja auch im Westen nicht gibt—hier springt allein die Gewerkschaftskasse ein) und analysiert die prinzipielle Gegensätzlichkeit der Interessen von Arbeitern und Bauern: Da letztere an hohen Preisen für die Agrarprodukte interessiert seien, sei die 'Solidarnosc Wiejska' eher eine Interessenvertretung als eine Gewerkschaft. Deutlich wird auf das Zunehmen der Kriminalität ab Mitte 1981 hingewiesen: '...wirkliche Kriminelle wurden als politische Gefangene bezeichnet und vom Mob befreit' (S. 34). Gierek wird insofern in Schutz genommen, als man ihm trotz aller Fehlkalkulationen nicht die Schuld an der Weltwirtschaftskrise in die Schuhe schieben kann. Die 'Solidarität' erscheint schließlich 'nicht als Partei des polnischen Realismus, sondern der Negation' (S. 51). Diesem allen folgt der Versuch einer historischen Einordnung des Geschehens und ein umfänglicher Anhang mit englischen Übersetzungen einschlägiger 'Solidarnosc'-Dokumente bis hin zur Deklaration von Radom (die nichtöffentlichen Verhandlungen auf diesem 'Solidarnosc'-Kongreß vom 11. Dezember 1981 werden zuvor im einzelnen kommentiert).

"Es ist wirklich überraschend, von einem exilpolnischen Journalisten, der noch dazu zugunsten der 'Solidarnosc' engagiert ist, ein so ausgewogenes Buch vorgelegt zu bekommen, das geeignet ist, hiesige Vorurteile über polnisch-amerikanische Oberflächlichkeiten zu korrigieren. Sicher stören die sentimental-reißerische, absatzorientierte Aufmachung und einige Ungereimtheiten, aber deutsche Journalisten und andere Verfasser zeitnaher Publikationen (die zwar nie frei von Fehlern sein können, aber für eine Information breiterer Schichten gebraucht werden) könnten sich am ruhigen, wenig enthusiastischen Stil Szymanskis ein Beispiel nehmen."

—F.G., *Jahrbücher für Geschichte Osteuropas*

"These are two very different books. *Candle for Poland* is written by a leading Polish writer exiled by Gomulka; it is well-written and for the general public. *Policy and Politics* is written by academics for academics, turgidly and of very uneven quality.

"Szymanski believes that 'if all the parties involved had had enough political wisdom,' the emergence of Solidarity need not have resulted in violent repression. The Communist party, in his view, should have coopted Solidarity as a junior party in governing Poland. 'If the Solidarity leaders had been given formal responsibility for the fate of their own country, they might have lost some of their revolutionary zeal' (p. 72). But Solidarity overreached itself, bringing down in the process all the freedoms gained during the previous 18 months. In its 469 days, Solidarity achieved gains unprecedented in the Eastern bloc. The climate of political opinion was changed. But Solidarity also brought about economic and political chaos and the clear danger of Soviet occupation. Solidarity went too far too fast; it never had time to mature politically, to gain seasoned, responsible leadership. 'Still, Solidarity has altered the Polish political system forever, with repercussions reaching throughout all of Eastern Europe....Solidarity was a great and glorious social experiment cut down in its prime, the massive outpouring of a repressed people' (p. 75).

"Szymanski reviews the role played by all major groups, including the Church, and concludes that General Jaruzelski has a 'short period of time' in which to act and introduce significant reforms before he, like Kania, Gierek, and Gomulka before him, is held accountable for his actions. Curiously enough, the author describes Lech Walesa as 'barely literate.'"

—Dr. Anthony T. Bouscaren, Le Moyne College

TEMPEST IN A TEAPOT (1983)

"To suggest that wars break out in unlikely places at unlikely times over unlikely issues is to state the obvious. Unfortunately, such conflicts have a way of escalating into larger and unmanageable affairs, becoming potentially dangerous when global adversaries like the United States and the Soviet Union are armed to the teeth and wary of each other's power. Although the U.S. and the U.S.S.R. were not directly drawn into the actual fighting in the Falklands, the world anxiously watched as a 20th century British Armada moved into the South Atlantic. When the disagreement over the islands broke out in serious warfare, many people were hard pressed to label who the 'bad guys' and 'good guys' were. For some it was easy to side with Great Britain, since Argentina had a reputation for oppression of human rights and a history of military dictatorships. For others, the action was simply an example of continual domination of the 'third world' by British imperialism.

"This book is a case study of the Falkland Islands conflict. It traces the historical basis of the claims of both countries, and serves to document the complex disagreement between Argentina and Great Britain over the territory. There is a review of the negotiations over the Island in the twenty-year period prior to the war, and a description of the domestic conditions in Argentina and Great Britain before the initial Argentine invasion in 1982. Also included is a lengthy description of the British mobilization and the Argentine defeat. Finally, there is a section which includes interviews with representatives of Great Britain and Argentina after the war.

160

It is in these latter discussions that one sees the importance of 'principle' when dealing with territory, even when the land in question may have marginal economic use.

"The authors demonstrate that in this dispute it is difficult to clearly establish who was right and who was wrong. Both sides have strong claims to the land, although the settlers in the islands are unwilling to accept Argentine sovereignty. The authors' thesis is that the dispute escalated into a war which neither side really wanted nor expected, and that a definitive solution is yet to be made. The book is a very useful undertaking, and while it is certainly not the last word on the subject, it does serve to illustrate the complexities of the conflicting claims and how both sides miscalculated. The book is objective. It shows how both governments exploited nationalism to justify military action.

"This book's title, if anything, is an understatement, and may mislead the potential reader. The authors recognize that this was not an affiar isolated from global politics. The U.S. and U.S.S.R. were involved by providing information secured by space satellite (the U.S. to Great Britain and the U.S.S.R. to Argentina). The United States and the Organization of American States convened meetings to deal with the problem. Both Argentina and Great Britain paid an enormous cost in lives, money, and war materiel, while the war also helped to re-elect a British Prime Minister and bring an end to military rule in Argentina (albeit perhaps temporarily).

"This book could be very useful in courses dealing with Latin American politics, international policies, or diplomacy. It contains maps of the Islands, pertinent U.N. and O.A.S. resolutions, draft agreements, diplomatic notes, extensive chronology from 1493 to January 1983, a list of Governors of the Islands, and a comprehensive bibliography."

—Dr. Wayne E. Johnson, Stephen F. Austin State University

A GUIDE TO SCIENCE FICTION AND FANTASY
IN THE LIBRARY OF CONGRESS CLASSIFICATION SCHEME (1984/1988)

"Included in this cataloguing guide, besides straight science fiction, is 'fantastic literature,' defined by Michael Burgess as 'including science fiction, fantasy (fantastic fiction), and supernatural horror, with peripheral coverage of utopian, gothic, and macabre literature.' Not included are the occult, futurism or UFOs. No specialist will be surprised by the extensiveness of the listings.

"Each section of the book is preceded by an introduction clarifying the author's method. He notes changes in style (the use of 'fantastic fiction' by the Library of Congress instead of the more common 'fantasy literature,' for example). The first section is 'Subject Headings,' which runs from 'Androids' through 'World War III' and includes dozens of subdivisions under 'Fantastic fiction,' 'Fantastic literature,' 'Ghost stories,' 'Horror tales,' 'Science fiction,' and more.

"Section II, 'Author Main Entries and Literature Numbers,' the bulk of the book, is 53 pages long and has some 2,700 names. The author entries reflect the changes from the second edition (1978) of the *Anglo-American Cataloguing Rules*

(AACR 2) and the literature numbers are those developed by the LC through mid-1984.

"The rest of the book is comprised of 'Artist Main Entries and Artist Numbers,' 'Motion Picture Main Entries and Classification Numbers'—the section on TV has one entry, *Star Trek*—and 'Classification Numbers,' followed by its own index.

"Michael Burgess is Chief Cataloguer at the California State University Library, San Bernardino, and he has brought to this guide his familiarity with Library of Congress classifications, cataloguing theory and practice, as well as the not-altogether-uniform-or-etched-in-stone changes resulting from AACR 2. He has, in addition, other publications to his credit, including *Science Fiction and Fantasy Literature.*

"This volume will help anyone seeking access to the science fiction and fantasy holdings of the Library of Congress."

—*AB Bookman's Weekly*

"Valuable as the May and Ballard volumes are, the most useful volume to be issued this summer is Michael Burgess' *A Guide to Science Fiction & Fantasy in the Lirary of Congress Classification Scheme....*I think that the highest praise I can give it is that I wish it had been available while I was working at the Library of Congress. Besides giving the subject headings which the LC has developed, as well as the classification numbers, Burgess provides a fifty-three-page, single-spaced listing of authors, indicating whether or not the LC holds their works and call numbers of the main author entries. The book does not do all of your work for you, but if you consult it before using the LC, it can provide an invaluable guide. A spot check indicates that is is thorough and accurate. Both libraries and individuals active in research need this volume. (I know from experience, incidentally, that the LC does not make interlibrary loans of its fiction. Perhaps more important, though I have not yet put it to the test, I imagine that Burgess will be of great help in finding titles held by the OCLC.)

—Dr. Thomas D. Clareson, College of Wooster

LORDS TEMPORAL AND LORDS SPIRITUAL (1985)

"This book is subtitled *A Chronological Checklist of the Popes, Patriarchs, Katholikoi, and Independent Archbishops and Metropolitans of the Monarchical Autocephalous Churches of the Christian East and West,* but is much more than a set of ecclesiastical lists. Within a small compass it gives a succinct historical sketch of every Eastern Church and jurisdiction and charts the relationships between them. The Christian West of the title is represented only by the Church of Rome; the Anglican and Lutheran Churches and the strange entourages of the *episcopi vagantes* are not mentioned. Western ecclesiastical pathology, however, is represented by 'the Renovated Church of Jesus Christ,' which produced an antipope successor to Pope John XXIII in 1963 in the person of Clement XV. Clement later starved himself to death during a hundred-days' fast, but a further antipope appeared in 1974 as a result of an internal split, Gregory XVII.

"There are some strange 'Orthodox' Churches in America, but nothing quite so lunatic as the Renovated Church of Jesus Christ, for if there had been we can be sure that Dr Clarke would have unearthed it. The lists he presents are the fruit of many years' research. Since his purpose was 'to record the chronology of each church as it perceives itself,' he first compiled lists from as many sources as possible and then sent them off to various church authorities for comment. The complexity of the task may be judged from the fact that no two lists ever agreed, even the 'official' list sometimes differing widely from those in the author's sources, and its success from the fact that some Churches accepted the lists the author sent them in preference to their own.

"The criterion for inclusion is autocephaly. Because of the fragmentation of the Eastern Churches for various historical reasons, this results in some seventy-five lists. There are, for example, five different patriarchs of Antioch, three of them in communion with Rome; there are five Armenian Churches, apart from the defunct Church of Caucasian Albania, each headed by a patriarch; there are seven different Ukrainian jurisdictions, not counting the uniates; and there are five independent Orthodox Churches in America besides the official Greek and Slav jurisdictions. The reader of this volume is provided with the means of distinguishing between them and examining their pedigrees. The Churches are arranged in alphabetical order by their primatial sees with brief histories and chronological checklists of patriarchs. This section is followed by an index, a bibliography, and a comparative table showing the equivalent forms of the various names in different languages.

"Dr Clarke, who is on the faculty of the California State University, says that he had originally intended to provide fuller information on the history of the various churches, their method of electing patriarchs, and the hierarchies still extant, but has held this material over for another book. Judging from this work, his fuller account is likely to be both fascinating and authoritative."

—Norman Russell, *Sobornost*

THE WORK OF COLIN WILSON (1989)
(as Editor)

"This first volume in Borgo's ambitious 'Bibliographies of Modern Authors' series introduces both the work of Colin Wilson and the Borgo bibliography series. Comprehensively designed and extensively annotated, the book provides an introductory essay, 'The Quest for Colin Wilson,' by Stanley, a chronology of publications and major events in Wilson's life through 1989, and substantive chapters devoted to Wilson's books, short fiction, nonfiction, introductions and afterwords, book reviews, other media appearances, and editorial credits. The final third of the text incorporates bibliographies of secondary materials (monographs, critiques, profiles and interviews, short bio-bibliographies, and other related items), miscellaneous entries, excerpts from critcial comments about Wilson's works, and a ten-page afterword, 'Inside Outside: Reflections on Being Bibliographed,' by Wilson. The volume is comprehensively indexed by title, subject, and author; in addition, items are listed chronologically and indexed by item number, allowing for frequent updating.

"Within each section, Stanley provides a wealth of bibliographical information. Section A, 'Books,' lists 96 books, giving full bibliographic citations for first and subsequent issues; in the case of Wilson's *The Outsider*, for example, this supplemental listing gathers 20 titles, includings translations into Arabic, Spanish, French, Finnish, German, Italian, Japanese, Korean, Dutch, Norse, Polish, and Swedish. The entries conclude with an 'Analytical Table of Contents,' 'Comments,' and 'Secondary Sources and Reviews' (over 40 listed for *The Outsider*). As a result of this kind of coverage, well over a third of the total pages in *The Work of Colin Wilson* are devoted to his novels, but other works are dealt with in as much depth and with as much precision.

"*The Work of Colin Wilson* also suggests that the series extends beyond the strict confines of science fiction and fantasy. Although Wilson has written fine SF novels—among them *The Mind Parasites* (item A20) and *The Space Vampires* (item A50)—entries range from philosophy to mainstream novels and books on criminology, biography, literary criticism, and music. Stanley's bibliography does justice to Wilson as a prolific and important contributor to contemporary letters, and simultaneously establishes the format for an important series of such studies. Borgo has published or announced annotated bibliographies of such writers as Brian W. Aldiss, William F. Nolan, Louis L'Amour, Stephen King, Orson Scott Card, Harry Harrison, and Ian Watson."

—Dr. Michael R. Collings, Pepperdine University

THE ARMS CONTROL, DISARMAMENT,
AND MILITARY SECURITY DICTIONARY (1989)

"This dictionary is a wonderfully concise and comprehensive resource on a very important topic. It provides a thorough and lucid set of definitions in a subject area which too frequently has been 'left to the experts.' In 268 detailed entries, the authors provide a wealth of information on such topics as the arms race, conventional and nuclear weapons, nuclear strategy, and disarmament. The entries are cross-referenced and an index is provided. Each entry provides definitions of words and concepts, as well as paragraphs on historical context and current significance. This book will be of great value to general readers as well as specialists, and will be indispensable in both academic and public libraries."

—Jennifer Scarlott, World Policy Institute, *Library Journal*

"Elliot (North Carolina Central) and Reginald (California State—San Bernardino) provide 268 systematically selected entries designed to complement by definition and organization those terms noted in standard texts on their topic. They have chosen to be discriminating rather than exhaustive in their selection, emphasizing primarily the US (e.g., entries for Army, Air Force), and drawing from the works of others (documented in 24 pages of notes). Their goal is the production of an accurate, concise, and objective lexicon in a readable format. With entry numbers affixed, items are arranged alphabetically within subject-matter chapters. Extensive cross-references are provided within or at the ends of entries; these may lead to other data included within the same or different chapters. The index to entry numbers features bold type for terms defined while subsidiary concepts are noted in standard type. Both more objective and less costly than David Robertson's *Guide to Modern Defense and Strategy*, this dictionary is suitable for public as well as academic libraries at all levels."

—M. J. Smith, Jr., Salem-Teikyo University, *Choice*

THE WORK OF ROSS ROCKLYNNE (1989)
THE WORK OF CHAD OLIVER (1989)
(as Editor)

"Two very different but also very respected writers of SF have their work listed and annotated in these two excellent samples of Borgo's ongoing bibliographical series. Rocklynne had only two books published, but a considerable number of short stories. Menville also went through his papers following Rocklynne's death and provides detailed information on the unpublished works. The volume on Chad Oliver contains, as well as the excellent bibliographical material, a long and interesting interview and an essay by Oliver. Both books are meticulously detailed, cover fiction, work in other media, even amateur publications. Each of the books in this series provides an excellent basis for research, as well as a checklist for people just interested in finding other work by the authors covered."

—Don D'Ammassa, *Science Fiction Chronicle*

THE WORK OF CHARLES BEAUMONT (1990)
THE WORK OF GEORGE ZEBROWSKI (1990)
(as Author/Editor)

"Updated versions of very comprehensive bibliographies of very disparate writers. Beaumont, whose fiction frequently inspired TV episodes, was primarily a writer of the supernatural and fantastic, while Zebrowski is more conventionally a writer of SF. Each book prints a very detailed lists of short and long fiction, essays, scripts, nonfiction, editorial credits and other information, and each includes an essay by the author covered. In Beaumont's case, it's a hard-to-find manuscript published posthumously. Two outstanding volumes in an outstanding series of author indices."

—Don D'Ammassa, *Science Fiction Chronicle*

AFTERTHOUGHTS

Harvesting the Vineyards of Obscurity

by Robert Reginald

So now the clock tolls forty-three. Ding dong, ding dong, half a life or more gone. I am conscious of time as never before. Opportunities missed. Chances wasted. Days and months and years passing by in an ever-increasing flood. But still a few roadmarks left along the way.

It's been a curious life. My father was an Air Force officer. We moved constantly. I remember the dusty, dirty, smelly streets of Izmir, the ragmen and the decaying fishing boats, the earthquakes, the jarring and exotic mix of East and West, of old and new, of poverty and wealth. Before my tenth birthday I had glimpsed pieces of Italy, Switzerland, Germany, France, Greece, and Austria—and California, Oregon, Massachusetts, Kansas, and several dozen other states. Of Fukuoka, my birthplace, I recall nothing.

Family was the only constant, that and my books. Friends could (and would) be left behind every three years or so, relegated to increasingly infrequent correspondence, rapidly fading from mind and memory. TV was nonexistent, and the radio waves were filled with alien sounds and languages. So I filled my life with words—fiction, nonfiction, whatever I could find, books by the hundreds. I devoured everything. And I wrote, slowly, tentatively, putting things together from the fragments I glimpsed around me.

I remember at the age of four or five copying words off my mother's kitchen appliances, in our old, two-storey house at Fairview, Massachusetts. Reproducing the words somehow made them more real. In Turkey I won second prize in an essay contest, to my utter astonishment. Evidently, the world was telling me, I had a talent of a sort. By my late grade school and early high school years I was working on school newspapers and compiling long lists of kings and monarchs.

Lists and compilations. Indexes and guides. Genealogies and family histories. Pieces and fragments. The roots of what I do go very deep, begin very early. It's self-evident in retrospect. Rearranging the world in some more logical order was my way of coping with the disruptions of a military (and social) life, of cleaning up a disorderly universe, and reworking it into something more palatable.

The making of bibliographies and reference volumes and genealogies (and, in my library work, the cataloging of monographs) seems to satisfy some basic need in me, and I have become, in these middle years of my life, fairly proficient at what

I do. I have developed an instinct for organization, an understanding of what and why and when and how to do things that is not easily described or passed on.

If bibliography is both a science and an art, as I believe it to be, it consists partly of technique (which can be taught), and partly of an esthetic sense born from the combination of experience and talent. One may acquire the latter only with time and seasoning and more than a little luck. I've been fortunate, I think, to have glimpsed even a small part of this.

"Of the making of books there is no end," saith the prophet—but a little voice keeps whispering *sotto voce* that we *do* end, all of us, sooner or later, and that our makings, our little explosions of creativity, will mostly end with us. The novels become *passé*, the verse old-fashioned, the bibliographies go out-of-date. Most of our reputations decline into obscurity (and few of us attain all that much notice even while we're still madly scribbling).

And yet, and yet...George and Jack and Bill and Jeff and Leonard and Robert and Brian and the rest (and I—*and I!*) write (have written, will write) our stories and novels and essays and even our bibliographies, and perhaps the world is a little better for them, by some infinitesimally fractional margin. Or so at least I tell myself on those days when the phone is jangling constantly, the bills are piling up, the irate authors are demanding to know when their overdue books will be published, and academe has gone crazy again.

One wonders at such times whether the effort has been worth the result. That's not a question I can easily or safely answer. There is a force within me, a madness, that drives me on, pell-mell, towards some unseen goal. Better not to know that end: there are no good endings, only less poor ones. I do know that I don't write for money, for I see very little of it; I don't write for fame, for I have found almost none; I don't write for academic advancement, because I ruin the grade curve, which doesn't endear me to my fellow professors; I don't seek public or private adulation, because only a handful of fellow bibliographers or editors or librarians understand even a fraction of what I've done or tried to do.

I do what I must, because the alternative is unacceptable in the overall scheme of things. And because some of what I produce is, in and of itself, good work, worthy of remembrance. If I appreciate Stokvis's magnificent three-volume opus—even if I am the only one who does—is he not in some sense still alive? The man may be dead, but his work goes on.

We who labor in the vineyards of obscurity know that there are many fine wines besides the "big labels," and that at least some of these vintages are worthy of sampling in their own right, even if they're not to everyone's taste. The work is its own reward, and if, as writer, one does not write first to please oneself, one's art (however that word is defined) must soon suffer irreparable damage. Caecilius Statius says: *"Serit arbores quae alteri seculo prosint."* I say: "Got a match?"

—Robert Reginald
San Bernardino, California
September 29, 1990-
September 29, 1991

167

AFTERWORD
Robert Reginald: Force Majeure
by Jack Dann

I'm three years younger in Germany than I am here in the United States. But here (and in England, too, alas) I'm also known as Jack Dunn, Jack Dawn, even Jack Danny. However, I should point out that these pseudonyms are not of my own creation. You see, even bibliographers can be careless. They err on spelling or on a birth date, the error goes into print, and other "researchers" then happily cobble their texts out of the mistakes of others.

And so the errors perpetuate, and I shall forever be younger in Germany and forever find that my stories and articles have been written by people with names that are (sometimes) very close to my own. For the record, I'm Jack Dann (really), no "ny," as in "Danny," unless you're referring to the state in which I live. And, for the record, I'm 46 years old, although, come to think of it, I should probably keep my mouth shut and keep German time. That makes me 43, which is a bit easier to live with.

If, however, you should require an accurate bibliography of my work, there is only one place you can go: to Rob Reginald's *Borgo Press*. Rob will not perpetuate errors. He goes to the sources, he researches, and he won't let facts see print unless they are accurate.

He's an "editor's editor."

I've known about Rob for years by reputation. As an anthologist, I found his work, especially *Stella Nova*, the *Cumulative Paperback Index*, and *Contemporary Science Fiction Authors* to be invaluable resources. But we tend to take such books for granted, useful as they may be. How many of us think of Marjorie E. Skillin and Robert M. Gay when we use *Words into Type*? When you're looking up a word such as "forwrecche" in the *Oxford English Dictionary*, do you think of F. J. Furnivall, or any of the other editors who brought its many volumes to life? For that matter, when you use Roget's *Thesaurus*, you don't really think about someone by the name of Peter Mark Roget...do you?

To be sure, Rob knew from the getgo that much of his labor would be in "the vineyards of obscurity" (his phrase). But he also felt that "the work is its own reward."

And we—readers, writers, editors, anthologists, critics, researchers—are the ones who reap that prodigious reward. Rob is a fashioner of finely honed tools, basic fundamental tools that we simply can't do without. Of course, we take those tools—those brilliant creations from "the vineyards of obscurity"—for granted, just as we do electricity and running water.

Perhaps this book might be thought of as a well-deserved celebration of someone who is willing to tend such vineyards for us. Thank you, Robert Reginald. We *do* know who you are!

* * * * * * *

Now the paragraph above could probably end this "short" Afterword (and I could go back to watching the Fall foliage around my pond), if, indeed, Rob were like most mortals.

Most of us strive and struggle to carve out a niche in our particular genre/discipline/profession and hope to gain some respect and even some well-deserved encomiums from our peers. But, of course, the kicker is that Rob is not like most of us. He is not only prolific (1,250 volumes in the last twenty years!), but he seems to be more than just one person. He is a publisher, anthologist, editor, librarian, bibliographer, cataloger, genealogist...but if you've read the excellent introduction by my friend Bill Nolan, you know all of that. As Bill says, Rob has written or edited sixty book so his own.

How does he do it all? Where does he find time to be a librarian at the ranking of full professor, take genealogical trips, run a major academic press, edit...and *write*. I think, perhaps, it even mystifies Rob, although I have several other friends blessed with the prodigious genius of productivity: one is Bob Silverberg, another is Barry N. Malzberg. Collaborating on fiction with Barry is like jumping on a train that is traveling full-bore. It's truly a vertiginous ride for a writer who considers four pages a day to be pretty good. And so it would be with Rob, I think.

To my mind, he is a writer first and everything else second. It's evident in the way he thinks, talks, and—most importantly—writes. I offer his own biographical "Afterword" as proof. I also have a piece of correspondence in hand which I believe might be illuminating.

Herewith Robert Reginald:

> What I do is rather different in one sense from fiction writing, although there are correspondences which seem obvious to me (but perhaps to no one else). I think there is a kind of *force majeure* behind all creative activity which defies logical explanation. Or, rather: we can describe it, even touch it, if you will, point out to strangers (the "hoi polloi") its peculiar characteristics with some great acumen (and at great length), but still never really understand exactly how it works. That such a creature exists I am convinced, but I am no better at roping it than any other of the bookaroos. Perhaps you will do better than I. All I can tell you is that I seem to spend an inordinate amount of time thinking about such things these days.

169

When editor, critic, and writer Damon Knight was asked to define science fiction, he said something to the effect that "It's whatever I point at." If you ask me to define the *force majeure* of creative activity, I can only do the same: point at it. Stand up, Robert Reginald. There is a man pointing at you.

—Jack Dann
Binghamton, New York
October 9, 1991

TITLE INDEX

"10-Millionth-Record Winner Strikes Back," B80

14 Official Blueprints, Star Trek, the Motion Picture, Rendered by David Kimble," B53

"15 Planets Discovered by Science Fiction Writers," B62

"18 Million Records Input Over 17 Years," K38

"9,000 Miles Later, They Found Her Roots," K14

"About Susan Wood," B111

"The Acclaimed Newcastle Forgotten Fantasy Library," F28

"The Adventures of Doctor Who, by Terrance Dicks," B49

"Afterthoughts: Harvesting the Vineyards of Obscurity," B133

"Afterword: Robert Reginald: Force Majeure," K56

Aladore, by Sir Henry John Newbolt," B66

"Alien, by Alan Dean Foster," B51

Alistair MacLean: The Key Is Fear, A6

"Anatomy of a Phenomemon," B1

Anatomy of Wonder (Barron), M14

Ancestral Voices: An Anthology of Early Science Fiction, A4

Ancient Hauntings, A7

"Ann Shadwick to Retire," B109

The Annotated Guide to Fantastic Adventures (Gallagher), G18

"Announcing Harlan Ellison's First NEW Book in Two Years!" F40

The Arms Control, Disarmament, and Military Security Dictionary, A44

"At Last, the Much Expanded SECOND EDITION!" F64

"Atreides, Haus, Gründung von," B82ad

"Atreides, Haus, Prominente Mitglieder," B83ad

"Atreides, Haus, und Imperiale Herrschaft," B84ad

"Atreides, House, and Imperial Rule," B84

"Atreides, House, Foundation of," B82

"Atreides, House, Prominent Members," B83

"Atreides, Minotauros (10059-10163)," B86

The Attempted Assassination of John F. Kennedy: A Political Fantasy, A5

"Author's Note," K30

The Autocephalous Orthodox Churches, D7/a

"Available Winter 1990/91: *The House of the Burgesses*, Second Edition," F55

"Awards," B23, B56

"Badger Science Fiction," H1

Bantam Books, M15

"Between the Planets, by Kurt Mahr," B26

Bibliographies of Modern Authors, D7/b

"Bibliography of Brian W. Aldiss," H7

"The Bibliography of Crime Fiction, 1749-1975, by Allen J. Hubin," B22

"A Bibliography of CSUSB Alumni Authors," E17

"A Bibliography of CSUSB Alumni Authors, Composers, and Playwrights: February, 1991," E18

"Bibliography of Jerry Pournelle," H8

"Bibliography of R. Reginald," H13

"Bibliography of R. Reginald 1984," H17

"The Big Lie," H19

Bio of an Ogre (Anthony), M17

"Bjo Trimble Bibliography," H9

Black Literary Studies, D7/c

Black Political Studies, D7/d

The Booke of the Rede Hand, IB5

"Books to Pep Up Every Collection," F5

Borgo Bioviews, D7/e

Borgo Cataloging Guides, D7/f

Borgo Family Histories, D7/g

Borgo Literary Guides, D7/h

Borgo Political Scenarios, D7/i

"The Borgo Press," B16

The Borgo Press, D7, M8

"The Borgo Press: 1989 Catalog Supplement," F50

"The Borgo Press: 1990/91 Catalog," F54

"The Borgo Press: Fall 1980 Library Catalog," F33

"The Borgo Press: Fall Catalog 1988," F49

"Borgo Press: Great Science Fiction & Fantasy Originals & Reprints," F29

The Borgo Press Newsletter, F23

"The Borgo Press: Order Form 1981," F36

"The Borgo Press: Order Form 1985," F42

"The Borgo Press: Order Form Fall 1980," F34

"The Borgo Press: Order Form Fall 1986," F45

"The Borgo Press: Order Form January 1983," F38

"The Borgo Press: Order Form Spring 1980," F31

"The Borgo Press: Spring/Summer 1982 Library Catalog," F37

"The Borgo Press: Stock List 1984," F39

"The Borgo Press: Stock List 1985," F41

"The Borgo Press: Stock List 1986," F43

"The Borgo Press: Stock List 1987," F46

"The Borgo Press: Stock List 1988," F47

"The Borgo Press: Summer 1990 Catalog," F53

Borgo Reference Guides, D7/j

Borgo Reference Library, D7/k

"Bring the Jubilee, by Ward Moore," B33

Brownstone Books, D7, M8

Brownstone Chapbook Series, D7/l

Brownstone Mystery Guides, D7/l

"Browsing in the Library," H18

Burgess & Wickizer, D7, M8

The Burgess Bulletin, D3

"Burgess Contributes Milestone Record," K18

171

"Burgess, Harrison and Etta (Enfield)," B115
"Burgess, Jacob L., Jr., and Lena (Morris) and Mayme (Corbin)," B116
"Burgess, Jacob L., Sr., and Maranda (Bell)," B117
"Burgess, James Sylvester, and Martha (Lawson)," B118
"Burgess, John H. and Martha," B119
"Burgess, John M., and Mary (Davis)," B120
"Burgess, M. R.," K16, K28
"Burgess, Michael," K27, K31, K33-K35, K39-K40, K42-K43, K45-K47, K49-K50, K52
"Burgess, Michael R.," K10
"Burgess, M(ichael) R(oy), 1948-   ," K13
"Burgess, Thomas F., and Sarah (Harris)," B121
"Burgess, Washington and Marietta," B122
"Burgess, William H., and Eliza (Bettis)," B123
"Burgesses in the 1790 Census," B124
"C. S. Lewis," G13
"Calibrations: *Golden Cities, Far*, edited by Lin Carter," B4
"Calibrations: *The Broken Sword*, by Poul Anderson," B5
"Calibrations: *The Well at the World's End*, by William Morris," B3
California Ranchos: Patented Private Land Grants Listed by County, A42
"California State College, San Bernardino Inputs Ten Millionth Record to OCLC Database," K19
California State College, San Bernardino Library Policy Manual, E1
Candle for Poland: 469 Days of Solidarity, A24, M6
The Centenarian (Balzac), M13
"Chuck Hillig's Primer for the New Age," F69
The Classic Years of Robert A. Heinlein (Slusser), M6
Clipper Studies in the American Theatre, D7/m
Clipper Studies in the Theatre, D7/m
"Comets Don't Slow Down," K54
"Coming December 1991!" F78
"Coming November 1991!" F77
"Coming Soon! The Moving Sequel," F48
"Commentary," B20, B25, B39, B45, B47, B48
"A Comparison of the Screen Treatment *Housebound* with the Motion Picture Version of *Poltergeist*," H16
"Completely Reset, Re-Edited, and Indexed!" F71
"*Conan*, by Robert E. Howard, L. Sprague de Camp, and Lin Carter," B35
Contemporary Science Fiction Authors, First Edition, A3
Contemporary Science Fiction Authors II, A18
Contemporary Science Fiction, Fantasy, and Horror Authors III, A76
"Cover, Arthur Byron," B126
"'CSB' Garners 10-Millionth OCLC Record," K20
CSCSB Library Policy Manual, Second Edition, E12
CSCSB Periodicals Holdings List 1974, E2
CSCSB Periodicals Holdings List 1976, E4
CSCSB Periodicals Holdings List 1977, E6
CSCSB Periodicals Holdings List 1980, E8
CSCSB Periodicals Holdings List 1981-82, E10
CSCSB Periodicals Subject List 1974, E3
CSCSB Periodicals Subject List 1976, E5
CSCSB Periodicals Subject List 1977, E7
CSCSB Periodicals Subject List 1980, E9
CSCSB Periodicals Subject List 1981-82, E11
"CSUSB Alumni Authors," E16
"CSUSB Librarians," E14
"CSUSB Library Faculty (June 1991)," E19
"CSUSB Library Staff Members," E15
"CSUSB Library Staff (June 1991)," E20
"*Cumulative Paperback Index, 1939-1959*: A Closer Look," K7
Cumulative Paperback Index, 1939-1959: A Comprehensive Bibliographic Guide to 14,000 Mass-Market Paperback Books of 33 Publishers Under 69 Imprints, A2, G1
"*The Cylon Death Machine*, by Glen A. Larson and Robert Thurston," B18
"The Dark Tower," IA4
"*Devil's Handmaiden*," B42
"*Dimension of Horror*, by Jeffrey Lord," B30
"Directory," B32
Discovering H. P. Lovecraft (Schweitzer), M6
Discovering Modern Horror Fiction (Schweitzer), G19
"The Dream," IA6
Dreamers of Dreams: An Anthology of Fantasy, A14
Earthdance: A Romance of Reincarnation (Connolly), G17
"Edward Burgess of Scott County, Kentucky—His Family and the Family Bible Record," B102
"Emperors of the Known Universe," B87
Essays on Fantastic Literature, D7/n
"Extensions of Remarks: New Book on Falklands War Recommended," B93, K26
"Fall Harvest, New and Exciting Books," F6
Fandom Directory No. 7 (Hopkins), D12
Fantasy Literature (Barron), M14
"*Fantasy Readers Guide, Number One: The John Spencer Publications*, edited by Michael Ashley," B46
"Fanthorpe, R(obert) Lionel," B94, B127
Far Rainbow; The Second Invasion from Mars (Strugatsky), M13
"Fiddling in Mañanaland," B105
"Fidel Castro Speaks!" F44
"Finis," IA1
"First Annual LTF Survey of CSU Librarians," B100
"First Book Publication!" F72
"The First Comprehensive Guide Published!" F73
"Foreword: It Was Twenty Years Ago Today," K55
"Forgotten Fantasy," K29
Forgotten Fantasy, Classics of Science Fiction and Fantasy, D2
The Forgotten Fantasy Library, D5
"Forgotten Fantasy Lives!" F7
"From One of America's Greatest Pulpsters! Now Available for the First Time!" F62
Full Frontal Poetry (Mallett et al.), M6
"*Futura Man, an Orphan in Time*, by R. G. Taylor," B55
Futurevisions: The New Golden Age of the Science Fiction Film, A34, G22
Galactic Central Publications, D7

"Gale Outside Editors: Full-Time Librarians Explore the Realm of Science Fiction and Fantasy," K36
"George Orwell's *1984*—How Close Are We," B14
"Ginaz, Haus," B88ad
"Ginaz, House of," B88
"*Golden Scorpion*, by Alan Burt Akers, a Second Opinion," B21
"The Gor Novels, by John Norman," B67
"Great Houses, The," B89
Great Issues of the Day, D7/o
Great Sky River (Benford), M1
Great Works & Rarities of Science Fiction & Fantasy (Levin), G7
"Greatly Expanded Second Edition!" F79
A Guide to Science Fiction and Fantasy in the Library of Congress Classification Scheme, A29
A Guide to Science Fiction and Fantasy in the Library of Congress Classification Scheme, Second Edition, A40
H. G. Wells (Crossley), G23
H. P. Lovecraft (Joshi), G10
Hal Clement (Hassler), G8
Hancer's Price Guide to Paperback Books, Third Edition, A52
"Harkonnen, Haus," B90ad
"Harkonnen, House of," B90
The Harlan Ellison Hornbook (Ellison), M16
"Harvesting the Vineyards of Obscurity," B133
Hasan (Anthony), M6, M17
"*Hasan*, by Piers Anthony," B68
"*Havoc in Islandia*, by Mark Saxton," B65
"*Hell's Bitch*," B29
"Herder and Herder Distributes Information Books and Newcastle Publishing," F2
"Herder and Herder: Fall 1971," F3
"He's a Superman of Letters," K3
A Historical and Critical Survey of the Science-Fiction Film (Menville), M6
"Hohe Häuser, Die," B89ad
The Holy Grail Revealed: The Real Secret of Rennes-Le-Château, A22, G26, M13
Horror Fiction in the Library of Congress Classification Scheme, A86
Horror Literature (Barron), M14
"*A House-Boat on the Styx*; and, *The Pursuit of the House-Boat*, by John Kendrick Bangs," B69
The House of the Burgesses, Being a Genealogical History of Edward Burges of King George and Stafford Counties, Virginia, with His Sons—Garner Burges of Fauquier Co., Virginia; William Burgess of Stafford Co., Virginia; Moses Burgess of Orange Co., Virginia; Reuben Burgess of Rowan Co., North Carolina, and His Grandsons, Edward Burgess of Culpeper Co., Virginia; John Burgess of Harrison Co., Kentucky; Henry Burgess of Fleming Co., Kentucky; Edward Burgess of Scott Co., Kentucky; John P. B. Burgess of Halifax Co., Virginia; Edward Burgess of Kanawha Co., West Virginia; William Burgess of Davie Co., North Carolina; Reuben Burgess of Davie Co., North Carolina; and Thomas Burgess of White Co., Tennessee—Together with Their Known Descendants Named Burgess, A26

The House of the Burgesses, Being a Genealogical History of William Burges of Richmond (later King George) Co., Virginia, and His Son Edward Burges of King George Co., Virginia, with the Descendants in the Male Line of Edward's Sons, Garner Burges of Fauquier Co., Virginia, William Burges of Stafford Co., Virginia, Edward Burgess, Jr. of Fauquier Co., Virginia, Moses Burgess of Orange Co., Virginia, and Reuben Burgess, Sr., of Rowan (later Davie) Co., North Carolina, Second Edition, A75
"Houses Minor," B91
"*I—Alien*, by J. Michael Reaves, a Second Opinion," B19
"'I Fear the Greeks...': An Introduction to the Life and Works of Robert Reginald," K24
I. O. Evans Studies in the Philosophy and Criticism of Literature, D7/p
If J.F.K. Had Lived: A Political Scenario, A23
"Imperatoren (Kaiser) des Bekannten Universums," B87ad
"Index," B54, B92
"An Inside Look at the Publishing Business," K4
Inside Science Fiction (Gunn), M6
"Interview: Robert Reginald," K12
"Interview with Michael Burgess (aka R. Reginald)," K22
"Introducing a New Magazine for the Discriminating Librarian...," F25
"Introduction: A Monumental Work," B112
"Introduction: About Susan Wood," B111
"Introduction: Comets Don't Slow Down," K54
"Introduction: Once Upon a Time," B64
"Introduction: The Ranchos of California," B103
"Introduction: The Stafford Connection," B114
"*An Introduction to the J. Lloyd Eaton Collection of Science Fiction and Fantasy*, by Clifford Wurfel; *Space Voyages, 1591-1920*, by Lynn S. Smith," B37
"Introduction to the Newcastle Edition," B6
"An Invaluable Research Tool for Student and Professor Alike!" F60
"It Was Twenty Years Ago Today," K55
"*Ivan Efremov's Theory of Soviet Science Fiction*, by G. V. Grebens," B60
J. G. Ballard (Brigg), G21
Jack London (Beauchamp), G16
"Jeff Rovin Bibliography," H10
John D. MacDonald and the Colorful World of Travis McGee, A12
King Solomon's Children: Some Parodies of H. Rider Haggard, A15
"Die Kleine Häuser," B91ad
"Kurtz, Katherine," B128
"Larry Niven Bibliography," H11
"*Legend in Blue Steel*, by Spider Page," B41
"Leonard Wibberley (1915-1983)," B79
"[Letter]," B126
"Librarians: Who We Are," B99
"Library Enters Computer Age, Part II," B98
"The Library Enters the Computer Age," B113
"*A Life for Kregen*, by Dray Prescot," B31
"Limericks," IB6
"*The Literature of Fantasy*, by Roger C. Schlobin, a Second Opinion," B59

"A Little Light Reading," C1, L13
"Looking Back on Films That Look Far Ahead," B12
Lords Temporal and Lords Spiritual: A Chronological Checklist of the Popes, Patriarchs, Katholikoi, and Independent Archbishops and Metropolitans of the Monarchical Autocephalous Churches of the Christian East and West, A33
Lords Temporal and Lords Spiritual: A Chronological Checklist of the Popes, Patriarchs, Katholikoi, and Independent Archbishops and Metropolitans of the Autocephalous Monarchical Churches of the Christian East and West, Second Edition, A64
Lost Race and Adult Fantasy Fiction: 69 Books, D9, F21
LTF Newsletter, D13
"'Luck of the Draw': Cal-State San Bernardino Adds 10,000,000," K17
"*The Man Whose Name Wouldn't Fit*, by Theodore Tyler," B2
Marion Zimmer Bradley (Arbur), G20
Mary Shelley (Phy), G27
"A Massive and Dynamic Work Which Will Become the Standard of Its Field," F76
"McAllister, Bruce (Hugh)," B95, B129
"Meet the Editor: Robert Reginald of Borgo Press," K23
"*Melusine; or, Devil Take Her!* by Charlotte Franken Haldane," B70
"Men and Women Who Claimed to Be God," H6
"Michael Lewis Cook," B108
The Milford Series: Popular Writers of Today, D7/q
"The Milford Series: Popular Writers of Today," F27
"Mir," IA5
The Missionaries (Compton), M1
"*Modern Science Fiction: Its Meaning and Its Future*, edited by Reginald Bretnor," B57
"A Modern Story of Guilt and Innocence—And the American Justice System," F57
"*Monk's Magic*, by Alexander de Comeau," B71
"A Monumental Work," B112
"*Motel of the Mysteries*, by David Macaulay," B44
Murder Was Bad: Mystery and Detective Fiction in Paperback Publishing, from the Pages of Paperback Quarterly, A69
Mystery and Detective Fiction in the Library of Congress Classification Scheme, A39
"Neb," H15
"*Die Neologismen in der Modernen Franzosischen Science-Fiction*, by Felix Scherwinsky," B58
"The Neustrian Cycle, by Leslie Barringer," B72
"New Book on Falklands War Recommended," A93
"A New Guide to the Work of a Rising Literary Star," F67
"A New Literary Guide to the Thinking Man's Detective!" F63
New Religious Movements Series, D7/r
New Science Fiction Voices (Elliot), M6
"New Second Edition!" F68

"A New Triumph from a Literary Master!" F52
"Newcastle Books in Print, 1974," F9
"Newcastle: Fall '75," F13
"Newcastle: Fall '76," F16
"Newcastle: Fall '77," F19
The Newcastle Forgotten Fantasy Library, D5
"Newcastle Publishing: Spring 1972 Catalog," F4
Newcastle Publishing Co., Inc., D4
"Newcastle Publishing Company, Inc.: 1977 Catalog," F18
"Newcastle Publishing Company, Inc.: Books for Fall 1974," F10
"Newcastle Publishing Company, Inc.: Books for Spring 1974," F8
"Newcastle Publishing Company, Inc.: Spring Previews 75," F12
"Newcastle Publishing, Publishers, Distributors, Importers: Fall 1979," F26
"Newcastle Publishing, Publishers, Distributors, Importers: Fall 1980," F32
"Newcastle Publishing, Publishers, Distributors, Importers: Spring 1980 Supplement," F30
"Newcastle: Spring '76," F14
"Newcastle: Spring '77," F17
"Nolan, William F(rancis)," B130
"Not Only Who Did It, But Why They Did It!" F74
"Now Available in Paper!" F70
"Now Available: The Flagship Volume of the Series," F51
"Now Available! *To Kill or Not to Kill: Thoughts on Capital Punishment*," F56
"Now...Two Great New SF Interview Collections...," F35
"Number Six — Studies in Judaica and the Holocaust," F66
"Obituaries: Michael Lewis Cook," B108
"*The Official Guide to Comic & Science Fiction Books*, by Michael Resnick," B36
Olaf Stapledon (Kinnaird), G24
"Once Atime and Long Ago," IB4
"One of America's Most Popular Writers!" F59
"One of England's Most Versatile Authors!" F65
"One of the Most Relevant and Burning Topics of Our Time!" F80
"One Small Step," G12
"Other Survey Results," B101
The Paperback Price Guide, First Edition, A20
The Paperback Price Guide, No. 2, A25
"*Paperbacks, U.S.A.*, by Piet Schreuders," B63
"*Paralittératures*, by Yvon Allard," B38
"Part Two: Directory," B32
"*Pavane*, by Keith Roberts," B34
"Peter Fitting on the Borgo Press: Two Reactions and a Note on *SFS*'s Reviewing Policy," B81
"Pfau Library Enters the Computer Age, Part One," B97
Phantasmagoria, A8
Philip K. Dick (Pierce), G9
Piers Anthony (Collings), G15
"The Pond," IA3
PQ-liar Perambulations: Studies in the History of the Mass Market Paperback, from the Pages of Paperback Quarterly, A71

"Predictions from Science Fiction," B13, B61
"Presenting New Worlds of Science Fiction & Fantasy...: Fall, 1978," F22
"Presenting New Worlds of Science Fiction & Fantasy...: Spring, 1978," F20
"Presenting New Worlds of Science Fiction & Fantasy...: Spring, 1979," F24
Price Guide to Paperback Books, Third Edition, A52
"*The Printed Book Catalogs of the Library of the State Historical Society of Wisconsin*," B11
"Psychologists Who Needed Help Themselves," H5
"Published by Members: Report of the Monitoring Committee," B7-B10
"The R. R. Bowker Company," H3
"R. Reginald," K1, K9
"*R. Reginald: Science Fiction and Fantasy Literature*," K21
"The Ranchos of California," B103
"Reading List," B125
"Reaves, J. Michael," B96
"Reaves, Michael," B131
A Reference Guide to Science Fiction, Fantasy, and Horror, A63
"Reginald, Robert," K5-K6, K8, K15, K32, K37, K41, K44, K48
"Reginald, R(obert), 1948- ," K2
Reginald's Science Fiction and Fantasy Awards: A Comprehensive Guide to the Awards and Their Winners, Second Edition, A58
"Reorganization Plan, CSUSB Library, October 1986," E13
"Revised and Expanded Second Edition: *The Beach Boys: Southern California Pastoral*," F58
"*Riddle of Stars*, by Patricia McKillip," B50
R.I.P.: Five Stories of the Supernatural, A9
"Robert Reginald: Force Majeure," K56
Robert Silverberg (Clareson), G14
"Roster of 'First Kentucky Ancestors': Henry Burgess," B104
"The Russians Are Coming! The Russians Are Coming...Again!" F61
San Bernardino County Studies, D7/s
"*Satan's Mistress*, by Tabatha Jervis," B27
Science Fiction: 61 Books, F11b
Science Fiction: 62 Books, D6, F11
"*Science Fiction: A Selected List of Books That Have Appeared in Talking Book Topics and Braille Book Review*," B52
Science Fiction and Fantasy (Levin), G4
Science Fiction & Fantasy Awards, Including Complete Checklists of the Hugo Awards, Nebula Awards, Locus Awards, Jupiter Awards, Pilgrim Awards, International Fantasy Awards, Ditmar Awards, August Derleth Awards, World Fantasy Awards, Eaton Awards, Gandalf Awards, British Fantasy Awards, John W. Campbell Memorial Awards, Milford Awards, Prometheus Awards, and Selected Foreign Awards, with a Complete Index to Winners, a List of Officers of the Science Fiction Writers of America from the Beginning of That Organization, a Checklist of World Science Fiction Conventions and Their Guests of Honor, and Detailed Statistical Tables, A21

Science Fiction and Fantasy Awards: A Comprehensive Guide to the Awards and Their Winners, Second Edition, A58
Science Fiction & Fantasy Book Review, D10, A19, M5
Science Fiction & Fantasy Book Review, Nos. 1-13, February 1979-February 1980, A19
Science Fiction and Fantasy Criticism, H14
Science Fiction and Fantasy Literature, a Checklist, 1700-1974; with, Contemporary Science Fiction Authors II, A18, G3, L7, L8
Science Fiction and Fantasy Literature, Supplement, 1975-1991; with, Contemporary Science Fiction, Fantasy, and Horror Authors III, A76, G28
Science Fiction & Fantasy Proofs and Review Copies (Levin), G5
"Scottie's Favorite Recipes!" F81
"Second Annual CSU Librarians Survey," B106
The Second Invasion from Mars (Strugatsky), M13
"The Short Fiction of Knowles," B73
Sidewinder Press, D7, M8
Sidewinder Reprints, D7/t
"Siridar-Dukes of Atreides Caladanides and Arrikides," B85
"Siridar-Herzöge Atreides, Caladanides, under Arrikides," B85ad
Sleepless Nights in the Procrustean Bed (Ellison), L12
"*So Love Returns*, by Robert Nathan," B74
"The Song of the Tin-Can Man," IB3
Space Log: A Chronological Checklist of Manned Space Flights, 1961-1991, A67
"*Space Lust*, bound with *Mixed Doubles*, by Cynthia Bellmore," B17
"*Spacedust One*, by C. C. Coffman," B40
"*Spacing Dutchman*, by Eric Vinicoff and Marcia Martin," B43
The Spectre Bridegroom, and Other Horrors, A10
St. Willibrord Studies in Philosophy and Religion, D7/u
St. Willibrord's Press, D7, M8
"The Stafford Connection," B114
"The Stairs," IA2
Star Drek, H4
Starmont Contemporary Writers Series, D7, M8
Starmont Mystery Guides, D7, M8
The Stars Were Ours: Science Fiction and Fantasy in Paperback Publishing, from the Pages of Paperback Quarterly, A70
The State and Province Vital Records Guide, A74
Stella Nova: The Contemporary Science Fiction Authors, A1, D1/1
Stephen King (Winter), G11
Stephen King As Richard Bachman (Collings), M6
Stokvis Studies in Historical Chronology and Thought, D7/v
"A Story from Yesterday's Headlines That's As Gripping As Any Adventure Novel!" F48b
Studies in Judaica and the Holocaust, D7/w
Sun Dance Press, D7
Supernatural & Occult Fiction: 63 Books, D8, F15

Survey of Modern Fantasy Literature (Magill), D11, M14
Suzy McKee Charnas, Octavia Butler, Joan D. Vinge (Barr et al.), G25
Tempest in a Teapot: The Falkland Islands War, A28
"Thaddeus Dikty," H20
They: Three Parodies of H. Rider Haggard's She, A16
"The Thief," H2
"*The Thing from the Lake*, by Eleanor Marie Ingram," B75
Things to Come: An Illustrated History of the Science Fiction Film, A13, G2
"Thinking about Genealogy: Part II, Comments and Further Thoughts," B107
"Third Annual CSU Librarians Survey," B110
"*Titans of the Universe*, by Moonchild/James Harvey," B24
Titles from the Back Room (Levin), G6
To Kill or Not to Kill: Thoughts on Capital Punishment, A54
The Trilemma of World Oil Politics, A57
Twentieth-Century Science-Fiction Writers, Third Edition, D14, M14
The Ugly Swans (Strugatsky), M13
"Unicorn & Son," F1
"Unicorn and Son," K51
Unicorn & Son, Publishers, D1, M8
"The University of Cosmopoli Tales, by Edward Heron-Allen," B76
Up Your Asteroid! A Science Fiction Farce, A11
"Utopias in Science Fiction," B15
"The Vengeance of Káthan Jolárson," IB2
"The Way of Sataphan," IB1
We Are All Legends (Schweitzer), M1
West Coast Studies, D7/x
Western Fiction in the Library of Congress Classification Scheme, A41
"Who Done It? Now You Can Find Out," F75
The Wickizer Annals: Wickizer, Wickiser, Wickkiser, Wickkizer, Wickheiser, A27
"Willis E. McNelly Bibliography," H12
"*The Wonderful Adventures of Phra the Phoenician*, by Edwin Lester Arnold," B77
The Woodstock Series: Popular Music of Today, D7/y
The Work of Brian W. Aldiss: An Annotated Bibliography & Guide, A61
The Work of Bruce McAllister: An Annotated Bibliography & Guide, A35
The Work of Bruce McAllister: An Annotated Bibliography & Guide, Revised Edition, A38
The Work of Chad Oliver: An Annotated Bibliography & Guide, A46
The Work of Charles Beaumont: An Annotated Bibliography & Guide, A36
The Work of Charles Beaumont: An Annotated Bibliography & Guide, Second Edition, A55
The Work of Colin Wilson: An Annotated Bibliography & Guide, A45
The Work of Dean Ing: An Annotated Bibliography & Guide, A56, M6
The Work of Elizabeth Chater: An Annotated Bibliography & Guide, A84
The Work of Gary Brandner: An Annotated Bibliography & Guide, A81
The Work of George Zebrowski: An Annotated Bibliography & Guide, A37

The Work of George Zebrowski: An Annotated Bibliography & Guide, Second Edition, A53
The Work of Harry Harrison: An Annotated Bibliography & Guide, A78
The Work of Ian Watson: An Annotated Bibliography & Guide, A48
The Work of Jack Dann: An Annotated Bibliography & Guide, A51
The Work of Jeffrey M. Elliot: An Annotated Bibliography & Guide, A30
The Work of Jeffrey M. Elliot: An Annotated Bibliography & Guide, Second Edition, A73
The Work of Joseph Payne Brennan: An Annotated Bibliography & Guide, A83
The Work of Julian May: An Annotated Bibliography & Guide, A32
The Work of Julian May: An Annotated Bibliography & Guide, Second Edition, A72
The Work of Katherine Kurtz: An Annotated Bibliography & Guide, A62
The Work of Louis L'Amour: An Annotated Bibliography & Guide, A59
The Work of Michael R. Collings: An Annotated Bibliography & Guide, A80
The Work of Orson Scott Card: An Annotated Bibliography & Guide, A77
The Work of Pamela Sargent: An Annotated Bibliography & Guide, A50
The Work of R. Reginald: An Annotated Bibliography & Guide, A31, K25
The Work of Raymond Z. Gallun: An Annotated Bibliography & Guide, A82
The Work of Reginald Bretnor: An Annotated Bibliography & Guide, A49
The Work of Robert Nathan: An Annotated Bibliography & Guide, A85
The Work of Robert Reginald: An Annotated Bibliography & Guide, Second Edition, A60, K53
The Work of Ross Rocklynne: An Annotated Bibliography & Guide, A47
The Work of Stephen King: An Annotated Bibliography & Guide, A68
The Work of William Eastlake: An Annotated Bibliography & Guide, A79
The Work of William F. Nolan: An Annotated Bibliography & Guide, A43
The Work of William F. Temple: An Annotated Bibliography & Guide, A87
"*World Without Mercy*, by William Voltz," B28
Worlds of Never: Three Fantastic Novels, A17
Xenos Books, D7
Les Xipéhuz; and, The Death of the Earth (Rosny), M13
Yesterday or Tomorrow? Questions of Vision in the Fiction of Robert A. Heinlein, A66
"Your Guide for a Tour of Other Worlds," K11
"*You're All Alone*, by Fritz Leiber," B78
"Zebrowski, George," B132
Zephyr and Boreas: Winds of Change in the Fiction of Ursula K. Le Guin, A65

www.ingramcontent.com/pod-product-compliance
Lightning Source LLC
LaVergne TN
LVHW011329080426
835513LV00006B/258